Innovation in Environmental Policy

New Horizons in Environmental Economics

General Editor: Wallace E Oates, Professor of Economics, University of Maryland

This important new series is designed to make a significant contribution to the development of the principles and practices of environmental economics. It will include both theoretical and empirical work. International in scope, it will address issues of current and future concern in both East and West and in developed and developing countries.

The main purpose of the series is to create a forum for the publication of high quality work and to show how economic analysis can make a contribution to understanding and resolving the environmental problems confronting the world in the late 20th century.

Published titles:

1. Innovation in Environmental Policy
   Edited by T. H. Tietenberg

Innovation in Environmental Policy

Economic and Legal Aspects of Recent Developments in Environmental Enforcement and Liability

Edited by

T. H. Tietenberg
Christian A. Johnson
Distinguished Teaching Professor
Department of Economics
Colby College
Waterville, Maine

Edward Elgar

Published by
Edward Elgar Publishing Limited
Gower House
Croft Road
Aldershot
Hants GU11 3HR
England

Edward Elgar Publishing Limited
Distributed in the United States by
Ashgate Publishing Company
Old Post Road
Brookfield
Vermont 05036
USA

A CIP catalogue record for this book is available from the British Library

Library of Congress Cataloguing in Publication Data
Innovation in environmental policy: economic and legal aspects of
    recent developments in environmental enforcement and liability /
    edited by T.H. Tietenberg.
        p.   cm. – (New horizons in environmental economics: 1)
      Includes bibliographical references and index.
        1. Environmental policy–United States.   2. Environmental law–
    United States.   I. Tietenberg. Thomas H.   II Series.
    HC110.E5I52   1992
    363.7'056'0973–dc20   91–39435
                                                                  CIP

ISBN 1 85278 588 8

Printed in Great Britain by
Billing & Sons Ltd, Worcester

Contents

List of Tables   vii

Acknowledgments   ix

Contributors   xi

  1. Introduction and Overview   1
      by Tom Tietenberg

PART I ENVIRONMENTAL ENFORCEMENT

  2. Federal Enforcement: Theory and Practice   21
      by Cheryl Wasserman

  3. Defining Efficient Sanctions   53
      by Kathleen Segerson & Tom Tietenberg

  4. Criminal Penalties   75
      by Mark Cohen

  5. Private Enforcement   109
      by Wendy Naysnerski & Tom Tietenberg

PART II ENVIRONMENTAL LIABILITY LAW

  6. Tort Law and the Deterrence of Environmental Pollution   139
      by Donald Dewees

  7. Natural Resource Damages from Oil Spills   165
      by Richard Dunford

  8. Lender Liability for Hazardous Waste Cleanup   195
      by Kathleen Segerson

PART III ASSESSING THE STATE OF THE ART

9. Environmental Enforcement 215
by Clifford Russell

10. Environmental Liability Law 223
by Susan Rose–Ackerman

References 245

Index 261

List of Tables

3.1 Administrative actions and criminal and civil referrals   68
     to the Department of Justice by USEPA

4.1 Justice Department prosecutions for environmental   78
     crimes by type of offense, 1983–90

4.2 Justice Department prosecutions for environmental   83
     crimes by type of offender, 1983–90

4.3 Criminal fines for environmental offenses pre– and   85
     post–Criminal Fine Enforcement Act of 1984 (firms
     sentenced between 1984 and Sept. 1990)

4.4 Regression analysis of fines and total sanctions,   94
     environmental offenses, 1984–90

4.5 Jail versus fines for 40 closely held companies   98

5.1 The geographic distribution of private enforcement   118
     actions

7.1 Comparison of natural resource damages under   180
     three liability schemes for four hypothetical spill
     scenarios

7.2 Hypothetical costs and liability for supertanker oil   185
     spills of various sizes (million dollars)

Acknowledgments

The essays in this book were originally presented at a conference held at Woods Hole Oceanographic Institution on April 12–14, 1991. That conference would not have been possible without the initiative and funding provided by the Marine Policy Center at Woods Hole Oceanographic Institution and the leadership and support provided by its Director, Jim Broadus.

Financial support to the editor is also gratefully acknowledged. A sabbatical fellowship from the Woods Hole Marine Policy Center and a research grant from Resources for the Future, Inc. made it possible for Tom Tietenberg to devote the time necessary to organize the conference and to guide the process of weaving the conference papers into a cohesive manuscript.

CONTRIBUTORS:

Mark Cohen is Associate Professor of Management at the Owen Graduate School of Management, Vanderbilt University. He was previously an economist at the US Environmental Protection Agency, the Federal Trade Commission and the US Sentencing Commission, where he recently served as a consultant analysing current sentencing practice and assisting in the drafting of proposed guidelines for the sentencing of firms convicted of corporate crimes. His research has focused on many different aspects of crime and regulation, and has appeared in both law and economics journals.

Donald Dewees is a Professor of Economics and a Professor of Law at the University of Toronto, and is currently an Associate Dean of the School of Graduate Studies of the University of Toronto. He teaches courses in environmental economics and in environmental law. His research interests and recent publications deal with the analysis of the effects of alternative regulatory policies and the relative effects of tort law and regulation in altering private behavior.

Richard Dunford is Assistant Director of the Natural Resource Damage Assessment Program at the Research Triangle Institute in Research Triangle Park, NC. He has led or contributed to assessments of natural resource damages from several US oil spills, including the *Exxon Valdez* oil spill in Alaska in 1989. Prior to joining RTI in 1986, he was a natural resource economist in the Department of Agricultural Economics at Washington State University in Pullman, WA.

Wendy Naysnerski is a Research Assistant at Industrial Economics, Inc., Cambridge. She formerly worked as a Research Assistant for Professor Tom Tietenberg who served as her supervisor for a Senior environmental enforcement practices. She presented a version of this paper at the Fourth National Conference on Undergraduate Research.

Susan Rose-Ackerman is Ely Professor of Law and Political Economy in the Yale Law School and Department of Political Science. She is the author of *Rethinking the Progressive Agenda: The Reform of the American Regulatory State* (1991), *Corruption: A Study in Political Economy* (1978), and (with others) *The Uncertain Search for Environmental Quality* (1974). Her research interests involve the overlap between public policy, administrative law and rational–actor models of politics.

Clifford Russell is Professor of Economics and of Public Policy and director of the Institute for Public Policy Studies at Vanderbilt University. His research has touched many areas of concern in environmental economics and policy, most recently problems of monitoring and enforcement, about which he has published a book and several papers. He is currently on the executive committee of the Board of the Tennessee Environmental Council, having served the Environmental Defense Fund in a similar capacity for a dozen years in the 1970s and '80s.

Kathleen Segerson is Associate Professor of Economics at the University of Connecticut at Storrs and currently an associate editor of the *Journal of Environmental Economics and Management* and the *American Journal of Agricultural Economics*. In addition, she is a member of the Board of Directors of the Association of Environmental and Resource Economists. Her work on pollution control and liability has been funded by the US Department of Agriculture, the US Department of Interior (through the Water Resources Institutes), and the Small Business Administration. She recently coedited a book on environmental risk and has published in numerous professional journals.

Tom Tietenberg is the Christian A. Johnson Distinguished Teaching Professor at Colby College in Waterville, Maine. He is the author of four books (including *Environmental and Natural Resource Economics,* a leading textbook, and *Emissions Trading: An Exercise* *in Reforming Pollution Policy)* and numerous articles and essays on environmental economics, law and policy. During the period 1987–8 he served as the elected President of the Association of Environmental and Natural Resource Economists.

Cheryl Wasserman currently serves as Chief, Compliance Policy and Planning in US EPA's Office of Enforcement, responsible for cross–cutting agency enforcement policy. She has held various policy and management positions in US EPA since 1972. She is the Executive Director of the Steering Committee on the State/Federal Enforcement Relationship, has published and delivered numerous articles and addresses in the US and international forums on environmental auditing and enforcement principles.

1. Introduction and Overview

Tom Tietenberg

Environmental policy has been (and will, no doubt, continue to be) shaped by an evolutionary process. As new problems are identified, novel approaches designed to resolve the identified problems are implemented.

In ecological systems survival of the fittest guarantees that any species which proves to be ill–suited for the surrounding environment fades from the scene, while more well–suited species prosper. Once all species have achieved a balanced co–existence with neighboring species the resulting climax equilibrium provides stability and continuity.

By contrast, ill–suited public policies can endure; no counterpart of the survival of the fittest principle governs the evolution of policy. Policies conveying large, concentrated benefits to a small segment of society may well provide strong incentives for that segment to maintain their existence even if the policies fail to serve some larger social purpose. If the excessive costs precipitated by the policy are diffused among a very large group of citizens, their incentives to oppose inefficient policies are small; each individual's stake in the issue is too small to take action. Add to this the tendency for the average citizen to be poorly informed about the details of any particular public policy and the likelihood of effective opposition is reduced even further.

The movement toward effective and efficient public policy therefore rests on distinguishing what is working from what isn't and acting on the basis of those findings. The effective niche for each component must be discerned in the light of experience. The ultimate boundaries of applicability of each policy can only be determined after analysing its successes and failures and isolating the factors which spell the difference. While the evolution of ecological systems is automatically shaped by natural forces, the public policy evolutionary process is discretionary, shaped primarily by trial and error.

Innovation in environmental policy has become commonplace. Recent innovations have enlarged the menu of policy instruments at our disposal as well as transformed the roles of the various institutions charged with implementing and enforcing this expanded menu.

Though both logic and experience suggest that the efficient mix of government policies for environmental management contains a carefully crafted blend of legislative, executive and judicial approaches, the relationships among these approaches have not been systematically studied. The economics literature concerned with cost–effective or efficient pollution control has traditionally devoted most of its attention to analysing the effects of legislative or regulatory policy instruments, such as emission taxes or emissions trading.[1] Recent contributions have expanded this focus to include the effects of monitoring and enforcement policies.[2]   With a few noteworthy exceptions the complementary role of the court system has not received analytical attention among experts in environmental policy in proportion to its importance in resource allocation.

This omission is unfortunate, particularly when the interdependence of regulatory and judicial approaches is taken into consideration.[3] Since judicial remedies can complement or substitute for more traditional regulatory approaches, an optimal policy mix cannot be established without taking these interdependencies into account.[4]

The need for environmental policy coordination among the policy–making bodies is acute. With the number and complexity of environmental risks growing and the presumption that regulatory agencies can and should be responsible for controlling these risks firmly imbedded in the minds of the public and Congress, regulatory agencies at the national, regional, and local level are overworked and understaffed. The plain truth is that it is simply not possible to forge regulatory solutions for all these risks in a completely timely and adequate fashion. Setting priorities is absolutely essential.

Developing a better understanding of the complementarity and substitutability of the regulatory and judicial roles could play a significant role in this regulatory priority setting by identifying those issues that are better handled by the courts. Having identified those areas where the net benefit of judicial activity exceeds that of regulatory activity, regulatory resources currently devoted to those areas could be usefully transferred to other areas where the regulatory approach is essential.[5]

Judicial approaches affect the style of as well as the substance of regulatory policy. By creating legal precedents which ensure that pollution damages inflicted on some other party will be borne by the polluter, for example, liability law can create incentives for efficient levels of precaution to be taken; by providing an alternative means of internalizing external costs judicial remedies can complement legislative and administrative remedies. At the same time damage payments can be used to mitigate or repair the damage or even to directly compensate those victims of pollution who are parties to the suit, an attribute not shared by traditional regulatory approaches.

Court remedies also provide powerful incentives to discover and disclose environmental risks that the litigants knew about or should have known about by imposing liability payments on those who breach the duty to disclose. In some cases court–inspired risk communication among the parties may be a more effective way of assuring the adequate generation and dissemination of information than expecting a regulatory authority to bear this burden.

Some of the characteristics which differentiate liability law from regulatory approaches are readily apparent. Because regulatory approaches focus on mandating specific desirable actions or prohibiting undesirable actions, they are by their very nature anticipatory. Liability rules, on the other hand, are imposed after–the–fact and, as a result, the remedy can be tailored more closely to the facts of each specific case.

The tendency for regulatory authorities to treat categories of industrial emitters as similar when their costs of control may not be similar is one of the well–known sources of extra costs in the traditional approach to regulation. One way to reduce this cost is to use liability law and regulations as complements in controlling some target risk.[6] The regulations assure that every source adopts the minimum acceptable practice, leaving the degree to which any individual emitter exceeded that practice to be controlled by the liability they would face for additional damages caused. When the circumstances are favorable, some of the best attributes of both approaches could be achieved by combining regulatory minimum practice standards with liability for damages. Regulatory costs could be reduced while ensuring that reasonable precautions would be undertaken even by "judgment–proof" firms.[7]

Courts also play a key role in the enforcement of environmental standards. Even the best–designed regulations would be ineffective if they were not enforced properly. An elegantly designed regulation which turns out to be difficult to enforce may, in practice, ultimately prove inferior to a rather more crude but enforceable alternative. Whether standards are properly enforced depends crucially on how the courts handle such issues as the constitutionality of surprise inspections, the treatment of bankrupt firms, burdens of proof, evidentiary rules and interjurisdictional pollution. Regulatory policies designed without taking these considerations into account are likely to be less effective than policies designed in full knowledge of the enforcement procedures dictated by the courts.

RECENT POLICY INNOVATIONS

Being in the midst of a dynamic evolutionary process in environmental policy presents unparalleled opportunities for understanding and influencing the shape of that process. In this book we single out for special scrutiny two areas of environmental policy experiencing rather dramatic changes—liability law and enforcement.

Enforcement

The enforcement of environmental laws has undergone some rather dramatic changes over the last decade. Civil and criminal monetary penalties have been imposed more frequently on violators and the size of the penalties has increased. Individuals, both corporate employees and officers, have become more common targets for penalties. Incarceration has not only become a more commonly imposed sanction, but the resulting jail sentences are longer. Finally, while enforcement responsibility has traditionally been exclusively vested in the public sector, recently private enforcement actions brought by environmental organizations have become a major force.

What effects are these innovations having on enforcement? Do they represent a move toward or away from efficiency? What is their appropriate niche?

Liability Law

Forcing those who create environmental risks to bear the costs of the damage caused by those risks can create incentives for efficient precaution. However, the legal doctrine used can make a big difference in whether the outcome is efficient or even approximately efficient. For example, the Superfund Act authorizes the use of "joint and several liability" which allows the government, in certain circumstances, to recover all of the contaminated site restoration funds from any subset of potentially responsible parties regardless of the magnitude of their individual responsibility for the problem. Analysis of this doctrine reveals that the incentives it creates are rather sensitive to the litigation strategy pursued by the government. Furthermore different litigation strategies imply different complementary regulatory policies.[8]

Once restricted mainly to the domain of common law, liability law has recently become imposed by statutes in a variety of new settings with a newly created set of accompanying procedures. The Comprehensive Environmental Response, Compensation and Liability Act has made liability law the chief vehicle for raising revenue to be used for cleaning up hazardous waste sites. Key aspects of this approach include the use of traditional common law doctrines in innovative ways and the use of stipulated economic valuation techniques to derive estimates of property damage to be used in compensating victims. The Oil Pollution Liability Act of 1990 has set in motion a similar approach for oil spills. How are these approaches working in practice?

As liability doctrines have assumed a more prominent place in environmental policy the set of potential defendants has been widened to include some parties which traditionally were immune from any financial responsibility. These now include individual officers within corporations, those acquiring land subsequently discovered to contain toxic wastes, and, importantly, banks that have lent money to those who have somehow been connected to a toxic waste site. While casting the net over a larger set of potentially responsible parties is unquestionably a good strategy for raising revenue, the incentives it has created for this expanded set of parties has not yet been systematically studied.

Defining the appropriate niche for these innovations in the totality of environmental policy is a timely issue. Not only has the interdisciplinary field of law and economics become increasingly sophisticated in its ability to use economic analysis to derive useful and meaningful insights about subjects previously considered only by lawyers, but, as illustrated above, recent innovations provide an opportunity to study for the first time how these approaches work in practice. The demand for synthetic integration is high and the methodological sophistication of the field has reached the point where it appears able to begin to fill that need. Experience with these approaches has proceeded long enough that we can learn something about what works and what doesn't. This book capitalizes on this confluence of disciplinary development and researchable innovations to discover and to communicate something about how these innovations in liability law and enforcement are working in practice.

OVERVIEW OF THE LESSONS LEARNED

In the first paper Wasserman provides an insider's view of the federal enforcement and compliance process and articulates her sense of the areas where those who hold the responsibility for implementing that process need help. The contrast among the various economic and legal theories of compliance with which she opens her paper serves to put the economic approach into larger perspective.

Wasserman continues by explaining how the government determines its enforcement strategy in practice and how this practice may deviate from the dictates of theory. Receiving particular emphasis in her discussion is how enforcement practices are shaped by relationships among federal and state enforcers as embodied in the US federal system of government. Her paper also makes clear that economic analysis can play a major role in determining the efficient deployment of enforcement resources, particularly in this period when the menu of enforcement options is expanding so rapidly.

As noted above, the menu of sanctions imposed for noncomplying behavior is one specific area of environmental enforcement that has undergone some rather dramatic changes over the last decade. Is this a case of progressive judicial evolution where a new enforcement structure has begun to fill an important, heretofore neglected, niche? Or is it a case of zealous enforcers going too far, producing a public appearance of effective enforcement that masks serious inefficiencies?[9] Why have individual sanctions become more important in the enforcement package? Why has criminal law received such recent emphasis?

Segerson and Tietenberg investigate these questions by reviewing and expanding the traditional theoretical literature on penalty structures and drawing out the resulting implications for environmental enforcement. Concerning the overall choice among the three judicial or quasi–judicial forms of enforcement, administrative proceedings are the least costly while criminal proceedings are the most costly, not only because the required standards of proof are higher, but because incarceration, a remedy available only with criminal proceedings, entails extra social costs. By itself this evidence would suggest that administrative remedies would be preferred to civil remedies and civil remedies would be preferred to criminal remedies unless these more costly proceedings offered compensating benefits. Segerson and Tietenberg find that the more costly forms of enforcement can, in certain circumstances, be justified, but these circumstances are unique and relatively rare.

The traditional penalty structure for managing environmental risks involves administrative or civil financial penalties imposed on organizations, not individuals. A belief that the corporate organization can be enlisted to the enforcement cause underlies the economic theory of deterrence for corporate crimes. Penalizing corporations for transgressions will, according to this presumption, lead ultimately to the internal identification of the individuals responsible for the transgressions.

Relying on a principal–agent analytical framework Segerson and Tietenberg point out that under the right conditions efficiency can be achieved with either (i) a monetary penalty placed on the corporation alone, without any penalty on the worker, or (ii) a penalty on the responsible individual, without any corresponding penalty on the firm. In other words, under ideal circumstances individual and organizational financial penalties are perfect substitutes. This is a powerful conclusion which supports both the traditional economic model of corporate harm and a good deal of current practice. It is also consistent with previous work showing that, when two parties have a contractual relationship, then the efficient outcome can be achieved by placing liability on either party, since through forward or backward shifting one party can always transfer costs to the other.

This analysis also isolates the conditions that would ensure the substitutability of corporate and individual penalties. First, the actions of the environmental workers should be observable so that wage structures can be used to penalize inefficient behavior and reward efficient behavior. Second, principals must have the ability to manipulate wages sufficiently that the proper correspondence with employee actions can be established. Third, the penalty or fine has to be set at the correct level. Finally, both the polluter and the worker must have sufficient assets to be able to pay the penalties that are imposed on them.

When those conditions are not fulfilled, traditional administrative and civil penalties on organizations do not produce efficient precautionary incentives. Inefficient situations could arise either when the polluting organization faces inefficient incentives (implying that even environmental risk managers who are pursuing the best interests of their employers will act inefficiently) or when the incentives facing environmental risk managers diverge from those facing the organization.

Segerson and Tietenberg suggest that when corporate and individual penalties are not perfect substitutes, more innovative penalty structures may be called for. Individual penalties and the greater expense associated with criminal penalties may be justified when the precautionary incentives associated with administrative or civil penalties on the organization prove inadequate to stimulate efficient precautionary behavior.

Segerson and Tietenberg suggest that when monetary penalties are clearly insufficient to produce the correct incentives, incarceration may be cheaper than putting up with a much higher level of environmental damage triggered by impaired incentives. A few well–publicized cases can set precedents that provide a large number of firms to take a more efficient level of precaution. Indeed, when an incarceration penalty works extremely well in deterring inefficient behavior, it would rarely need to be imposed. While the additional expenditures associated with trying these few cases may well be very high on a per–case basis, the additional precaution achieved from all firms recognizing those precedents and reacting to them will very likely be enormous. The costs and benefits of these remedies cannot be examined merely in the context of a single case.

While the Segerson–Tietenberg analysis has identified several possible roles for both individual and criminal penalties in environmental enforcement, it remains true that these roles are limited, not dominant. Individual and criminal penalties should complement, not replace, the dominant strategy—civil and administrative penalties against organizations.

One aspect of the penalty structure investigated by Segerson and Tietenberg is the role for criminal penalties in deterring environmental contamination. Cohen's paper examines the empirical evidence on the use of this particular sanction.

Following a review of the criminal penalty provisions of environmental statutes, Cohen highlights the growing trend away from the traditional legal standard of requiring criminal intent and towards the prosecution of negligence, strict and vicarious criminal liability offenses– not only for corporations,but for corporate officers as well. He then summarizes the evidence for individuals and organizations convicted of environmental crimes at the federal level.

* Nearly 100 federal indictments for environmental crimes are brought per year.

* About 70 per cent of criminal indictments are against individuals, with the remaining 30 per cent against organizations.

* Although most firms prosecuted for environmental criminal activity are small, closely held firms, about 12 per cent have publicly traded stock and 40 per cent are large enough to have either $1 million in sales or 50 or more employees.

* The median criminal fine for an organization

convicted of a federal environmental offense is
$50,000. However, in the past few years, a
significant number of fines have been in the
$500,000–and–up range,

* About 30 per cent of individuals convicted along
with their corporate employers received jail time,
for an average length of 7 months, while 54.5 per
cent of individuals convicted without a corporate
defendant received jail time, for an average length of
18 months.

* The most important explanatory variables when
estimating criminal fines and total monetary
sanctions are the amount of monetary harm (clean
up, etc.) and the seriousness of the environmental
hazard. Some evidence suggest that larger firms
receive more stringent sanctions.

Cohen is able to test empirically some of the implications of the
Segerson–Tietenberg analysis. Contrary to the traditional economic
model, in his total sample he finds that the courts treat individual and
corporate liability as complements, not substitutes. Larger corporate
fines are associated with higher likelihoods that individual co–
defendants have been convicted and sent to jail. One possible
explanation for this result is that it reflects unobservable measures of
the severity of the offense. In a restricted sample of closely–held
companies, he finds that corporate fines and jail sentences for the
owners *are* substitutes. Finally, although his study was unable to
distinguish firms based upon their ability to pay, Cohen reports on
another study encompassing all corporate crimes that finds higher
rates of both individual criminal liability and incarceration when the
firm cannot afford to compensate for the harm it caused. This is also
consistent with the Segerson–Tietenberg results.

In 1984, Congress established the US Sentencing Commission,
which was given the task of writing mandatory guidelines for judges
to follow when sentencing federal criminals. The first set of
guidelines, which went into effect late in 1987 for offenses committed

after November of that year, are expected to increase both the incarceration rate and jail times.

The new sentencing guidelines give prosecutors a powerful new weapon to fight environmental crimes. However, like all weapons, these guidelines have the potential to cause unintended harm. One of the key questions yet to be answered is whether these more stringent criminal sanctions result in "overdeterrence" for firms that are already making a good–faith effort to comply with environmental laws. Has the use of the criminal sanction transcended its efficient domain? Only time will tell.

Creative penalty structures are far from the only source of innovation in the enforcement field. Another major innovation involves authorizing an expanding role for nongovernmental organizations in enforcement. While the role of nongovernmental organizations in environmental policy is growing rapidly, our analytical understanding of the causes and consequences of this emerging role has not kept pace. In the 1970s, Congress authorized private organizations to seek injunctions (and in some cases penalties) against firms violating the terms of their environmental operating permits. The analysis in the Naysnerski–Tietenberg paper show how varying remedies, limitations, and reimbursement procedures can affect both the level and patterns of litigation activity as well as the compliance consequences. A database containing information on 1205 cases is used to infuse empirical content into the analysis.

The Naysnerski–Tietenberg analysis suggests that private enforcement provides two specific sources of hope for improving the enforcement process. If the government monopoly on enforcement can be challenged, private enforcers could complement public enforcers, producing greater compliance and, quite possibly, a more responsible public sector. Since the value of private enforcement is greatest when public enforcement is not very effective, the significant challenge to regulatory policy posed by ineffective public enforcement can be turned into an opportunity. Furthermore, when private enforcers are entitled to attorney fee reimbursement, the financial burden of enforcement is transferred to those who create the need for it. Limited public resources need not be a barrier to effective enforcement.

Naysnerski and Tietenberg also find that citizen suits have offered a

distinctly superior form of enforcement whenever public enforcement agencies seem reluctant to enforce pollution violations
committed by public facilities. Private enforcers have no such lack of
will to pursue public polluters and therefore would presumably be
able to produce compliance faster for this important class of
polluters.

Adding private to public enforcement would represent an
unambiguous move toward cost–effectiveness only if the emission
standards were cost–effective. Blending private enforcement with
emissions trading would not only encourage cost–effective compliance
with the standards, but it would provide an additional inducement for
high marginal cost firms to trade, making for a more active market.
In this case the coexistence of private enforcement and emissions
trading produces a policy which is greater than the sum of its parts.

According to Naysnerski and Tietenberg, however, private
enforcement does not flourish in all environments. If it is to fulfill its
promise, certain preconditions must be satisfied. The most important
of these involve establishing a reasonable burden of proof and
allowing for the reimbursement of legal fees, including justifiable
attorney fees. Examples of US laws which satisfy these preconditions
are presented.

While regulation has played the dominant role in environmental
protection in the past, will that necessarily be the case in the future?
In the related area of product liability, for example, the role for tort
law has expanded considerably, and is now assuming a much larger
burden for assuring reasonable levels of risk. Is environmental law
likely to be the setting for the next major expansion of tort law? And
would a greatly expanded role for tort law in the totality of the
environmental program represent good public policy?

Focusing on both the necessary conditions for a plaintiff to succeed
and the compatibility of the resulting incentives with efficient
deterrence, the Dewees paper examines the evidence. He concludes
that equivalent expansions in environmental law are unlikely and,
with one exception (property damage), that a large expansion of the
role of tort law would not make good sense for public policy.

Including in his analysis both common law doctrines (nuisance,
trespass, strict liability, and negligence) and the emerging use of tort–
based statutes (such as the US Comprehensive Environmental

Response, Compensation, and Liability Act of 1980) to impose cleanup costs and damages on responsible parties, Dewees demonstrates a number of significant barriers to the initiation of suits by injured parties. These include difficulties of proving causation, statutes of limitations and the legal costs of bringing suit. Because these barriers reflect important, reasonable attributes of the tort system, eliminating them would only introduce a new set of problems.[10]

Dewees argues that tort law does have a unique niche to fill, however. It is most effectively employed for local pollution problems involving a single pollutant causing very substantial damage. He further argues that it should not be expanded into most of the traditional areas of air and water pollution involving multiple pollutants and large numbers of both polluters and victims. Despite their inherent deficiencies regulatory remedies are still superior for that type of problem. This normative conclusion is apparently consistent with the current experience in the US and Canada where the major expansions in tort law have involved compensation for property damaged by hazardous wastes, precisely the type of case where Dewees believes tort law can be an effective approach.

The effectiveness of liability law in deterring inefficient damage to the environment even in this limited setting depends on its ability to internalize the external costs imposed by any damage that does occur. Once it becomes clear to polluters that they will be responsible for those costs, taking all cost–justified precautionary measures becomes part of the strategy to minimize private costs. How effectively these costs are internalized depends crucially on the procedures for calculating and imposing *ex post* assessments of environmental damage.

Previous experience with applying this particular approach to oil spills, a case which would appear to lend itself to a liability approach, has been less than encouraging. On 17 March 1978 the *Amoco Cadiz*, an oil transport ship, travelling in a bad storm, lost steering control, and after unsuccessful towing attempts, drifted onto the rocks off the shore of Portsall, France, on the Brittany coast. Ultimately, the ship broke in two and discharged 220,00 tons of crude and 4,000 tons of bunker fuels along the coast of a resort area, two months prior to the opening of the tourist season.

Damaged parties went to court in the US to seek damages. In 1990 the trial judge, now retired from the bench, summed up the situation:

> So here we are, twelve years after the accident, eleven years after the suit was filed, with the plaintiffs in possession of an enormous judgment and subject to enormous legal fees without one cent having changed hands. The case marches onward to the Court of Appeals with each principal party expected to appeal those aspects of the final judgment with which they disagree. This raises the possibility, almost unimaginable, but very real, that the whole case could have to be tried again. (McGarr, 1990)

One means of dealing with the inherent legal complexity of the use of liability to control oil spills is to standardize (by statute and regulations) the procedures. Since the Oil Pollution Control Act of 1990 represents the latest in a series of US statutes establishing the official procedures for determining the magnitude of the damage and the process by which assessments are levied, its passage offers an excellent opportunity to characterize and evaluate the evolution of damage assessment procedures and the extent to which they can provide both a timely and effective response to the problem posed by oil spills. How have the procedures changed over time? What are the crucial issues? Has the evolution represented an unambiguous move toward efficiency? How do these damage–assessment procedures affect the potential role for liability law in the efficient deterrence of oil spills?

Dunford begins his examination of these issues by reviewing the damage assessment regulations promulgated by the Department of Interior to implement CERCLA and showing how the 1989 *Ohio* decision in the US Court of Appeals modified these rules. Whereas the initial regulations had allowed damages to be calculated as the lesser of restoration costs and diminution–of–use values, the 1989 decision gave clear priority to restoration costs (even when they exceeded diminution–of–use) and expanded the scope of permissible damages by putting nonuse values on an equal footing with use values. In this respect the evolution has meant a clear increase in the magnitude of damages to be included in the assessment.

Although increasing damage assessment liability in theory, Dunford also notes that the Oil Pollution Act (OPA) of 1990 puts limits on the liability of responsible businesses for cleanup costs and damages in general and it operationalized an Oil Spill Trust Fund that will cover cleanup costs and damages in excess of these liability limits. So even though OPA increases spillers' gross damage assessment liability for many oil spills, the Oil Spill Trust Fund may pay for a substantial portion of this liability. Consequently, OPA may actually *reduce* some spillers' liability relative to their pre–passage liability, an outcome that Dunford concludes is most likely for larger spills.

Liability law has the virtue that it raises revenue while providing incentives to take precautions and to increase the available information on the magnitude of the risk posed. In the United States, for example, CERCLA assigns the liability for cleaning up contaminated waste sites to "potentially responsible parties". Recently the definition of potentially responsible parties has been expanded to include both purchasers of contaminated property and banks when they foreclose on a piece of contaminated property (thereby becoming its owner).

As a practical matter this implies that the number of possible parties from whom cleanup costs could be recovered has been expanded. While the additional revenue generated by this expansion is clearly a benefit in cleaning up the sites, some questions about the incentive effects are also raised. What effect does this expansion of the definition of potentially responsible parties have on the incentives of sellers? of buyers? of lenders? Can an efficient set of liability sharing rules be defined? What would they look like?

To shed light on this important issue Segerson constructs a three–part analysis of the problem. In the first part she examines the incentives of the buyer and seller to conduct an environmental assessment in order to ascertain the actual level of contamination. The key, she discovers, is the extent to which the seller is judgment–proof (i.e. unable to pay the assessed liability). If the seller bears the full liability of dealing with the contamination, no liability should be shifted; the seller would conduct an assessment if, and only if, the assessment were cost–justified. If the seller were somewhat, but not completely, judgment–proof, transferring some liability to the buyer would make sense. For example, if the likelihood that the buyer will be judgment–proof exceeds the likelihood that the seller would be judgment–proof once he sells the property, the incentive for the buyer to conduct an environmental assessment can be made efficient by imposing a larger share of the liability on the buyer whenever an assessment was not done. However, the share of this liability which should be borne by the buyer to preserve efficient incentives is a function of the relative likelihood that the buyer and seller will be judgment–proof. In general it is not efficient to either transfer all liability to the buyer or to transfer it only when no environmental assessment has been done.

Recognizing that the land market will provide a means for feedback effects while allow for a certain amount of liability shifting, Segerson examines the incentives to transfer the property from buyer to seller in a setting which allows buyer and lender liability. Would the expansion of the definition of potentially responsible party discourage the flow of the property to its highest valued user? She finds that if sellers cannot reduce their liability by selling (skipping town with the proceeds, for example), incentives to buy/sell will be efficient if all liability remains with the seller (no transfer to the buyer or the lender). On the other hand, fully transferring liability to the buyer and subsequently to the lender in the event of foreclosure would be efficient, if and only if, the probability that the seller is not judgment–proof (assuming he retains title) is the same as the corresponding probability for the buyer (under equity financing) or the buyer/lender combination (under debt financing).

Despite the fact that the expansion of liability to buyers and lenders was apparently undertaken as a means to tap more and deeper pockets in search of revenue, Segerson concludes that efficiency provides no general justification for absolving lenders from liability in the case of foreclosure. Because the very act that transforms the lender into an owner (foreclosure) also indicates a judgment–proof problem on the part of the buyer (which undermines the buyer's incentives), lender liability may well have some role to play.

The last two essays provide a stimulating, personal, post–conference assessment of the state of the art from the vantage point of two of the major contributors to the field. These closing contributions not only provide some useful context for the other essays in this volume, but a good foundation for future research as well.

Taken together these essays provide a number of useful lessons for defining the niches for each of these innovative approaches to environmental protection policy. Not surprisingly, no dominant solution emerges, but each innovation does seem to have an enduring, if limited, role to play. The key is to assure that the domain of application for each innovation coincides with its domain of maximum usefulness. While we have learned a great deal which can help to tailor these innovations, much remains to be done.

NOTES

1. For a survey of this literature see Bohm and Russell (1985), Hahn (1989), and Tietenberg (1990).
2. For a review of this literature see Russell, Harrington, and Vaughan (1986) and Russell (1990b).
3. One excellent study of the interdependence of liability law with regulatory approaches for controlling accidents is Shavell (1987b).
4. For economists this notion of a policy interdependency which crosses jurisdictional lines will have a familiar ring since the coordination of monetary and fiscal policy plays such a prominent role in economic stabilization.
5. One example of how Congress has not only recognized the substitutability of judicial and regulatory approaches, but has acted upon this recognition in writing legislation occurred when the Amendments to the Superfund Act were passed. Economists uniformly lamented the fact that the proposed waste end taxes were eliminated and replaced by a less-targeted way of raising the money to finance the Superfund. Completely overlooked in those initial discussions was the fact that this law allows the government to collect revenue for restoring the designated contaminated sites by suing the potentially responsible parties responsible for creating the site. The precautionary incentives created by this use of liability law to raise revenue may in principle be as efficient as any actual set of waste end taxes may have been, but whether or not it has been is examined by several papers in this book.
6. This argument is suggested in Shavell (1984b).
7. Judgment-proof firms are those not having an incentive to take precautions under liability law since for one reason or another they may be immune to liability assessment. For an analysis if dealing with this problem see Shavell (1986).
8. These issues are explored using noncooperative game theory in Tietenberg (1989).
9. Some evidence suggests that overzealous use of criminal prosecution has occurred in some states. One study found: "Urged by public pressures to criminally charge whenever possible, a predisposition to the criminal enforcement side of the civil vs. criminal enforcement dichotomy exacted some cost in terms of lower prosecutorial success rates."See Rebovich (1987,183).
10. The excessive deterrence created when polluters are penalized for contamination incidents caused mostly or entirely by others is an example of one such problem.

PART I
Environmental Enforcement

2. Federal Enforcement: Theory and Practice

Cheryl E. Wasserman

INTRODUCTION

Compliance is essential to the success of any environmental program. However, there is little empirical data on how best to gain broad–scale compliance with environmental laws. Comparatively little in the traditional economics literature deals with the subject of compliance, and still less with environmental compliance and enforcement: what works, what does not work, in what circumstances, and why. This paper reviews the theories that federal, state and local regulators and law–enforcement personnel draw upon in implementing enforcement programs, how the realities of implementation differ from theory, and the need for further research by environmental economists and those in related social science disciplines.

WHY COMPLIANCE AND ENFORCEMENT MATTER

In the early 1970s much of the attention of US government officials at the federal, state, and local levels was devoted to standard–setting and to permit–issuance. While enforcement was undertaken as a basic element of each environmental program, it first began to assume its place as the subject of significant policy interest and priority in the later 1970s and the 1980s. This, in large part, reflects a natural evolution in the programs, shifting their focus to field implementation once requirements were put in place and it also reflects the introduction of statutory penalty authorities in the latter part of the

1970s. The extent of compliance and the effectiveness of enforcement efforts are important for several reasons.

Effectiveness
Compliance is critical to realizing the benefits envisioned by environmental policy, statutes, regulations, standards, and permits. The vast regulatory apparatus we have put in place to protect public health and the environment amounts to empty words and deeds without compliance. It is the regulatory bottom line. All of the cost–benefit or cost–effectiveness studies that go into assessing the best regulatory route become meaningless if the costs and benefits do not play out as predicted, usually with assumptions of full compliance.

Efficiency
Environmental economics, among other things, seeks to identify the most efficient solution to achieving desired public health and welfare benefits. If regulations and permit conditions are designed to be economically efficient, inconsistent enforcement will lead to economically inefficient results.

Equity
A consistent enforcement response provides an element of fairness to the regulatory process that would be missing if those who failed to comply benefit at the expense of those who do, or if regulatees who do not comply are treated very differently depending upon their location and circumstance.

Credibility
The rule of law and credibility of our governmental institutions require that laws be taken seriously. The expectation that violations will generate a predictable and proportionate enforcement response is essential to the credibility of our regulations. Support for escalating enforcement response to known violations and following through until compliance is achieved, are essential to the credibility of government regulations. It is the ultimate test of the public will to see programs through to full implementation.

BASIC THEORIES ON COMPLIANCE AND ENFORCEMENT

Several operative theories underlie environmental enforcement; some are explicit in guidance and policy, while others can be surmised from practice through observation. All are interrelated. This discussion first distinguishes between compliance and enforcement. Second, it presents the theory of deterrence which is fundamental to enforcement strategies, along with the contributions of economic theory. Third, it discusses other theories or assumptions about what motivates compliance behavior, and their implications for more efficient and effective compliance and enforcement programs.

Compliance is defined as the ultimate goal of any enforcement program. Compliance is essentially a state of being, when a regulated source is achieving required environmental standards, regulations, or permit conditions by meeting expected behaviors in processes and practices. Enforcement is defined as a set of legal tools, both informal and formal, designed to compel compliance.

The term 'enforcement response' usually applies to those agency actions specifically intended to convey legal sanction and/or penalty. Traditional enforcement programs encompass compliance monitoring and both informal and formal enforcement responses. Recently, the broader range of both coercive and cooperative techniques used to effectively change or deter source behavior are being tied together into comprehensive compliance strategies for each of the major environmental programs and their components.

Deterrence, perhaps the most important underlying theory of enforcement, is used somewhat differently in the literature than in practice. According to the concept of deterrence, a strong enforcement program deters the regulated community from violating in the first instance. Specific deterrence is deterring an individual violator from violating again. General deterrence is deterring the broader regulated community from violating. The literature on what is necessary to create deterrence identifies four elements: (i) a credible likelihood of detection of the violation; (ii) swift and sure enforcement response; and (iii) appropriately severe sanction; and (iv) that each of these factors be perceived as real (Charlton, 1985).

Deterrence is viewed in practice as creating a multiplier effect for each enforcement action, the magnitude of which depends on the strength of each of these factors. The multiplier effect is important. No enforcement program can provide sufficient presence all of the time for all violations. It is therefore generally held that an enforcement program must rely upon and to some extent develop a complying majority and devote its resources to addressing the remainder that do not comply. In contrast, pure deterrence theory as described in the literature would have us distrust "voluntary compliance", that it is only the direct threat of some legal action and sanction that motivates a source to comply.

Economic theory as it has been applied to enforcement is compatible with and indeed could be said to quantify the principles of deterrence theory. Both describe the would–be violator as an amoral, rational calculator. Economic theory argues that each source calculates whether it is in its economic self–interest to comply or to violate requirements. This economic calculus compares the cost of coming into compliance with the likelihood of getting caught multiplied by the penalty of violating. Economic self–interest could also take into account future liability, the economic value of a negative impact on the firm's reputation if caught, etc., but at bottom it comes down to dollars and cents.

Neither pure deterrence theory or its economic complement addresses the broader array of motivations that may explain compliance behavior, such as societal norms, moral values, sense of professional conduct, etc. Because compliance behavior is just that, behavior, it cannot readily be predicted and is more likely the result of complex motivations, only some of which are rational, reasonable, and economically motivated. That is not to say that economic theory and analysis is without merit or potential value here. It is to say that environmental economics as applied to enforcement is not a simple matter.

The behavioral school of compliance theory argues that, at least for corporate compliance, individuals within a firm are motivated less by conscious decisions based on profit/loss than by motives of personal advancement, by fear of corporate sanction, or by social influence through an individual relationship with the regulator/inspector, peers, and/or social and moral norms.[1] The literature takes two approaches to this more behavior–driven compliance. One group presents the business firm or regulatee as a political citizen, postulating that enforcement is not cost–effective because of its high transaction costs, and that it is really not necessary in most instances, given the inherent willingness of sources to comply with the law. This school argues for a more cooperative approach to gaining compliance, and to the promulgation of rules that are perceived as reasonable, since those motivated by citizenship will not obey rules perceived as arbitrary or irrational. Another group in the literature focuses less on cooperation than on sanctions, arguing that, because fines and penalties are unlikely to be sufficiently high to overcome the low likelihood of detection and are not coming directly out of the individual's pocket, criminal sanctions, with the threat of personal incarceration, or other sanctions adversely affecting individuals within an organization, are far more powerful tools to gain compliance (Diver, 1977).

The literature presents a third potential image of the violator, that of the incompetent, with violations stemming from a failed organization or procedure. Under deterrence theory, the threat of sanction is the best motivation to establish proper systems and internal controls to motivate against the safety of blissful ignorance. Those who advocate cooperation, argue that a strong enforcement response is inappropriate here. As to what truly motivates preventive behavior, there will soon be new literature on corporate culture and how it might affect compliance behavior.[2]

Some recent enforcement research is derived from game theory and operations research to develop a framework for predicting behavior. Borrowing from economic literature, it adds situational variables to reflect a variety of possible motivations to comply, given complex regulatee and regulator relationships (Filar, 1985).

In summing up what these theories of enforcement mean for enforcement practice and analysis, two factors should be kept in mind. First, perception is as important or even more important than reality. In 1971, Chester Bowles, of the wartime Office of Price Administration, suggested that there will always be 5 per cent of individuals who will violate no matter what, 20 per cent who will comply no matter what, and 75 per cent who will comply only if the violators are punished and/or the requirements are perceived as nonarbitrary. The perception of a strong enforcement effort, of the willingness to pursue sanctions and to escalate enforcement action can be created by the manner in which government enforcement actions are taken, as well as by the actual number and results of actions themselves. While one cannot create perceived action from inaction, in the annals of military history many successful battles have been won where a small number of troops have created an image of a formidable fighting force, thereby demoralizing and successfully competing against superior forces. A successful enforcement effort cannot be correlated to quantification of action and result; a multiplier effect must capture these other factors or theory is likely to paint an unrealistically gloomy portrait of what it would take to do the job.

Second, enforcement strategies must reflect a mix of these theories, to both stroke 'em and poke 'em, to both promote and coerce compliance. Any stage in the process will always raise a question of timing and mix of enforcement response versus technical assistance, and whether they should be sequenced or provided simultaneously. The answers may vary greatly depending upon the nature of the requirements, the level of public support and technical know–how, but given human nature, it would seem that enforcement would be a strong constant throughout.

ENFORCEMENT PROGRAMS: THEORY, REALITY, AND OPEN QUESTIONS

The strategies currently in use at the US Environmental Protection Agency and its counterparts at the state and local levels generally address the following elements:

* establishing program priorities and identifying the regulated community;
* promoting compliance within the regulated community;
* monitoring compliance within the regulated community;
* responding to violations including timeliness and appropriateness of the enforcement response;
* imposing civil penalties and other sanctions for non–compliance;

* clarifying roles and responsibilities of federal and state or local agencies; and
* evaluating results and establishing accountability.[3]

Each element of a compliance strategy is reviewed below in terms of the current operative theory used by government officials, what we know of practice and how it differs from theory, and finally, what questions should be addressed in further research to lead to more cost–effective compliance and enforcement program design.

Establishing Program Priorities and Identifying the Regulated Community

Environmental requirements now cover virtually every activity involving production, transportation and consumption in our society. Keeping up with the most recent developments in environmental policy is more than a full–time task. The number of Federal Register pages devoted to environmental requirements has grown geometrically and plant–specific permit requirements are now reflecting the complete environmental life–cycle from storage of raw materials of production to disposal of process waste products. As difficult as it is for the regulated community to keep up with these requirements, it is even more difficult for environmental officials to ensure compliance is achieved and to take the necessary enforcement actions. Therefore, priorities must be set to focus enforcement activities.

In theory, enforcement priorities should simply take into account the environmental risk posed by failure to comply, much as we do when devising standards and regulations. However, enforcement poses more complex challenges for priority–setting, and must consider the need to enforce requirements essential to preserving the integrity of the regulatory scheme (such as testing, monitoring, reporting, and record–keeping requirements, violations of which may not pose significant risk but may mask more significant environmental problems), and the need to enforce previous enforcement agreements and orders to preserve the integrity of enforcement itself.

There are further complications. A requirement which, if violated, may pose a very high environmental risk may be one for which the regulated community has a strong incentive to comply, for example, if there is liability for damages through other institutions. This might arguably make it a low enforcement priority. Also a violation may be one which has a very low risk of occurring given the reliability of the control system, or may be one for which only a small percentage of the regulated community is out of compliance.

Enforcement priorities are currently defined through several vehicles. At a very broad level, annual Agency Guidance specifies program priorities. EPA has placed a premium on fully integrating enforcement into every aspect of program implementation. More specifically, enforcement priorities are further established in program measures of success which accompany the annual guidance, defining what constitutes Significant Non–Compliance (SNC) in each program (Strock, 1991a). How effectively the Significant Non–Compliers are returned to compliance is a measure of success. In addition, other program areas need an enforcement presence, but not necessarily through coverage of all violations. In such aspects of the program, enforcement initiatives may be designed to send a clear message to the regulated community. Enforcement initiatives are targeted and concentrated enforcement actions timed to have a maximum deterrent impact through press coverage, and packaged to gain economies of scale in preparing cases for litigation.

In practice, the environmental programs have not been entirely successful in effectively establishing priorities based upon risk or on the need for deterrence. In the hazardous waste program, for example, the SNC list focused priorities at land–disposal facilities on all groundwater–related violations, thus including some minor violations of these requirements. The air program has placed a high priority on violations of pollutant standards in areas exceeding national ambient air quality standards for that pollutant. However, the air program also has included as SNC violations of any national new source performance standard. Therefore, the failure to conduct a performance stack test upon starting up a new source in an attainment area, has had the same priority as a violation of volatile organic compound (VOC) requiréments in an ozone nonattainment area, even if federal or state officials have reason to believe the source is in compliance. While refinements are being made, a priority setting scheme is never fully satisfactory at the national level. Federal officials are currently working with EPA Regions and the states to adjust more successfully national priorities to local circumstances.

Further, priority setting has, until very recently, reflected the fragmented nature of environmental laws and organizations. In its Four Year Strategic Plan and Agency Vision Statements, the Administrator of EPA has placed increased emphasis on multi–media and cross–program priority–setting to enhance environmental risk reduction and deterrence through, for example, geographic, pollutant, industry, company and/or facility targeting, and through increased emphasis on multi–media and cross–program inspections, enforcement settlement agreements, and cases.[4]

In a more detailed setting, priorities are also established in those programs which must address continuing compliance and operations and maintenance violations, e.g. air and water. Because no pollution control system can operate in one hundred percent compliance one hundred percent of the time, these programs establish priorities by setting limits on actionable violation levels. This does not mean that any violations are countenanced but rather, that given the large numbers of violating sources, limits must be set. Because these limits are for management purposes only, they do not apply to citizen suits, and citizen suits have been effectively brought for violations at lesser levels which were not being addressed by regulatory agencies. Many reformers argue that such definitions should formally distinguish "exceedances" from "violations", and take into account what is statistically and realistically achievable in practice.

In reviewing enforcement priorities it is important to recognize that an enforcement response happens late in the enforcement process. Faced with violations, most government agencies would prefer to respond in some manner. Therefore, setting correct priorities at the beginning of the enforcement process, i.e. strategies for detecting violations through targeted inspections, can best assure that agency resources are focused on the most important problems. This issue is addressed later, in the section on Monitoring Compliance.

Promoting Compliance within the Regulated Community

Compliance promotion is that set of activities which promote rather than coerce compliance, such as offers of assistance, information exchange, and the like. The theory that underlies most compliance monitoring and enforcement programs is that the best way to promote compliance is to enforce the law; a corollary is that ignorance is no excuse under the law. Nevertheless, compliance programs at the federal and state level offer a range of programs to disseminate information and provide technical assistance to the regulated community. While it is broadly held that the threat of enforcement is the best motivation for regulatees to avail themselves of these sources of information and assistance, state and federal officials undertake these compliance promotion activities to build a complying majority, and tap the broadest range of motivations to comply. One research issue that emerges is the efficiency of dollars spent promoting compliance versus enforcing requirements, and the proper balance between the two. In practice, compliance promotion activities have been the least well funded and the most expendable activity in enforcement programs, although some would argue that each time an inspector visits a facility it is and should be used as an opportunity to inform, offer assistance, and convey credibility to the regulatory scheme.[5] In recent years, however, with regulatory activities reaching ever smaller and more numerous sources, providing information to the regulated community (i.e. on the requirements for compliance, on why the requirements are important, on what is required to comply, and the consequences of noncompliance) is viewed as essential by federal and state regulators. A notable exception reflecting a trend in the opposite direction is the fact that until quite recently compliance promotion activities were the primary response to municipalities for safe drinking water and municipal treatment–plant operating violations. The low levels of enforcement against these sources was ineffective and EPA has shifted its emphasis to introduce more vigorous enforcement.[6] In the case of safe drinking water, Congress has also had a hand in this transition by requiring, in the recent Amendments, enforcement for all violations, a goal which both EPA and states will have difficulty fulfilling.

Another compliance promotion issue, and perhaps the most fundamental, concerns the form and nature of regulations and permits and how "enforceable" they are. Concerns for compliance must begin with the design of a requirement. Our economic analysis techniques need to take more into account the institutional costs of realizing the benefits of regulation through enforcement and the likelihood of source compliance given the regulatory design. These implications have not been given full weight in assessing its economic efficiency or effectiveness. Several factors are pertinent.

Clarity
Clear, simple requirements tailored to a source are most amenable to compliance by the source, monitoring by governmental officials, and enforcement. Tradeoffs must often be made between the simplicity of a regulatory scheme and the efficiency of that scheme.

Stringency
One tradeoff that is often made in designing requirements is between the stringency of a requirement and long–term reliability of the control approaches upon which the requirement is based. For example, 80 per cent control may be 99 per cent reliable whereas 95 per cent control may be 80 per cent reliable. Given an understandable reluctance by industry to invest in new and unproven technology, from an enforcement point of view it makes sense to favor the more reliable option and rely upon accepted industry practice. Nevertheless, many of our statutes seek the best available control or force technology and enhanced reliability in use. This is not to say that the technology–forcing strategy is necessarily less efficient or effective in the long run, particularly where market failures are inhibiting desired change, but rather that high rates of compliance will take a longer time to achieve and that projected costs and benefits should take this need for greater enforcement into account.

Form of regulation
Individualized permit or other requirements versus general rules of applicability. Rules of general applicability in theory can be easier to communicate to the regulated community, can be easier for inspectors to master, and can offer more standardized enforcement responses. However, individually tailored requirements make the facilities or sources far more aware of requirements and the permit specifically interprets how they apply. Therefore, although more complicated to monitor, and more costly administratively, tailored permits can lead to higher levels of voluntary compliance.

Type of standard. Regulatory requirements generally fall into one of several groups: ambient standards, mass rate or output standards, technology standards, work practice standards, and information requirements. Ambient standards, concentrations most related to health and welfare benefits, must be translated to enforceable requirements that pertain to an individual source. This can be accomplished through technology or performance requirements. Technology requirements are far simpler to enforce and understand from a compliance standpoint; however, they are economically inefficient since they do not allow more cost–effective substitutions. Performance standards, while more economically efficient, are enforceable only to the extent that the technology exists to monitor performance reliably.

Regulatory scheme
Environmental requirements can be developed along three somewhat interrelated models.

Liability. Many environmental laws and requirements start from the basic rights of individuals not to be subject to harm to their person or property from the actions of others. Liability systems establish norms of behavior over time as legal action is pursued against those who have caused harm. The difficulty with liability–based systems is that the social norms of behavior are defined after the harmful act is taken, so those taking action receive little advance notice, and they place little emphasis on prevention unless the magnitude of potential liabilities and likelihood that action will be brought begin to drive people to avoid them. These systems require competent advocates for those who are harmed, with adequate resources to pursue legal action. Recent Securities and Exchange Commission requirements for disclosure of even potentially material environmental liabilities and public reporting requirements for toxic releases greatly enhance the liability approach. Enforcement of these requirements is critical to their success in leveraging liability to achieve reductions in environmental risk.[7]

Command and control. Most environmental requirements, as described in this paper, can be characterized as command and control, that is, the government prescribes desired behavior and proscribes undesirable behavior. This provides more certainty as to what behaviors, i.e. processes, pollution control, and practices, are required to do from both the government's perspective and those who are subject to requirements. The disadvantage of command and control approaches is that they sometimes impose solutions which may not be the most economical within a community or within a facility's operation to gain an equivalent result. They also set limits within which desirable behavior is promoted and generally do not encourage facilities to do more than is minimally required to comply with requirements.

Market–based approaches. These approaches often build upon and supplement command and control approaches by introducing market forces to encourage greater pollution prevention and more economical solutions to environmental problems. These approaches include:

* Fee systems which tax emissions, effluent and other environmental releases, or tradeable permits to induce sources to reduce emissions to save money;
* Tradeable permits which allow companies to trade allowable emission rights under existing permits to other companies. By reducing emissions or releases below levels required by existing permits, the facility can create marketable rights and economic value. Such systems require clear rights that are tradeable, and equivalent environmental impact after trading occurs.
* Offset or Bubble approaches which allow a facility to seek a form of variance or adjustments from specific requirements within the same process and facility if the adjustments would lead to the same environmental result. It is called a bubble because the regulators essentially place a bubble around the facility and offer the adjustments if the same results would occur "within the bubble".

Market–based systems still require enforcement if they are to be effective. Potential buyers and sellers of emission rights must be assured that they have an accurate accounting of the rights they are purchasing. Fee systems must enforce the basis for the calculated fee and collection of the fee. Offset or bubble approaches still require initial definition of requirements and enforceable adjustments known to and possibly approved by regulators. Often market–based approaches require inspectors to review more records, e.g. of transactions and adjustments to permit limits, in preparation for and during inspections. They also require accurate means for sources to monitor and assess levels of environmental releases.

Monitoring Compliance

Compliance monitoring encompasses all those activities undertaken by the regulated community or government officials to collect information on and assess the compliance status of regulated sources of environmental pollution. Several purposes underlie compliance monitoring strategies used by environmental regulators. The first is that self–awareness and self–monitoring will lead generators of pollution to take essential preventative and corrective action to maintain compliance. The second is that a credible likelihood of detection by government regulators is an essential prerequisite to deterrence. Two other purposes served by compliance monitoring are: to provide the evidence needed to support enforcement actions for identified violations, and to provide reliable statistics on the progress in implementing environmental requirements.

Source self–monitoring and inspections are the most important approaches to monitoring compliance. Ambient monitoring and aerial surveillance are used, but rarely. In theory, compliance monitoring should be a statistically valid indicator of compliance; the methods should be the same as those on which the standard was based; and the methods should be reliable and cost–effective.

In practice, source self–monitoring is not as widespread as regulators would like. First, the development of cost–effective monitoring devices has lagged behind regulatory developments. Source monitoring is used extensively in the water NPDES program for all dischargers and for groundwater protection from hazardous– waste disposal and storage tanks, but to a far lesser extent in the air program, where continuous emission monitors are expensive and, until recently, were not reliable. At the federal level, the Paperwork Reduction Act seeks to limit the information requests of industry and states. Sometimes compliance monitoring requirements and other related reports are sacrificed at the expense of information needed to develop sound regulatory proposals.

Increasingly, some US laws are introducing self–certification of compliance by senior industry officials as an adjunct to self–monitoring and reporting. The value of self–certification lies in the personal liability of senior management for false reporting which enhances the attention it gains. Such requirements need to be backed up by clear guidance and procedures which define the basis for the self–certification. Self–certification of compliance also may be designed to include reports of violations and efforts to correct them. Most significantly, no agency can afford to conduct unlimited inspections. The challenge is therefore one of priorities and the allocation of scarce inspector resources.

To date, priority schemes for inspections have been unsophisticated. They have tended to focus on one element of the program, the need for breadth of coverage, rather than on targeting inspections on those sources and violation types most likely to yield the greatest benefit from enforcement action. Environmental inspection programs for air and water have typically called for inspections of the major sources, generally defined by size and potential environmental impact, at least once per year, biennially for minor sources. In the hazardous–waste program the past focus has been on land disposal facilities.

Times are changing, however. States and many EPA Regions have argued successfully that, given limited resources, meeting national requirements for minimum inspection frequency has prevented them from visiting individual sources that are more likely to be having problems or which locally pose a greater risk. Recently, the programs have been providing more flexibility in the tailoring of inspection strategies to local needs. Also the introduction by EPA later this year of the Integrated Data for Enforcement Analysis (IDEA) capability with its on–line instantaneous access to compliance profiles for virtually all environmental programs should revolutionize inspection and enforcement targeting schemes (Bryan, 1991b). Some applied statistical techniques have also been used to assess how inspection resources can be used more efficiently and effectively. In response to a GAO report and inquiries from Congress, the air program has been developing some alternative models for directing inspections (Johnson, 1987).

A study by Duke and Northwestern University economists (Magat and Viscusi, 1987) may serve to reinforce the importance of inspection targeting to enforcement. Correlating federal and state inspections with reductions in effluent in 75 pulp and paper plants over several years, they identified a statistically significant reduction in effluent after a 4–6 month lag, with little recidivism, following inspections during the period 1977–85. In the view of this author, further analysis of this data would be desirable, especially on the effects of different types of inspection, the effect of subsequent enforcement action, and the effects of alternative internal management approaches/corporate culture on source compliance behavior. None of the analysis done to date has provided a sense of the value of compliance–monitoring information.

Government officials are constrained from imposing an undue burden on the regulated community through required monitoring of their ongoing compliance. The questions that must be addressed are: what is information worth, and who should pay for it? While economic theory would seem to support a source paying for compliance monitoring as the operating cost of doing business and the cost of running the pollution control devices, regulators need better ways to build costs and benefits into the justifications for and contents of proposed requirements.

What are less easy to address from the perspective of environmental economics are the costs and benefits of multi–media or cross–program versus single program inspections. The recent emphasis on pollution prevention and a growing concern for the regulation of the whole process stream are changing the perceived benefits of multi–media inspections. Given the costs of multi–media inspections (e.g. possible reduced deterrence from fewer site visits, increased training needs for inspectors and increased demands on inspection planning, including potential delays on–site if a single plant manager must provide inspector access to processes and records in many media), under what circumstances does it make sense for enforcers to inspect interrelated processes to ensure the most efficient outcome from the regulatory scheme and from enforcement actions?

Given that work practices are often related to general management, can any economic indicators be developed that not only correlate well with a plant's environmental performance, but also suggest where such approaches might be most beneficial? Finally, an issue related to behavior theory and compliance monitoring is whether source self–monitoring should be reported on an exceptions basis or whether complete reporting of all data should be routinely required.

Responding to Violations: Timely and Appropriate Enforcement Response

The concept that enforcement response should be timely and appropriate to the violation is now a key component of current enforcement theory and practice. Swift and sure response is one of the three elements that traditional deterrence theory would deem essential to success. The concept was introduced operationally at the federal and state levels in 1984 through the Policy Framework for State/EPA Enforcement Agreements and program–specific implementing guidance.[8] The Policy Framework was the product of a steering committee of state and federal officials from all EPA programs charged with defining expectations, roles, and relationships for an effective national enforcement program.

The Policy Framework defines timeliness as specific points in time by which there should be an initial response to a violation, formal enforcement action (i.e. when informal means are not effective in returning the violator to compliance after a specified period of time), and more broadly as timely follow through and escalation in the event of the violator failing to comply, until full physical compliance has been achieved.

The Policy Framework also defines "appropriate" enforcement response as having three elements. First, there is the appropriate level of formality of enforcement response. An initial violation can be addressed through a full range of informal and formal enforcement tools such as phone calls, site visits, warning letters, notices of violation, formal administrative complaint and/or proposed law suit. Any and all approaches that the government official believes will be most cost–effective are acceptable unless and until compliance problems extend beyond a specified period of time and have not been resolved, i.e. at a certain point in time the response should be formal.

The Policy Framework defines formal action as a law suit or formal administrative response, i.e. it is independently enforceable, defines the violation, defines the required response and a date certain for achieving full physical compliance. In particular, court–imposed action may be essential where a violator's schedule to comply exceeds a statutory deadline.

The second and third elements of an "appropriate" enforcement response suggest that it should correct the violation and should include a penalty or other sanction as appropriate to create the necessary deterrence against future violations by that source or other sources.

The Policy Framework sets a priority on first meeting timely and appropriate enforcement response for Significant Non–Compliers. Recognizing that requiring timely and formal enforcement action for all violators would overburden limited resources, the Policy Framework only encourages federal and state officials to meet it for non–SNC violations. Furthermore, the concept is used to establish appropriate state and federal roles in delegated or approved states. Under most statutes EPA retains parallel enforcement authority following delegation or approval of a state program. According to the Policy Framework, if the state is pursuing timely and appropriate enforcement response, EPA will generally defer to the state (unless it requests EPA action or there is a national legal or program precedent). However, once the time frames are passed, EPA will take action if, after discussions with the state, it determines that the state is not moving expeditiously.

The timely and appropriate enforcement response system is built on the willingness of government officials to follow through on less–costly enforcement responses and to escalate responses in a timely manner that gives weight and force to lesser responses. Each higher–order enforcement response carries with it a multiplier effect in its deterrent value. Initially, to build credibility, officials may be forced to utilize more costly formal administrative or judicial action. When a track record is established, the expectation is that in most instances a simple notice will send violators scrambling to resolve quickly a compliance problem or negotiate its resolution cooperatively.

How has this policy worked in practice? At the time of writing,

EPA reports have been prepared annually on timeliness and appropriateness of state and federal enforcement response for fiscal years (FY) 1986–90 (Bryan, 1991a). Since the introduction of the policy, states have increased significantly their use of formal enforcement and the use of penalties in enforcement actions. For example, in the air program in the first year, states increased their use of penalties in enforcement actions from 69 per cent to 92 per cent and maintained a level of about 90 per cent with a drop this past year to 73 per cent. In the hazardous waste program, states went from 33 per cent of enforcement actions with penalties to 79 per cent In the water permit program it has remained at about 73 per cent.

The studies have found that the concept of enforcement being "timely and appropriate" is widely accepted as an important measure of the effectiveness of the enforcement effort, but that in many cases both EPA and the states are still wide of the mark in meeting their goals. The RCRA target for formal enforcement response was 135 days for high priority violations, the NPDES goal is within two quarters of the SNC violation, and the air program is only 120 days.

Recognizing that differences among these programs exist in the way they define the target universe of Significant Non–Compliers, the time frames the programs established as goals, and the enforcement tools available, the water permit program, with the longer time frames, was able to increase steadily its ability to meet its timely and appropriate criteria from 75 per cent in FY 1986 to 85 per cent in FY 1990. Public drinking water system enforcement increased timeliness from FY 1987 to 1990 from 38 per cent to 61 per cent The hazardous–waste program was able to increase its record in meeting its timeliness goals from 29 per cent in FY 1986 to 39 per cent in 1989, the states showing the best performance increasing from 25 per cent in FY 1986 to 45 per cent in FY 1990. The air enforcement's timeliness goal, representing the shortest time frame, has hovered around 25 per cent from the beginning, reflecting in part some fundamental problems in enforcement authorities, enforceability of requirements, a languishing of enforcement awaiting revisions to the Clean Air Act and the promise of new administrative enforcement authorities to support more timely response than sole reliance on court suits.

Some of the generic reasons for failing to take timely or

appropriate enforcement response include inadequate resources, cumbersome enforcement procedures — particularly a lack of simple administrative penalty authorities — and/or a reluctance to pursue formal enforcement action.

At this juncture, the need for research on what should constitute timely and appropriate enforcement response is acute. First, we do not have a good feel for the impact or cost–effectiveness of the various forms of enforcement response. This analysis is complicated because the cost–effectiveness of less expensive responses is dependent on the use of more costly and onerous responses. In a dynamic system, how much escalation to the more costly forms of enforcement such as law suits or administrative orders do we have to pursue to bolster less–costly responses?

Second, the value of timeliness of response should be assessed against the severity of sanction. As our legal systems seek to balance individual rights against the government's need for action, there is a natural tradeoff between sanction and timeliness. Some interesting applications of decision theory and economic models have been used in Superfund settlement cases. These cases involve huge sums of money. The models address whether the government should continue to negotiate, sue, or settle, given the strength of the case, its value and needed deterrence (Guerci, 1987).

Further, our legal systems for formal response are complex, in part to safeguard personal property and freedoms from unwarranted government intrusion. Nevertheless, there is room for reform. How much is it worth to society to reduce and streamline these procedures, and at what cost to society in terms of guarantees of certain rights? How much should we be willing to invest in more administrative law judges and the like to speed the processing of appeals on administrative complaints and thereby to speed the environmental results? These questions are all amenable to economic analysis.

Imposing Civil Penalties and Other Sanctions

Civil penalties and other sanctions such as criminal conviction, shut–down of operations, sewer bans, etc., play an important role in enforcement actions. The imposition of a sanction is a critical third element in deterrence theory. In the past, many enforcement actions merely set forth tailored compliance agreements detailing remedies and schedules for correcting the violation. However, it is now generally recognized that if the polluter expects no consequence from noncompliance (except having to meet with government officials to agree to do what was required in the first place), he has little incentive to undertake any costs of compliance before getting caught. This has proven to be true even when it is broadly understood that clean–up costs will increase substantially if violations are not corrected early and where actual cost savings from compliance activities has been realized.

The Policy Framework for State/EPA Enforcement Agreements addresses three aspects of current operating theory related to civil penalties and other sanctions. First, as noted above, each environmental program is to identify where a penalty or sanction is essential for an enforcement response to be effective, recognizing that penalties cannot easily be sought in each and every case. In such cases, if a state enforcement action contains no penalty or sanction, EPA will seek to pursue its own penalty case to fulfill this need for consistency and broad deterrence on a national basis. The complexity of our enforcement procedures are proportionate to the potential severity of the sanction. Judicious application of penalties is sought not only because of the cost (in time and resources) of seeking penalties, but also due to the fact that penalties are more hotly disputed by violators than either the fact of the violation or needed remedies. It should be noted that requiring sanctions in all cases of a certain type emphasizes general rather than specific deterrence. In some instances the equities of an individual case could argue against a penalty. Current policy would identify certain violations where sanctions are a must, placing more emphasis on looking beyond the good–faith efforts of an individual violator in order to set an example and create an incentive for others to do all they can to comply and avoid a penalty.

The second issue addressed in the Policy Framework is the level of a civil penalty. Economic theory has been most directly used in enforcement in this area. According to the theory embodied in the 1977 Clean Air Act Amendments' Section 120 Administrative Penalty authority and in EPA penalty policies, the recovery of the economic benefit of noncompliance is essential to deter would–be violators from seeking economic gain by deferring the required expenditures on environmental pollution controls. The theory has much appeal. EPA first adopted it formally as a minimum desired level of penalty in 1984 (US Environmental Protection Agency, 1984a). (Note that the penalty policies not only call for recovery of the economic benefit of noncompliance, but also add a gravity component reflecting the severity of the violation, its potential harm, the compliance history of the violator, etc.) Several states have also adopted penalty policies which articulate this philosophy (Environmental Law Institute, 1986). However, many states do not share the view that it is necessary to recover the economic benefit of noncompliance to deter violations. Indeed most states simply invoke the maximum statutorily permissible penalty level and proceed to negotiate from there, sometimes, but not always, based upon penalty policies that are graduated to reflect the severity of the violation and compliance history of the violator. According to EPA policy, state enforcement actions should attempt to recover economic benefit at a minimum, but this is not now required. EPA will seek to take its own enforcement action to recover additional penalties if a state penalty is grossly deficient under the circumstances. The criteria for this determination include whether the penalty bears any reasonable relationship to the seriousness of the violation, and/or economic benefit gained by the violator.

The issue of penalty or sanction is perhaps the most sensitive issue in the state/federal enforcement relationship. If compliance can be achieved more expeditiously by a violator who is willing to agree to a schedule and remedial actions, but who will dispute proposed penalties or sanctions, many states would prefer to forgo penalties or to agree to a lesser penalty amount than would EPA. This ignores questions of equity, fairness and effectiveness in the context of general deterrence created by a penalty.

Third, the Policy Framework explicitly recognizes that non–monetary sanctions can have a more powerful deterrent effect than monetary penalties, and that those will be acceptable substitutes. The Policy calls for national guidance as to what alternative sanctions would be acceptable for this purpose. This includes sewer bans, pipeline severance, permit revocation, and incarceration, all of which impose some economic cost. In relating theory to practice, addressing first the issue of whether a penalty or other sanction is sought, EPA seeks a sanction or penalty in a high percentage of its formal enforcement responses where this authority exists (over 90%), and the percentage has been increasing.

In the municipal compliance arena for water discharge requirements, states and EPA joined forces to implement a National Municipal Enforcement Policy which stressed enforcement and stiff fines regardless of the availability of construction grant subsidies for building municipal treatment plants. This Policy turned around years of reluctance on the part of both federal and state officials to seek stiff penalties against municipalities. Many states and EPA pursued tough enforcement and high penalties under this Policy and achieved significant increases in compliance, and increased willingness on the part of municipalities to settle cases.[9] Nevertheless, a legitimate question remains whether municipal penalties have an effect comparable to the deterrent effect of penalties imposed on industry given the nature of municipal finance. Several research questions remain to be answered: Where do monetary penalties make a difference? How is that difference in behavior manifest? Would other sanctions be more effective?

The second area of actual practice involves EPA's success in recovering the economic benefit of noncompliance as advocated by theory. Reported penalty levels in years prior to the 1984 EPA Penalty Policy, which strengthened the provisions setting recovery of economic benefit as a floor (where the concept is applicable), made recovery of economic benefit suspect. However, following the Policy, improvements in the models used to calculated economic benefit and national reporting of results have corrected the situation, In the 1985 Fiscal Year alone, EPA imposed one third of all penalties of its entire 10–year history and penalty levels were more like what one would expect from the economic models. Since then, penalty levels have increased geometrically, with Fiscal Year 1990 representing a 74 per cent increase over FY 1989.[10] A recent GAO study confirmed documentation of recovery of economic benefit by EPA in 88 per cent of judicial cases, but was unable to find sufficient documentation in administrative cases or other judicial cases to pass judgment (US General Accounting Office, forthcoming). Realistically, some of the huge sums that emerge from the very

successful EPA model used to compute economic benefit cannot be
sustained in all settlement negotiations, although the courts have
upheld EPA policies and citizen groups have used it very effectively
in some significant court cases.[11] While the policy itself seems to
have widespread support, the calculation of economic benefit
continues to be disputed by violators, most recently with a challenge
to the manner in which the discount rate is calculated. This continues
to be fertile ground for financial analysts and economic theorists.

Despite the likely failure fully to recover the economic benefit of
noncompliance until FY 1985, air and water programs had
"reportedly" achieved fairly high rates of compliance (Wasserman,
1984). The evidence suggests that something else is driving
compliance besides a simple economic decision. (Note that deliberate
economic decisions not to comply are subject to criminal prosecution
as willful noncompliance.) This is particularly significant given that
the expected cost according to the economic equation (the probability
of a penalty multiplied by the expected penalty amount) can be quite
small due to what is often a low likelihood of discovering a violation.
What is not clear, however, is what other factors are motivating the
behavior of noncompliers and how they can be addressed.

Unfortunately, the systematic use of sanctions beyond those
associated with monetary penalties has not yet been subjected to
rigorous empirical analysis. The author would postulate that among
other factors, substantial liability imposed by Superfund for past
waste disposal practices that were otherwise legal at the time, and the
increased application of criminal sanctions to corporate officials
described below, are at least two powerful forces at work influencing
compliance decisions by firms.

Criminal sanctions are viewed by many as the most effective
deterrent in the environmental enforcement arsenal, particularly by
those who favor the behavioral models of compliance. Indeed,
environmental crimes have gained substantial public support as
compared to other crimes.[12] Criminal sanctions are increasingly
being sought by federal EPA, the Department of Justice and the
Federal Bureau of Investigations and in a growing number of state
programs. It is, however, generally valid only for intentional
circumventing of the law, for negligence under the Clean Water Act,
and in all instances of unpermitted dumping into our waterways under

the Safe Rivers and Harbors Act. A growing number of cases where jail terms have been meted out (223 years of incarceration, before suspension of sentence, in the past four years alone) have begun to change some corporate management ethics (Strock, 1990c). Pronounced policy on compliance with environmental laws and general compliance programs is no defense (nor a mitigating factor for sentencing purposes) for corporate officials charged with the criminal wrongdoing of their employees. Courts will only consider environmental programs with strong oversight and follow–through for the specific activities in question. This seems to be having a significant effect on prevention of violations through internal compliance systems and employee compliance incentives within a firm.

Further, EPA is seeking to tap these internal corporate incentives by introducing environmental audit provisions into consent decree negotiations in cases where a clear pattern of environmental management problems or a pattern of a given type of violation within a company has become apparent,[13] and it is a required consideration in sentencing by judges under the new Sentencing Guidelines. (US Sentencing Commision, 1991). This creative sanction is also supported by the behavior–theory schools which would advocate establishing, to the extent possible, self–policing and internal control systems within a company, tied to environmental compliance. This policy has been supplemented by a campaign by EPA to illustrate by case example the benefits to industry of sound environmental management and periodic environmental auditing.

EPA is also making increasing use of its Contractor Listing authority. A listed company/facility is deprived of the right to be awarded federal government contracts as long as it is on the list. This is mandatory for successful criminal cases under the Clean Air and Clean Water Acts and discretionary applications for facilities with continuing violations under these statutes. The sanction has offered significant economic leverage in several difficult compliance cases. In addition, EPA is placing increasing emphasis on the use of enforcement settlements to leverage more widespread compliance, e.g. publicity surrounding its enforcement actions, and to achieve broader environmental results, e.g. pollution–prevention agreements or supplemental environmental projects designed to mitigate damages or control pollution more than is required.[14]

Clarifying the State/Federal Relationship

Enforcement must be viewed as firm, effective, and fair on a national basis. In 1984 EPA and the states drew up a Policy Framework for implementing State/EPA Enforcement Agreements which set forth clear roles and responsibilities in enforcement. The Policy clarifies the expectations for good performance in implementing a strong enforcement effort, and establishes protocols for advance notification and consultation on all inspection and enforcement matters. In addition, it establishes the importance of consistent national reporting of key indicators to assess how effectively the national compliance and enforcement program is being carried out.

A key principle was the introduction of timely and appropriate enforcement response criteria and the definition of what is required in the form of a sanction. If a state is not getting what it should through its enforcement program, EPA will. The ideal of presenting a unified face to the regulated community, and consistency in response has been widely regarded by both industry and state and federal officials alike as essential steps toward a more effective enforcement program.

Recent evaluations show that these Agreements have had a positive impact despite philosophical differences between EPA and some states which will have to be worked out over time. Any assessment of improved efficiencies and effectiveness in enforcement response must take into account the role of state and local governments and whether it is efficient or explainable given different roles and responsibilities, that EPA is responsible for about 30 per cent of formal enforcement actions nationally, but handles less than 10–30 per cent of inspections under the delegatable/approvable programs.

Evaluating Performance and Accountability

Formal reporting and accountability systems for all environmental enforcement programs set forth five key indicators of performance: (i) the rate of compliance, (ii) the progress in addressing Significant Non–Compliers and returning them to compliance, (iii) the number of inspections (or number or percentage of facilities inspected), (iv) the number of administrative actions taken, and (v) the number of civil and criminal judicial enforcement actions taken. In addition to these indicators, efforts are made each year to assess whether enforcement by both federal EPA and states has been timely and appropriate, and trends in federal penalty practices. Furthermore, EPA internally assesses the extent of compliance with consent decrees and any follow–up action taken.

Increasing attention has been paid to issues such as penalty collection and state penalty assessment practices or other sanctions, but at the time of writing no systematic data have been collected. Further, Congressional, federal and state officials are continuing to seek meaningful environmental measures of success. Some initial attempts were made to attribute environmental results to enforcement actions, but it is difficult since a large portion of the benefits of a single enforcement action reside in the deterrence or multiplier effect it has on widespread compliance, not just the direct environmental benefits.[15]

The traditional economic literature would have us examine only the likelihood of having a violation detected and the amount of penalties imposed in reviewing the performance of our enforcement programs. The author would like to see more realistic measures of program effectiveness developed and applied.

THE CHALLENGE TO ENVIRONMENTAL ECONOMISTS

In conclusion, compliance with and enforcement of our environmental laws should be a central issue for environmental economists, but the economics of enforcement has received little attention to date. The economic literature has made a great contribution to the issue of monetary penalties, with the theory that enforcement programs should recover the economic benefit of noncompliance. The theory is widely regarded as a basic tenet of enforcement programs at the federal and state level. Nevertheless, theory does not always equal practice. While it is worthwhile to base our penalty assessment practices upon this theory, we must recognize that compliance motivation and the realities of an enforcement program are far more complex than this simple theory adequately addresses.

The challenge to environmental economists is to provide analysis of empirical data on compliance and to develop practical decision tools and techniques that can be used by state and federal officials to make this increasingly difficult task more cost–effective and efficient from the design of regulations, through compliance monitoring and promotion strategies to enforcement response and accompanying sanctions. The issues are well defined; the answers are not.

Environmental economists will face several difficulties in meeting this challenge. The first is the fact that data have not been conveniently collected in one data base, nor is it systematically compiled over time. This should change significantly over the next year as the IDEA capability becomes publicly available. Enhanced use of enforcement data systems will force improvements in data quality as bad or missing data in these systems become impediments to its practical use. Much has changed in the world of data management over the past five years. The first two reports on Federal Civil Penalty Practices were painstaking for the author's staff who labored through hundreds of manual calculations in developing data sets on penalty trends and statistics. This information is now computerized. Soon, data on facility–specific inspection activities, self–monitoring reports, administrative and judicial enforcement actions will be accessible through one user–friendly system. In the future, environmental impact data which might be correlated to specific facility compliance may also be available.

The second, and perhaps greater, difficulty is the fact that compliance results cannot be explained by economic theory alone. The challenge here is to draw from other disciplines and empirical studies of decision–making within the regulated community to derive a more complete understanding of compliance behavior.

It is surprising that environmental economic research and applications in enforcement and compliance monitoring have been limited to date, given the potential payoffs in enforcement and compliance for learning something more about the economic efficiency of our environmental regulations and standards. What information is needed by environmental regulators or by the regulated community on compliance and enforcement that environmental economists can deliver? The following list of issues is proposed for further research:

Compliance motivation

What motivates compliance? under what circumstances? What is the effect of the form of the requirement i.e. performance, technology or work practice standard, permit or general regulation? the cost and availability of technology?

What is the effect of corporate culture and management systems design on compliance? What is the effect on environmental compliance of the competitive environment/of reputation, in different economic markets?

Are firms which are financially unsound less likely to comply? What are the implications for targeting of enforcement given the likely difficulties in collecting large penalties from marginal firms which may not be able to pay?

Compliance practices

What are the quantifiable benefits of specific environmental management practices? What are the costs to regulated entities of past, present and future noncompliance?

How can liability costs be better incorporated into internal economic decision making? What algorithms can be used by company managers (financial managers, engineers and plant managers) to factor future environmental liabilities (both compliance–related and risk–related) into internal decision-making? How can activities which have short–term costs (environmental auditing, waste minimization) be better presented to show long term benefits?

Compliance monitoring

What is the value of information on compliance in different settings given the risks to the environment and public health from a violation and its probability of occurring?

Who should pay for compliance monitoring? What are the implications for types of inspections? for required compliance self–monitoring and reporting in regulations and permits? for research and development on compliance monitoring techniques?

How frequently and what kind of inspection should be undertaken, at what facilities, to maximize deterrence and provide accurate compliance statistics within a given budget?

Enforcement response
Given the environmental risks from noncompliance, how much should governments spend to ensure high levels of compliance? What are the multiplier effects and cost–effectiveness of individual enforcement response options, given their interdependence? in different contexts?

Sanctions
How effective are alternative sanctions in providing the necessary disincentive to non–compliance, in what settings?

Is the sanction equitable, and fair in addition to being effective?

What are the effects on competition and markets of uneven enforcement? How consistent does national enforcement need to be?

What levels of penalty should be imposed for reporting and record–keeping violations? (The economic theory of recovering the costs of noncompliance does not work well here.)

Do high penalties and enforcement actions targeted at a few influential actors within the regulated community have a greater deterrent impact than lesser penalties imposed on a larger percentage of violators? How does either approach compare in terms of equity, cost–effectiveness, etc.?

Tax policies, technical assistance and subsidies
What are the effects of tax policies and capital markets on

compliance? What are the compliance implications of alternative policies?

NOTES

1. See Charlton (1985), Scholtz (1984), Kagan and Scholtz (1984), D. T. Miller (1985), Meidinger, Boyer, and Thomas (1987), and Edwards and Kuusinen (1989).
2. The United States Environmental Protection Agency has been funding several years of research at Tufts University on corporate culture and environmental protection. Reports are not available at the time of writing.
3. See US Environmental Protection Agency (1984b), Wasserman (1984), and Wasserman (1990).
4. US Environmental Protection Agency (1990a), and US Environmental Protection Agency (1991a).
5. In fact, EPA's hazardous–waste program and the Blackstone Project being undertaken by the State of Massachusetts are experimenting with promotion of pollution prevention through their inspectors. See Dillard and Manik (1990) and Gigliello (1990).
6. See 49 Federal Register 3832 (January 30, 1984), and Strock (1990c).
7. Item 303 of Regulations S–K, Management's Discussion and Analysis of Financial Condition and Results of Operations (MD&A release), Securities Act Release No. 22427 (May 18, 1989); 54 Federal Register 22427 (May 24, 1989).
8. Barnes (1986) and Wasserman (1987).
9. Infra, note 6
10. Ludwiszewski (forthcoming), Strock (1990a), Reich (1989) and Adams (1988).
11. *U.S.* v. *Roll Coaster* Cause No. IP-89-828C (S.D. Ind. March 22, 1991) as example federal case.
    SPIRG v. *Hercules* 29 ERC 1417 (D.N.J. 1989). *SPIRG* v. *AT&T Bell Laboratories* Civil No. 84-1087 (D.N.J. 1985). *Chesapeake Bay Foundation* v. *Gwaltney of Smithfield, Ltd*, 611 F. Supp. 1542 (E.D. Va 1985), Aff'd 791 F. 2d 304 (4th Cir. 1986) Cert. on unrelated issue, S.Ct. No. 86-473. The Supreme Court held that the penalty could not cover past violations, which did not reject economic benefit but significantly reduced the calculated amount in this case. See 890 F2nd 690 (4th Cir 1989).
12. See US Department of Justice (1984), in which 60,000 people were asked in a public opinion poll to rank the severity of particular crimes. Environmental crimes ranked seventh after murder but ahead of heroin smuggling and skyjacking.
13. 51 Federal Register 25004 (July 9, 1986). See also Adams (1986), Wasserman (1989), Arthur D. Little, Inc. (1983, 1984, 1985) and US Environmental Protection Agency (1986).
14. Strock (1991b, 1991c) and US Environmental Protection Agency (forthcoming).
15. See the case studies in Strock (1990c).

3. Defining Efficient Sanctions

Kathleen Segerson & Tom Tietenberg[1]

INTRODUCTION

The enforcement of environmental laws has undergone some rather dramatic changes over the last decade. Civil and criminal monetary penalties have been imposed more frequently on violators and the size of the penalties has increased.[2] Individuals, both corporate employees and officers, have become more common targets for penalties.[3] Finally incarceration has not only become a more commonly imposed sanction,[4] but the resulting jail sentences are longer.[5] Is this a case of progressive judicial evolution where a new enforcement structure has begun to fill an important, heretofore neglected, niche? Or is it a case of zealous enforcers going too far, producing a public appearance of effective enforcement that masks serious inefficiencies?[6]

The traditional economics literature creates a presumption that sanctions against individuals and toward criminal law are inefficient. In one of the clearest statements of this position Posner suggests that all white–collar crimes should be punished by civil monetary penalties on the organization rather than by imprisonment of individuals (unless imprisonment is necessary to coerce payment of the fine).[7] According to this view all sanctions, including jail sentences, have an equivalent monetary value. When this value is collected through a civil monetary sanction on the organization, collection costs are low and society receives a payment. Imprisonment of individuals, on the other hand, imposes high costs on society (prisons, guards, and the lost production of the prisoner, for example) and society receives no transfer comparable to the revenue from the fine. If the organization can internally sanction employees, any level of deterrence achievable by a particular jail sentence can be achieved by a fine of the appropriate magnitude on the corporation at a lower net social cost. Among the monetary sanctions civil penalties are preferred to criminal fines because they involve lower transactions costs (e.g. lower burdens of proof).

In this essay we examine this presumption against individual and criminal sanctions by inquiring into some specific aspects of the application of individual sanctions in environmental law. We argue that in certain specific circumstances that are common in the environmental context the incentives of employees and firms may diverge in ways that are not easily correctable by traditional internal, performance–based employment and compensation policies. In such a context, the presumption that corporate monetary sanctions should predominate is tempered somewhat. Individual penalties in general and jail sentences in particular do appear to have their own limited niche in environmental enforcement if efficient precautionary incentives are to be preserved.

THE INSTITUTIONAL CONTEXT

When confronted by a violation of the law involving the environment, the United States Environmental Protection Agency can respond by initiating (i) an administrative proceeding, (ii) a civil judicial proceeding and/or (iii) a criminal proceeding. These are not mutually exclusive. Civil and criminal proceedings can be pursued in parallel under the appropriate circumstances.[8] These three different enforcement strategies place different burdens on the enforcement agency and offer different remedies. Since these differences play an important role in defining optimal enforcement strategies, we shall briefly note their essential characteristics.

Administrative Proceedings

The bulk of EPA's enforcement activity is handled through administrative enforcement mechanisms.[9] Essentially the government has created a quasi–independent judicial system within the executive branch to resolve cases without going to court. This alternative is typically much cheaper for all parties than court proceedings, but it is somewhat less protective of the violator's rights and the menu of available remedies is somewhat limited.

Adjudicatory proceedings are presided over by an administrative law judge, in the case of a formal proceeding, or a hearing or presiding officer in the case of an informal proceeding. Adjudicatory proceedings can be used not only for directed relief (a command to undertake or to cease specific activities), but also to impose monetary penalties.[10] In most cases the decision of the judge or presiding officer is a recommendation to the EPA Administrator rather than a final decision. The Administrator's decision is final unless appealed.[11]

Civil Proceedings

Civil proceedings are conducted within the court system rather than within the administrative agency. Because EPA does not have authority to take cases to court, all civil (and criminal) cases must be referred to the Department of Justice for action. The Department of Justice has discretion over whether or not it chooses to take a case and has the responsibility for prosecuting any chosen case.

While the potential remedies are similar for administrative and civil proceedings (typically directed relief and/or civil penalties and restoration costs), the higher burden of court proceedings is sometimes justified by the nature of the case. Courts have more latitude in assigning punitive damages, can resolve difficult points of law and can establish precedents which lay the groundwork for future cases. Parties frequently resort to out–of–court settlements as a means of resolving the complaint without the resource burdens associated with a full airing of the issues in a courtroom.

Criminal Proceedings

Criminal proceedings share with civil proceedings the characteristic that they are conducted within the court system and that both the final decision to prosecute and the implementation of that decision rest with the Department of Justice, not EPA. Differences between civil and criminal litigation involve procedures for gathering evidence, the available remedies and the standards of proof necessary for a favorable verdict.

Gathering Evidence

In criminal cases investigators may search the person or the person's property seeking evidence of alleged criminal activity only with the consent of the person or after obtaining a warrant. A warrant will only be issued when sworn testimony demonstrates "probable cause" that a crime has been committed and that the search is necessary to obtain evidence of a crime. Though warrants are also required in civil cases, the "probable cause" standard for obtaining a search warrant in a criminal case is far more stringent than for a civil warrant.

Criminal investigators can also use the substantial subpoena powers granted to a grand jury as a means of gathering evidence. While indictments must be brought by grand juries to proceed with a felony case, grand jury indictments are not necessary to prosecute misdemeanors. As a practical matter government attorneys frequently seek grand jury indictments for misdemeanors as well, since the subpoena powers associated with that process are so broad and such a useful means of gathering evidence.[12] A witness who fails to respond to a grand jury subpeona is subject to immediate arrest and the proceedings are secret.[13] Even the alleged criminal's lawyer cannot attend. Broad subpeona powers greatly facilitate evidence–gathering by forcing informed but reluctant witnesses to talk and by allowing the government to build its case without revealing its hand to the defense until the actual criminal trial has begun.

Defining Environmental Crimes

The government does not have a free hand in deciding whether a particular violation should be pursued administratively, civilly or criminally. Not all environmental incidents involving a violation can be prosecuted as if they were criminal activity. How is the border between noncomplying behavior and criminal activity defined?

In addition to environmental activities which clearly fall under conventional criminal statutes (murder, fraud, etc.) and can therefore be prosecuted under those statutes, environmental statutes have singled out two distinct types of activities as criminal: (i) falsification of records, monitoring information, or any of the other documentary evidence upon which effective regulation depends, and (ii) violations which fulfill the *scienter* requirement.

Self–monitoring is the lynchpin of much regulatory activity. The only way regulators can effectively keep track of compliance is by scrutinizing reports submitted by the permittees. Because violations recorded in the reports can trigger expensive enforcement actions, violators always face a temptation to falsify the reports. Improper documentation leads to ineffective enforcement. Recognizing the pivotal importance of reliable self–monitoring, Congress imposed criminal liability for falsifying records.[14]

Scienter is Latin for knowledge. According to the *scienter* requirement the violator must have "knowingly" violated the law. Some evidence of conscious wrongdoing or criminal intent must be present. Recently Congress added "knowing endangerment" as a separate category of *scienter* which would call forth the most severe criminal penalties. The boundary between a "knowing" and a "knowing endangerment" violation is usually crossed by placing human life or limb in jeopardy.[15]

Standards of Proof

One main differentiating characteristic of criminal enforcement involves the very high standards of proof that must be met by the prosecutor to secure a conviction. In the American system defendants are presumed innocent until proven guilty and the procedural cards are stacked as to ensure this outcome.

"Beyond a reasonable doubt", the most stringent standard, is required in criminal cases. While this standard does not require the prosecutor to eliminate all doubt, for any lingering doubt to be considered "reasonable" the trier of fact must find support for it in the facts of the case as presented.

Remedies

Another distinguishing characteristic of criminal enforcement involves the menu of remedies available to the successful prosecutor. In addition to financial penalties, which are available under both civil and administrative proceedings, jail sentences are only available in a criminal proceeding. These jail sentences can be (and have been) handed out to corporate executives for environmental crimes even if they were not personally involved in the activity producing the damage.[16]

While many of the monetary payments levied under civil proceedings can be deducted from the corporation's income tax or covered by insurance, neither civil nor criminal fines receive this favorable treatment.[17] Typical payments that could be deducted from taxes or covered by insurance include clean–up or restoration costs, and damage payments to victims.

THE DESIGN OF EFFICIENT FINES[18]

We believe that the key to understanding why a range of penalties is necessary in environmental law lies in specifying the relationship between the upper–echelon corporate managers, those most closely accountable to the stockholders, and the employees responsible for the day–to–day management of environmental risk. As noted by others (e.g. Sykes, 1981, 1984; Kornhauser, 1982; Newman and Wright, 1990), this relationship affects the impacts of alternative fine schedules since payments imposed on one party can potentially be "passed on" to the other party. For example, if wages can be varied with the number or size of accidents that occur, then firms facing large penalties for large damages can pass those penalties along through reductions in the employee's wage. Likewise, employees facing large individual penalties can demand higher wages as compensation for the services they provide the firm. The efficient design of fines in this context then hinges on the answers to the following questions: (i) what are the implications of this pass–through for the incentive affects of alternative fine structures? (ii) when is such pass–through unlikely to occur? and (iii) how do various limitations on pass–through affect the efficiency of alternative fine structures?

In order to identify a fine structure that yields efficient incentives, it is first necessary to define what is meant by efficient incentives. In economic terms, "efficiency" requires the maximization of net social benefits from a given activity, here the operation of the firm. Net social benefits entail two components. The first is the net benefit (benefit minus production cost) from consumption of the output that the firm produces. The second is the expected external environmental damage from the operation of the firm. Net social benefits then equal the net benefit from consumption minus the expected environmental cost.[19]

If the actions of both the firm and the worker can affect damages, then to ensure efficiency both must be chosen to maximize net social benefits. Suppose the firm's decisions are limited to the size of the operation of the firm, with a larger firm creating a greater potential for environmental damages. The worker, on the other hand, determines the level of care (or precaution) with which the firm's day–to–day operations are conducted. Efficiency then requires that (i) the production level be set at a level where the marginal benefit from the firm's output equals the marginal cost of producing that output, including any increase in expected environmental damages due to expanded production, and (ii) the level of precautionary actions be set where the marginal cost of additional precaution equals the marginal reduction in expected environmental damages.

Given the definitions of efficient output and care, an efficient fine structure is then one that induces the firm and the worker to choose those levels when pursuing their own self–interests. In general, a fine structure can take one of three forms: a fine only on the firm, a fine only on the worker, or fines imposed on both the firm and the worker. Which fine structure is efficient hinges on the potential for pass–through via the wage contract.

The Case of Perfect Pass–Through

As noted above, perfect pass–through requires that (i) the firm be able to penalize the worker through reduced wages whenever the firm incurs high penalties as a result of the worker's actions, and (ii) the worker be able to demand higher wages from the firm whenever it is subject to individual penalties for environmental damages. In the first instance, the firm is able to pass its penalties backward to the worker, while in the latter case the worker is able to pass its penalties forward to the firm.

Since backward pass–through or shifting requires that wages vary with penalties imposed on the firm, the firm must be able to link wages to the actions of the worker either directly (through perfectly observing or monitoring the level of precaution taken by the worker) or indirectly (by inferring that level of precaution from the resulting environmental damages). Likewise, since forward shifting requires that wages vary with the penalties imposed on the individual, the individual must be able to link his wage demands to the actions of the firm that determine environmental damages (and thus the penalties incurred). This requires that wages vary with, for example, output, so that workers at large firms with higher potential damages (*ceteris paribus*) are compensated by higher wages if individual penalties are imposed. Thus, in order for both forward and backward pass– through to be possible, wages must depend on both the decisions of the individual (his choice of care, either directly or indirectly) and the decisions of the firm (e.g. its output level or overall safety policies).

Suppose that such a wage contract is possible. For example, the worker's wages are based on the firm's safety record (number and severity of accidents), or the worker receives bonuses for safety innovations as well as, possibly, compensation for the increased risks of expanded output. In this case, efficiency can be achieved from a fine on the firm alone, a fine on the worker alone, or a combination of fines on both the firm and the worker that sum to the total amount of damages. Such a result is consistent with previous analyses of liability in the presence of contractual relationships (Shavell, 1980; Segerson, 1990) and can be explained as follows.

Consider first the case of a fine on the firm alone. If each additional dollar in penalties that the firm incurs implies an additional dollar reduction in wages, i.e. if the penalties are passed backward to the worker, then in choosing his level of care, the worker will consider the impact that choice will have on the level of penalties. If penalties are set equal to damages, then his choice will reflect the impact of care on potential damages and he will be induced to choose a level of care that balances the marginal benefits of increased care with its marginal costs.[20] Thus, despite the fact that he faces no direct penalties, the worker will choose an efficient level of care because of the indirect effect of the firm's penalties on the wage rate. Likewise, in choosing its level of output (or any other variable affecting environmental damages), the firm will consider the impact of that choice on the wages that it must pay. In other words, if higher levels of output *ceteris paribus* imply higher levels of damages and thus higher penalties, the worker will demand a higher wage as compensation for these higher penalties that he bears indirectly through backward shifting or pass–through.[21] Thus, despite its ability to shift costs backward to the worker, the firm is still induced to consider the impact of its decisions on the penalties it faces and thus on the environmental damages that result from its operations. As a result, the firm would make its choices efficiently.

A similar story can be told for the case where a penalty is imposed on the worker but not on the firm or where the two parties "split" the damages. Again, the ability to shift costs forward and backward leaves each party facing the correct incentives, thereby inducing each to make the efficient decisions. This suggests that, when perfect forward and backward pass–through are possible, corporate and individual penalties will be perfect substitutes. In other words, either can be used to induce efficient incentives. The choice between the two should therefore hinge not on their incentive effects but rather on other considerations such as administrative or transaction costs and risk sharing.

Imperfect Pass–Through

In many cases of environmental risk, the conditions outlined above under which perfect pass–through or shifting would occur (and thus corporate and individual fines would be perfect substitutes) are unlikely to hold. One class of environmental risks that seem to preclude effective internalization through wages are those where damages are not discovered until long after the actions that caused them were taken. For example, surreptitious dumping of chemicals may not be discovered for a very long time. Likewise, health effects from prolonged exposure to chemicals may not be discovered until years after exposure has ceased. This time lag means that the options open to the firm are limited. Employees may be fired, but generally back wages cannot be garnished. The corporation may reduce future payments (e.g. raises and promotions) for the worker, but it has few levers it can pull to assign retrospective damages. In addition, with significant time lags it is possible that the worker will no longer be employed by the firm, in which case the firm can do little to the worker other than possibly damage his reputation.

Relating wages to the scale of operations seems less problematic for organizations although it is not clear how often it is done for environmental risk managers. While some managers routinely receive corporate bonuses based on firm performance, this is generally based more on a desire to motivate employees to increase their productivity than a demand by employees as compensation for increased expected individual penalties. Furthermore, these bonuses are typically given to managers who are seen as being more in operations; environmental risk managers are less likely to participate in this type of compensation package.

For at least one important class of polluters the flexible wage assumption appears particularly unrealistic.[22] Employees at public facilities usually face rather rigid, civil–service wage schedules. The individual plant manager has little flexibility in structuring wages to facilitate the achievement of environmental objectives. If the plant manager is unable to institute a wage schedule that makes environmental managers at public facilities accountable for their actions, a crucial link in the chain has been broken.[23]

When penalties can be shifted forward (from the worker to the firm) but not backwards (from the firm to the worker), then individual penalties are efficient while corporate penalties are not. Imposing a penalty on the individual induces the worker to take an efficient amount of care. In addition, since the worker's wage varies with the risk of penalties, through forward shifting he can induce the firm to make efficient risk–related decisions. Thus, both the worker and the firm are induced to behave efficiently. The same is not true, however, when penalties are imposed on the firm alone. While the firm will be induced to make decisions efficiently, it has no way of ensuring that the worker does likewise. Thus, when wages cannot be based directly or indirectly on the actions of the worker, the use of individual fines is preferred (in terms of incentives) to the use of corporate penalties.

The opposite is true when backward, but not forward, shifting is possible. In this case, corporate penalties alone are efficient while individual penalties are not. Basing wages on the worker's actions allows the firm to shift its expected penalties back to the worker so that the effects of the worker's actions will be internalized. However, if wages are not tied to the firm–level decisions, the worker has no means of shifting the external effects of those decisions back to the firm. Thus, the wage contract can be a substitute for direct penalties on the worker but not for direct penalties on the firm.

When neither forward nor backward shifting is possible, then neither party can use the wage contract to influence the actions of the other. The contractual relationship is then independent of the environmental risks and the problem reduces to the case of a "joint tort".[24] To ensure efficiency in such cases, each party must face its own penalty equal to its incremental contribution to damages. In our context, this implies that both corporate and individual penalties should be used simultaneously to ensure correct incentives.[25]

The above results imply that, as the costs of enforcement to violators rise, we would expect the amount of internal monitoring to increase. In essence the amount of expenditure on internal monitoring should be related to the amount of money it could ultimately save in reduced penalties and wages to its employees. The larger are the penalties and compensating wage differentials, the more it pays to spend on internal monitoring. In the absence of systematic evidence we are forced to rely on anecdotal evidence, but that does seem to support the implication. Environmental auditing has become a booming field for consultants.[26] According to the EPA definition, "Environmental auditing is a systematic, documented, periodic and objective review by regulated entities of facility operations and practices relating to meeting environmental requirements." The expense of enforcement has apparently reached the point when an ounce of prevention really is worth a pound of cure. Some corporations have even transformed their organizational structure to facilitate internal monitoring of environmental risks.[27]

Inadequate Penalties

If either type of monetary penalty is not set at the appropriate level, efficient levels of precaution are not taken, even with observable actions and flexibility in setting wage schedules. In general the total sanction should be a multiple of the harm where the multiple is equal to the inverse of the likelihood that a violation will result in a monetary sanction.[28] When the probability of detection is very low, the consequent efficient penalty should be a very high multiple of the actual harm done. Whenever sanctions fail to meet the expected damage, they will fail to produce efficient deterrence unless the private settlements and reputational losses are sufficiently large to offset the difference. Enforcement activities with a very low probability of detection will not be well served by monetary sanctions unless the courts tend to impose sanctions that are sufficiently high.

Inefficiently low penalties can result either from penalty determination procedures or from statutory limits. In many cases courts are reluctant to assess penalties that are many times the harm.[29] Kraakman (1984, 882) points out two reasons why penalty determination procedures may lead to inefficiently low penalties. First, specific legal doctrines (such as retribution) that underlie determination of the level of sanction seek an equivalency between the amount of harm inflicted and the punishment. Second, courts are reluctant to apply large sanctions if they pose a significant risk of bankruptcy for the target firm.

Examples of statutory limits on civil penalties are not hard to find. Penalties for violations of the Clean Water act are limited to $25,000 if imposed by an informal administrative hearing, but the limit rises to $125,000 in a formal hearing.[30] Civil penalties are limited to $5,000 per violation in the Federal Insecticide, Fungicide and Rodenticide Act.[31] Furthermore, both the Toxic Substances Control Act and the Clean Water Act require the Administrator to take into account the "ability to pay" of the violator in determining the appropriate penalty.[32] It is not hard to imagine that even judges not faced with this statutory mandate could well tailor the penalty to the wealth of the violator.[33]

Monetary criminal penalties can provide a measure of correction to limits on monetary civil penalties since the limits on criminal monetary penalties are higher for several statutes. For example, civil penalties under the Federal Insecticide, Fungicide and Rodenticide Act are limited to $5,000 per offense, but the limit for a criminal penalty is $50,000.[34] Violating the Resource Conservation and Recovery Act's "knowing endangerment" provision could trigger a penalty up to $250,000 for an individual or $1,000,000 for an organization.[35] Furthermore when the acts defining the offences have not established the limits, the much higher limits authorized by the Criminal Fine Enforcement Act of 1984 apply.[36] Criminal penalties also add the threat of incarceration, either as a substitute penalty or as an addition to the monetary penalty, for responsible parties within the organization.

Insufficient Assets

Insufficient assets are another potential source of inefficiency in the use of either individual or corporate fines. Though long recognized as a source of inefficiency in tort law remedies (e.g. Shavell, 1986, 1987), insufficient assets can undermine the efficiency of the use of financial penalties in enforcement as well. Furthermore, introducing individual penalties provides a new source of concern about the problem of insufficient assets since individuals typically have fewer assets than the organizations that employ them.

Insufficient assets change the nature of taking environmental risks by curtailing the size of the penalty that would have to be paid. When firms have insufficient assets to pay the fine, their downside risk is truncated.[37] Thus, even if the courts were routinely imposing an efficient level of monetary sanctions, the polluter with insufficient assets to comply with the court's mandate would face insufficient incentives.[38]

THE CRIMINAL SANCTIONS ALTERNATIVE

What can be done when a firm's or an individual's assets are insufficient to cover the efficient penalties that would be levied on them or when the actual penalties are below the efficient levels? One possibility is to use incarceration to fill the gap left by unenforceable or inadequate fines. With the use of incarceration, two extra social costs are introduced: (i) the dollar equivalent of the direct disutility (or lost income) from a jail sentence for the worker, which is a monotonically increasing function of the number of years spent in jail, and (ii) the social costs of incarceration, including the costs of providing capital (prisons), labor (guards and support personnel) and raw materials and services (uniforms, food). Neither of these costs exist with a fine. Therefore as long as any specific level of deterrence achieved by incarceration could be also achieved by a fine, fines dominate (e.g. Polinsky and Shavell, 1984). However, when fines do not ensure sufficient incentives, incarceration may have a role to play. When considering incarceration rules in the context of environmental risks, the following question arises: Should an individual who undertakes a great deal of care still be subject to incarceration if an accident occurs? Or should the possibility of incarceration be reserved for cases where the level of care was "criminally" low? This distinction is similar to the distinction in tort law between the use of a strict liability rule (liability regardless of the level of care) and a negligence rule (liability only for failure to exercise "due" care). While such a distinction has not been made in previous economic analyses of incarceration (e.g. Polinsky and Shavell, 1984; Shavell, 1987a), it is crucial in analysing the role of incarceration in ensuring efficient incentives. An incarceration rule based on strict liability principles will not generally yield efficient care, while a rule based upon negligence principles can.[39]

The inefficiency that can arise from a strict liability approach to incarceration can be explained as follows. The private costs of incarceration are only the opportunity costs of the worker's time. The social costs, on the other hand, are the opportunity costs plus damages and the direct costs of incarceration. Thus, private costs are less than social costs and incarceration cannot induce efficiency. Contrary to what has been thought, however, the inefficiency of incarceration here does not stem from the mere existence of direct incarceration costs. Even if jails are costless to operate, the problem remains. As long as the opportunity costs of the time spent in jail is included in the measure of social losses, as is typical in models of incarceration (e.g. Polinsky and Shavell, 1984; Shavell, 1987a), the private costs will still be less than the social costs and a strict liability–based incarceration rule cannot be structured so that private and social costs are equal even at the margin.[40] As a result, the worker will choose a care level that is less than efficient. A similar result holds for the decisions of the firm.

It is possible for a strict liability approach to incarceration to be efficient if individuals incur sufficient reputational costs from incarceration. Reputational costs serve to increase the private costs of incarceration without affecting social costs, thereby bringing private and social costs closer into line. If reputational costs are sufficient to offset fully both damages and the direct costs of incarceration, then efficient incentives can be achieved. However, for environmental risks with large potential damages, it seems unlikely that reputational costs could be sufficiently high to ensure efficiency.

Note, also, that the potential inefficiency of incarceration cannot be eliminated by simply coupling incarceration with fines. If the worker's assets are insufficient or the efficient fine would exceed a statutory limit, then in the relevant range the worker will view the fine as fixed at its maximum level (equal to his assets or the legal limit). The existence of the fine will then have no effect on the worker's marginal incentives. Thus, in the absence of sufficient reputational costs, marginal social costs will continue to exceed marginal private costs and an insufficient amount of care will be chosen.

These conclusions regarding the inefficiency of incarceration hinge on the strict liability form of the incarceration "rule" that is considered above. In contrast, it is possible to base an incarceration rule on negligence principles. Suppose, for example, that a jail sentence is imposed if an accident occurs and care was less than the due standard. (No sentence is imposed if the worker took sufficient care.) Assume that the due standard of care is set equal to the socially efficient level of care.

Under these conditions the worker can be induced to choose the efficient level of care by an incarceration rule that imposes an appropriate jail sentence if and only if the worker's chosen care level was less than this standard. The length of the jail sentence should be set sufficiently high so that the cost of the jail sentence to the individual (discounted for the probability that it will be imposed and any resulting reputational costs that would be incurred) exceeds any private gain that would have been realized by choosing a lower level of care. In other words, the sentence should be set sufficiently high that it will not be "worth it" for the individual to act carelessly. Note that the efficient penalty is independent of the level of damages. Instead, it is determined by the size of the penalty necessary to deter inappropriate behavior. Clearly, the greater the private benefit of inappropriate behavior, the larger the jail sentence must be to deter it. Likewise, the smaller the probability that it will be imposed, the larger the necessary penalty.[41] Positive reputational costs also reduce the required sentence.

Although a negligence standard for criminal penalties no doubt sounds like an unrealistic proposal to those familiar with the use of criminal penalties in nonenvironmental settings, this concept has recently been applied. According to Section 1319(c)(1) of Title 33 of the US Code negligent violations of Clean Water Act provisions can now trigger criminal penalties. Fines of up to $25,000 per day and 1 year in prison are authorized for a first offense with higher penalties authorized for repeat offenders. Such an approach could promote efficiency under the right conditions.

SUMMARY AND CONCLUSIONS

Among the three judicial or quasi–judicial forms of enforcement administrative proceedings are the least costly while criminal proceedings are the most costly, not only because the required standards of proof are higher, but because incarceration, a remedy available only with criminal proceedings, entails extra social costs. By itself this evidence would suggest that administrative remedies would be preferred to civil remedies and civil remedies would be preferred to criminal remedies unless these more costly proceedings offered compensating benefits.

Table 3.1   *Administrative actions and criminal and civil referrals to the Department of Justice by USEPA*

Action	FY81	FY82	FY83	FY84	FY85	FY86	FY87	FY88	FY89
Admin	1107	864	1848	3124	2609	2626	3194	3085	4136
	(90)	(87)	(91)	(92)	(89)	(87)	(90)	(87)	(91)
Civil	118	112	165	251	276	342	304	372	364
	(10)	(11)	(8)	(7)	(10)	(11)	(9)	(11)	(8)
Criminal	0	20	26	31	40	41	41	59	60
	(0)	(2)	(1)	(1)	(1)	(2)	(1)	(2)	(1)
Total	1225	996	2039	3406	2925	3009	3539	3516	4560

Notes: FY refers to Fiscal Year
The numbers in parentheses represent the proportions of the total multiplied by 100.

Source: Office of Enforcement, *Enforcement Accomplishments: FY 1989* (Washington, D.C.: United States Environmental Protection Agency, 1990):Appendix.

As Table 3.1 confirms, the distribution of federal enforcement actions conforms to this expectation. Administrative proceedings comprise about 90 per cent of federal enforcement actions. Since 1982 criminal referrals have held steady at about 1 or 2 per cent of the total. Interestingly, the number of criminal actions has kept pace with the overall increase in enforcement actions, but has not exceeded it. Thus, while the number of criminal proceedings has been growing, this seems more of a reflection of the general increase in enforcement than any tilt toward criminal enforcement.

The traditional penalty structure for managing environmental risks involves administrative or civil financial penalties imposed on organizations, not individuals. A belief that the corporate organization can be enlisted to the enforcement cause underlies the economic theory of deterrence for corporate crimes. Penalizing corporations for transgressions will, according to this presumption, lead ultimately to the internal identification of the individuals responsible for the transgressions.

Under the right conditions efficiency can be achieved with either (i) a monetary penalty placed on the corporation alone, without any penalty on the worker, or (ii) a penalty on the responsible individual, without any corresponding penalty on the firm. In other words, under ideal circumstances individual and organizational financial penalties are perfect substitutes.

These circumstances include the following. First, the actions of the environmental workers should be observable so that wage structures can be used to penalize inefficient behavior and reward efficient behavior. Alternatively, wages that are tied to the environmental performance of the firm must be possible. Second, firms must have the ability to manipulate wages sufficiently that the proper correspondence with employee actions can be established. Third, the penalty or fine has to be set at the correct level. Finally, both the polluter and the worker must have sufficient assets to be able to pay the penalties that are imposed on them.

These conditions are not always fulfilled. Inadequate precautionary behavior occurs with traditional administrative and civil penalties on organizations when the incentives facing those entrusted with the responsibility for managing environmental risks are not consistent with efficient behavior. This could occur either when the polluting organization faces inefficient incentives (implying that even environmental risk managers who are pursuing the best interests of their employers will act inefficiently) or when the incentives facing environmental risk managers diverge from those facing the organization.

The polluting firm would face inefficient incentives as a result of incorrectly imposed monetary penalties or insufficient organizational assets to pay any assigned penalties. Even when organizational incentives are efficient, individual incentives might arise from difficulties in monitoring employee performance or difficulties in structuring compensation systems capable of harmonizing the interests of employees and owners. Individual and/or criminal penalties can provide a measure of correction for each of these sources of inefficiency.

For example, when individual assets are insufficient to pay the magnitude of penalties necessary to ensure efficient incentives, incarceration provides an available, if costly, alternative. However, care must be taken to structure an appropriate incarceration rule. For example, a rule based on negligence principles may be more efficient than one based on strict liability. In this case, the length of the sentence should be determined by what is necessary to deter inappropriate behavior rather than by the level of damages that result from that behavior. Such an approach to incarceration may fill an important niche in environmental enforcement.

In addition, incarceration may be cheaper than putting up with a much higher level of environmental damage triggered by impaired incentives. A few well–publicized cases can set precedents that persuade a large number of firms to take a more efficient level of precaution. Indeed, when an incarceration penalty works extremely well in deterring inefficient behavior, it would rarely need to be imposed. While the additional expenditures associated with trying these few cases may well be very high on a per–case basis, the additional precaution achieved from all firms recognizing those precedents and reacting to them will very likely be enormous. The costs and benefits of these remedies cannot be examined merely in the context of a single case.

While we have identified several possible roles for both individual and criminal penalties in environmental enforcement, it remains true that these roles are limited, not dominant. We would expect individual and criminal penalties to complement, not replace, the dominant strategy — civil and administrative penalties against organizations.

NOTES

1. The authors wish to acknowledge helpful comments from Mark Cohen, Cliff Russell, Carol Jones, and Jim Opaluch.
2. From its creation through fiscal year 1989 the United States Environmental Protection Agency has imposed $185.9 million in civil penalties. In FY1989, $34.9 million in civil penalties were assessed, $21.3 million in civil judicial penalties (the second highest in agency history) and $13.6 million in administrative penalties (an all–time record). See US Environmental Protection Agency (1990, 18).
3. For an examination of how courts have begun to expand individual liability for corporate environmental violations see Cordiano and Blood, (1990c, 18).
4. The number of criminal cases referred to the Department of Justice by EPA rose from 0 in fiscal year 1981 to 60 in fiscal year 1989. US Environmental Protection Agency (1990c, Appendix).
5. Starr and Kelly (1990, 10096).
6. Some evidence suggests that overzealous use of criminal prosecution has occurred in some states. One study found, "Urged by public pressures to criminally charge whenever possible, a predisposition to the criminal enforcement side of the civil vs. criminal enforcement dichotomy exacted some cost in terms of lower prosecutorial success rates."See Rebovich (1987,183).
7. Posner (1980, 409–18). See also Polinsky and Shavell (1984, 89–99).
8. This is an important aspect. It implies that the appropriate enforcement choices even for individual cases should not be framed in terms of "which approach" but rather what combination of approaches should be employed.
9. The rules governing these procedures can be found in Sections 554 and 556 of the Administrative Procedures Act and EPA's Consolidated Rules of Practice, 40 CFR Part 22.
10. Allowing penalties to be imposed in administrative proceedings, as opposed to reserving that power for the courts, is relatively recent. For water pollution control this power was conferred by the Federal Water Quality Act of 1987. 101 Stat 46 codified at 33 USC §1319.
11. All final administrative orders can be appealed to the US courts.
12. For a detailed description of how these powers can be used see Riesel (1985, 6).
13. Some limited subpoena powers are available for civil cases, but penalties against a noncomplying witness can be levied only after a time–consuming and expensive hearing. In addition information provided by witnesses subpoenaed in a civil case cannot be kept secret if it falls within the scope of the other side's discovery requests.
14. Under the Clean Air Act, for example, criminal liability can be imposed for making any false statement, representation, or certification in a document filed or required to be filed under the Act as well as for falsifying, tampering with, or knowingly rendering inaccurate any monitoring device. 42 U.S.C. § 7413(c)(2).
15. For example in the Clean Water Act a violation becomes a "knowing endangerment" when it "places another person in imminent danger of death or serious bodily injury". 33 U. S. C. §1319(c)(3)(A).
16. See, for example, *United States* v. *Johnson & Towers, Inc.* 741 F. 2d 662 (1984) where middle–management officers were held criminally liable when a foreman and a service manager of a vehicle repair shop allowed methylene chloride and trichlor-ethylene to enter the Delaware River.
17. For a detailed description of the tax treatment of enforcement payments see Slavitt (1990).
18. For details regarding the results discussed in this section, see Segerson and Tietenberg (1991).
19. This formulation assumes that society is risk neutral, an assumption we make throughout. If society were risk neutral, net social benefits (or "welfare") would

depend not only on expected damages but also on other moments of the distribution of damages.

20. This assumes that all of the costs of care, such as the disutility from having to be more careful, are borne by the individual worker.

21. The worker will thus effectively shift some of the penalty back to the firm through forward shifting. The net effect of the combination of forward and backward shifting is that the worker ultimately bears any increase in the penalty attributable to his choosing a level of care less than the efficient level. More specifically, the worker indirectly bears a penalty equal to $D(x,a^*)-D(x,a)$ where D is the level of damages, x is the actual output level of the firm, a^* is the efficient level of care, and a is the worker's actual choice of care. See Segerson and Tietenberg (1991) for details.

22. For evidence that public polluters are an important part of the problem, see Stanfield (1987, 762–6).

23. Objective functions which differ from private firm counterparts offer another possible reason why public polluters may not respond efficiently to monetary penalties. Yet the literature seems to suggest that the divergence of bureaucratic objective functions from private objective functions may not be quantitatively important. See Lyon (1990, 198–220), and Oates and Strassman (1978, 283–91).

24. See Tietenberg (1989), Miceli and Segerson (forthcoming), and the references cited therein for a discussion of joint torts.

25. As Cohen points out in his contribution to this volume, the simultanteous application of corporate and individual penalties is quite common in practice.

26. According to Frank J. Priznar, the Executive Director of the Institute for Environmental Auditing, "Environmental auditing has proliferated in use and matured in complexity as a tool for detecting and preventing environmental problems." See Priznar (1990, 10179).

27. Soon after the oil spill from the Exxon Valdez, the Exxon Corporation announced that it had created a new position, the Vice President for Environment and Safety. The first incumbent, Edwin Hess, serves as an environmental watchdog and reports directly to the President. He attributes the new visibility of environmental concerns in Exxon corporate decision–making directly to the losses incurred by the corporation in the aftermath of the spill. See Sullivan (1990a, B12).

28. See Polinsky and Shavell (1979, 880–891).

29. See also the evidence on the size of civil penalties in Russell (1990b, 252–3).

30. 33 U.S.C.§ 1319 (g)(2).

31. 7 U.S.C. § 136(l) (a).

32. 15 U.S.C.§ 2615(a) (1) (b).

33. Tailoring the magnitude of the fine to the wealth of the violator can be optimal, but not in the sense conveyed by these statutes. In a model imbedding enforcement costs, but ignoring both marginal deterrence and alternative penalty structures, it has been shown that optimal fines should be equal to the wealth of low–wealth individuals, but be less than the wealth of others. See Polinsky and Shavell (1989).

34. 7 U.S.C. §136(l)(a)(1) and §136(l)(b)(1)

35. 42 U.S.C. §6928 (e).

36. For individuals these limits are now $250,000 for a felony or a misdemeanor resulting in death or $100,000 for a misdemeanor not resulting in death. See 18 U.S.C. § 3623.

37. Insufficient enforcement attention to the problem of insufficient assets could create an incentive to set up underfunded subsidiaries for the sole purpose of keeping environmental risks away from the parent corporation. This has apparently happened in the United States according to evidence presented in Ringleb and Wiggins (1990).

38. In some ways the problem of insufficient assets might even be more severe in enforcement than in tort law. Most tort law damages paid to individuals and costs incurred in cleaning up sites are insurable, providing another source of assets to be tapped. Fines, however, are typically not insurable, particularly criminal fines which fulfill the *scienter* requirement.

39. See Segerson and Tietenberg (1991) for a detailed derivation of this result. Note that it is in direct contrast to the standard results from the economic analysis of torts, where it is well-known that in unilateral care cases efficient care by an individual can be induced through either strict liability or negligence. See, for example, Shavell (1980).
40. Note that this inefficiency does not arise in the models of Polinsky and Shavell (1984) and Shavell (1987a) since they consider only discrete choices problems (whether to undertake the activity or not) where marginal incentives are not an issue.
41. These results are consistent with the results obtained by Shavell (1987a).

4. Criminal Penalties

Mark A. Cohen

INTRODUCTION

Although the Refuse Act of 1899 made it a criminal offense to discharge any refuse into navigable waters,[1] it appears that actual criminal enforcement of environmental regulations is a relatively new phenomenon. Few environmental offenses were prosecuted until the early 1970s, when prosecutors "rediscovered" the Refuse Act's strict liability provisions (Carter, 1980, 583–4). Even then, in the entire decade of the 1970s, only 25 criminal environmental cases were prosecuted at the federal level (Habicht, 1987).

The 1980s brought about significant changes in criminal enforcement. EPA established an Office of Criminal Enforcement and the Justice Department established an Environmental Crimes Unit in 1981. Congress further upped the ante by reclassifying environmental crimes from misdemeanors to felonies in the mid–'80s (Starr and Kelly, 1990). The number of prosecutions has since skyrocketed, to over 100 per year during the past few years. Perhaps even more significant is the fact that over 150 years of actual jail time have been served by the 380 individuals convicted in these cases (Hutchins, 1991).

Apparently little controversy surrounds the use of criminal sanctions for "midnight dumpers" who illegally dump hazardous wastes. At the other extreme, the advisability of using the criminal statutes against a corporation held vicariously liable for negligent actions taken by an employee has triggered a heated debate.[2] At the heart of this debate is the purpose of the criminal law.

This chapter reviews the current state of knowledge concerning the actual use of criminal enforcement of environmental regulations in the US. After reviewing both the legal theory and practice of criminal liability for environmental offenses, we examine recent empirical evidence on sanctions imposed on both individuals and firms convicted of environmental offenses. We also focus on the current debate over the drafting of sentencing guidelines for environmental crimes.

CRIMINAL LIABILITY FOR ENVIRONMENTAL OFFENSES

Although this chapter is not intended to be a legal treatise on criminal liability for environmental offenses, a brief overview of criminal liability will assist the reader in understanding the policy implications of using criminal sanctions to enforce environmental regulations.[3] A crime (as opposed to a tort or administrative violation) generally involves intent, is publicly enforced, and does not require actual victim harm. In contrast, a tort does not require intent, is privately enforced, and the plaintiff must establish damages (Coffee, 1991). Whereas torts generally involve the compensation of victims and are designed to deter the tortfeaser, crimes require punitive sanctions and are designed primarily to punish.[4] Administrative violations are similar to crimes in that they are generally publicly enforced and do not require actual damages. However, administrative violations are not generally predicated on intent, and remedies are generally designed to restrict (or require) certain future actions. Although civil penalties might be levied, they are often designed to take the monetary gain away from offenders, and are not generally designed to punish.

Many legal scholars argue that the single distinguishing characteristic of a crime should be "moral culpability" (Hall, 1943). That is, torts involve the "essentially non–moral character of negligence...[compared to the]...essentially moral aspects of the conditions of responsibility in the criminal law" (Coleman, 1985, 326).

For example, in the case of the *Exxon Valdez* oil spill, although there was little question that the firm was liable under tort law for damages caused to private property, the question of criminal liability was much more controversial. Indeed, the focus of the debate was primarily over whether or not Exxon was morally culpable for the spill. While Exxon claimed the spill was an accident, the government sought criminal charges under the theory that Exxon "had reports that Hazelwood was not competent...[and thus]...culpability went beyond simple negligence to a much higher degree". Commenting on Exxon's plea to criminal charges, the prosecuting attorney claimed that it "reflected the moral sensibilities of the community" (Crovitz, 1991).

There are two main bodies of criminal law related to environmental violations. The first type of violation involves the general criminal statutes, such as conspiracies, mail fraud or false statements to the government. In a few instances, firms have also been charged under RICO. The second category includes all of the specific environmental statutes that include criminal provisions.

Virtually all environmental statutes now include criminal provisions. They generally fall into two distinct categories: (i) "strict liability" or "public welfare" offenses, and (ii) those requiring some degree of "knowing," "willful" or negligent conduct. Although legal theory tends to require some degree of intent or moral culpability before labeling an incident a "crime", in practice, it appears this distinction is not followed for many environmental offenses.

The original Refuse Act of 1899 was a "public welfare" offense, imposing criminal liability on any party who discharged refuse into navigable waters. However, most of the subsequent environmental legislation has failed to impose such a strict liability standard. Instead, the Clean Water Act provides for criminal sanctions when a discharge is "willful" or "negligent". The latter term is broad enough to allow prosecutors to charge firms with criminal negligence for failure to adequately prevent accidental oil discharges as in the case of the Exxon Valdez. In contrast, the Clean Air Act does not contain a criminal negligence provision. Instead, the violation must be "knowing" in order to be criminal. Not surprisingly, there have been fewer criminal prosecutions under the Clean Air Act than under the Clean Water Act (see Table 4.1).

RCRA also imposes a "knowing" standard for violations that include illegal storage, transportation, treatment, disposal or recordkeeping violations. CERCLA contains a strict liability standard for failure to notify authorities of either a release of a hazardous substance or the existence of an unpermitted hazardous–waste disposal site. This CERCLA provision might be used in hazardous–waste cases that are difficult to prove as "knowing" violations. However, since CERCLA violations are only misdemeanors, this has apparently not been the charge of "choice" for prosecutors. Moreover, the case law now appears to define "knowing" broadly enough to include knowledge of the hazardous nature of the pollutant — not just knowledge of an actual violation. In one case, the fact that the defendant did not know (or even have reason to know) that the facility lacked an EPA permit was not an adequate defense.[5]

Table 4.1 Justice Department prosecutions for environmental crimes by type of offense, 1983–90

Statutory violation	Number	Percent
RCRA and/or CERCLA	347	50
Clean Water, Safe Drinking Water, Refuse Act	184	25
Title 18 (e.g. false statements)	83	12
Toxic Substances Control Act	40	5
Clean Air Act	26	4
FIFRA (pesticides)	18	3
Miscellaneous	5	1
Total	703	100

Source: Hutchins (1991).

Other laws that include criminal provisions are TSCA, the Safe Drinking Water Act, and FIFRA. These laws generally require some *mens rea* component, either a "knowing" standard or through actual falsification of records. However, FIFRA also "provides that criminal liability may be vicariously imposed upon principals without any additional required mental state, for the acts, omission, or failures of their officers, agents, or employees" (Riesel, 1985).

In general, the "knowing" standard requires a lower burden of proof than the "willful" standard, "since the individual with knowledge need not intend or desire the result to occur, so long as he is substantially certain it will occur. On the other hand, knowledge is a more difficult standard to prove than negligence since the negligent violator need only have known there was a substantial risk that the unlawful conduct would occur, or have failed to exercise due care to avoid the unlawful result" (Riesel, 1985).

Under Federal law, corporations can be held criminally liable for virtually any illegal actions by their agents or employees that take place within the scope of their employment — even if their actions were in direct conflict with company policy or management orders. The only requirement is that the "corporation exerts some control over persons or events responsible for a criminal violation" (Riesel, 1985).

Corporate officers may also incur criminal liability for the actions of their employees — even if they did not participate in the criminal activity themselves. For statutory violations requiring some degree of "knowledge" or "willful" conduct, individual liability will generally be applied to corporate officers who somehow fail to prevent, authorize or tacitly acquiesce in a crime ("Individual Liability...", 1989).

However, for "public welfare" (i.e. strict liability) or "negligence" statutes, individual criminal liability might be established solely on the basis that the officer was ultimately responsible for the activity — even if that responsibility was delegated. The precedent–setting case was US vs. Park, where the president of a supermarket chain was held criminally liable for his firm's failure to clean up rodent–infested food warehouses. Criminal liability was imposed despite evidence that Park personally sent a memo to subordinates ordering them to clean up the warehouses after receiving civil citations from FDA inspectors. The fact that his employees failed to follow orders was not a defense ("Individual Liability...", 1989).

According to the former head of the Justice Department's Environmental Crimes Unit, "it was his policy while in the government to prosecute the highest–ranking corporate officer with any responsibility for overseeing environmental compliance" (Abramson, 1989). Thus, in 1988 three corporate officers working at the Philadelphia headquarters of Pennwalt Corporation were indicted following an accidental tank rupture and chemical spill at its Tacoma, Washington, plant. Although charges were later dropped, according to the government prosecutor, "we were charging corporate officers for passive negligence as distinguished from active negligence — they failed to take a proactive role in establishing preventative maintenance plans for their facilities adequate to protect against this kind of situation."[6]

As a former US Attorney noted, "the decision whether to proceed criminally or civilly is a discretionary judgment". The key factors prosecutors allegedly use to determine which approach to take are (i) knowledge or intent, (ii) harm associated with the offense, (iii) gain to the offender, (iv) continued violations after repeated EPA notifications, and (v) strength of the evidence (Habicht, 1987). Note also that parallel civil and criminal cases may be pursued.

Although this section has only scratched the surface of the legal theories of criminal sanctions, when coupled with the chapter by Segerson and Tietenberg (this volume), it does provide some basis to compare legal and economic theories of the criminal law. The key difference between traditional legal and economic theories is their treatment of the purpose of criminal sanctions. Economists oftentimes assume that the only difference between criminal and civil sanctions is incarceration. A dollar fine costs the firm one dollar whether it is called a "cleanup cost", "restitution", "civil penalty", or "criminal fine".[7] Segerson and Tietenberg (this volume) explicitly derive the need for jail solely on the basis of the inadequacy of monetary penalties to deter unlawful behavior. On the other hand, legal theorists often assume there is a moral component to the criminal law that is absent from civil liability. In theory, one can test these differing views by examining the effect of various sanctions on the firm.[8]

Empirical Evidence on Sanctions for Environmental Crimes

Given the rather recent trend towards criminal enforcement of environmental regulation, it is not surprising that few if any empirical analyses of criminal sanctions have been undertaken. Moreover, it is not easy for outside researchers to collect data on environmental prosecutions. Virtually no readily accessible data is available at the state level. Although EPA publishes a semi–annual summary of all federal indictments stemming from its referrals to the Justice Department (US Environmental Protection Agency 1990b), that listing does not include many environmental prosecutions initiated by the FBI. It also excludes a lot of factual information on the nature of the offense and the offender.

To date, the only comprehensive summary statistics available on criminal enforcement of federal environmental statutes are quarterly summaries provided by the Justice Department's Environmental Crimes Section (Hutchins, 1991). Although these statistics are often reported in the popular press through Justice Deptartment press releases and speeches, the raw data are not available to researchers. Instead, we are left with a summary that is of only limited value to understanding trends and/or the potential impact of criminal sanctions. For example, we are told that in FY 1989, there were 107 convictions resulting in $12.7 million in fines and 37 years of actual jail time served. However, we do not know how many of those convictions were corporations versus individuals, nor how many individuals received a jail sentence.

This lack of solid data on corporate criminal prosecutions and sanctions is not unique to the environmental area, and became evident to the US Sentencing Commission when they began the task of drafting guidelines for sentencing organizations convicted of federal crimes. In order to support their drafting effort, the Commission collected court documents on corporations and their individual codefendants from US District Courts around the country. The first stage of this data collection involved firms sentenced between 1984 and 1987 (Cohen, 1989), with a later follow–up of 1988 cases added. More recently, I collected publicly available information on 1989–90 cases, and compared them to the two earlier time periods (Cohen, 1991a).

The remainder of this section summarizes these data on criminal sanctions for environmental crimes. Before proceeding, three caveats are in order. First, since there are differences in the three data sets (both in the number of variables collected and in the sampling method employed), they cannot always be combined for purposes of analysis. Second, since these data were originally collected to analyse corporate sanctions, individuals convicted of environmental crimes are included here *only* if they were indicted along with a corporate codefendant. At this point, we do not know whether the offenses charged and the sanctions imposed against individuals indicted personally are any different from those imposed against individuals who are indicted along with their corporate entities. Finally, the fact that these data focus on federal convictions does not necessarily mean that sanctions are less stringent for criminal offenses prosecuted at the state level. Although we do not have any summary data on state prosecutions or sanctions, significant jail terms have been reported in the press.[9]

Distribution of Offenses and Offenders

Table 4.1 provides a percentage breakdown of all Justice Department prosecutions since 1983. Approximately 50 per cent of prosecutions have been RCRA or CERCLA violations — primarily the illegal disposal of hazardous wastes. The second largest category (25 per cent) is for Clean Water Act violations. The remaining categories include false statements (12 per cent), Toxic Substances (5 per cent), Clean Air Act (4 per cent) and FIFRA (3 per cent). Most cases are settled by guilty pleas. Trials constitute about 12 per cent of all convictions, and *nolo* pleas about 5 per cent.

Most federal criminal prosecutions of organizations involve small, closely held corporations. About 12 per cent of the firms sentenced for environmental offenses during the 1984–1990 time period were publicly held, with about 40 per cent being large enough to have either $1 million in sales or 50 or more employees.[10] A recent trend seems to involve the prosecution and conviction of larger companies for corporate crime (Cohen, 1991a). Since a good portion of this trend can be attributed to recent cases involving the major defense contractors, we do not know if it will continue. However, given recent statements by Justice Department officials concerning their prosecutorial objectives and the apparent trend towards criminalizing regulatory noncompliance and prosecuting strict liability offenses, it would not be surprising to see the proportion of large companies increasing even further. Although no such trend is evident in environmental cases, given the small sample size, it is virtually impossible to determine whether or not any such trend exists.

As shown in Table 4.2, about 70 per cent of indictments for federal environmental crimes are against individuals — with the remaining 30 per cent being corporations. About 70 per cent of these corporations had individual codefendants.[11] The majority of individuals indicted for environmental crimes are either owners or presidents (35 per cent) or corporate officers, vice presidents or directors (17 per cent). Management and supervisory personnel constitute another 29 per cent, with the remaining 19 per cent being nonsupervisory personnel.

Table 4.2 *Justice Department prosecutions for environmental crimes by type of offender, 1983–90*

Offender position in company	Total	Ave. per year	% of indictments	% of individuals
Corporations	222	28	32	——
President/Owners	168	21	26	35
V.P./Director/Corp. Officers	82	10	12	17
Management	68	9	8	14
Supervisory	71	9	10	15
Nonsupervisory	92	12	13	19
Total	703	89	101	100

Source: Hutchins (1991).

MONETARY SANCTIONS FOR CONVICTED ORGANIZATIONS

This section will analyse monetary sanctions imposed against organizations convicted of environmental crimes.[12] Since firms convicted of environmental crimes may receive many sanctions other than the criminal fine, two types of monetary sanctions will be analysed — criminal fines and the "total sanction". The "total sanction" is defined to include all *government*-imposed sanctions such as federal criminal fines, restitution, administrative penalties, state criminal or civil fines, cleanup costs ordered to be paid by the offender, voluntary restitution made known to the judge prior to sentencing, *and* court-ordered payments to victims or other third parties. The latter would include payments that are made as part of a formal plea agreement. It does *not* include nonmonetary sanctions or private settlements made to victims that are not part of the criminal settlement agreement. Nor does it include costs incurred by the offender for legal fees, cleanup, etc. that are not part of the overall legal settlement.

The above definition of "total sanction" is less than satisfactory, since it does not reflect the total monetary cost to firms convicted of crimes. However, these estimates are nearly always impossible to obtain. Two oil spill cases of interest will illustrate the difficulty of estimating the real monetary impact.

In 1988 Ashland Oil accidentally discharged more than 500,000 gallons of oil in the Monongahila River near Pittsburgh. The firm was ordered to pay $2.25 million in federal criminal fines and agreed to pay $4.66 million to Pennsylvania. The latter amount included reimbursement for state cleanup expenditures as well as civil penalties. Thus, the federal criminal fine was $2.25 million, while the total criminal sanction was $6.91 million. However, Ashland also paid over $44 million in civil settlements, $11 million in direct cleanup costs and reportedly spent over $5.25 million in legal and administrative fees to handle the various class action suits filed against it.[13] If one were interested in the true monetary impact of the spill on Ashland, these latter costs would have to be included.

In June 1989 Ballard Shipping and the captain of one of its oil tankers pleaded guilty to the negligent discharge of 300,000 gallons of heating oil after a tanker ran aground. Apparently, the tanker "did not have on board the required harbor pilot, someone who is familiar with local waters".[14] The federal judge imposed a criminal fine of $1 million, with $500,000 of that amount suspended if paid to Massachusetts. It also called for reimbursement of Coast Guard cleanup expenditures, estimated to be $2 million. The state agreement called for a payment of $3.2 million to compensate for natural resource damages, $1 million to reimburse for cleanup costs and $500,000 to fishermen who lost business due to the spill.[15] Thus, although the federal criminal fine was $500,000, the total sanction was $7.7 million. Unlike the Ashland case, I have included payments to third parties here, since they were part of the agreement with the government.

Table 4.3 reports on the monetary sanctions for 115 firms sentenced for environmental crimes between 1 January 1984 and 30

Table 4.3 *Criminal fines for environmental offenses pre– and post–*
Criminal Fine Enforcement Act of 1984 (firms sentenced
between 1984 and Sept. 1990)

	Pre–1984 Fine Act	Post–1984 Fine Act
Fine up to $10,000	11 (34%)	22 (26%)
$10,001 – $25,000	5 (16%)	9 (11%)
$25,001 – $50,000	11 (34%)	17 (20%)
$50,001 – $100,000	3 (9%)	9 (11%)
$100,001 – $500,000	2 (6%)	19 (23%)
$500,001 – $1,000,000	0	5 (6%)
Over $1,000,000	0	2 (2%)
Total number of firms	32	83
Mean criminal fine	$49,986 *	$182,332 *
Median criminal fine	$27,500 *	$50,000 *
Maximum criminal fine	$600,000	$2,250,000
Mean total sanction	$108,786*	$443,882 *
Median total sanction	$35,725	$63,859
Maximum total sanction	$1,000,000	$7,700,000
Number of firms with convicted individuals	15 (47%)	46(55%)
Number of firms with convicted individuals who were jailed	7 (44%)	18 (38%)
Number of individuals jailed	10	22
Average months jail time for jailed individuals	3.5	6.75

* Difference is statistically significant at $p < .05$

September 1990. These firms represent approximately 75 per cent of all corporations sentenced for environmental offenses at the federal level during this time span. Crimes committed after 1 January 1985 are subject to substantially higher statutory maximum penalties.[16] Since there is some evidence that judges responded to these higher statutory maximum fine levels by increasing the average criminal sanction (Cohen, 1991a), Table 4.3 distinguishes between those firms sentenced under each statutory maximum regime.

As shown in Table 4.3, firms sentenced under the Criminal Fine Enforcement Act of 1984 received more punitive sanctions than firms sentenced under the old law. The average corporate fine increased from $49,986 to $182,332, while the median fine increased from $27,500 to $50,000. Similarly, mean total sanctions increased from $108,786 to $443,882, while median total sanctions increased from $35,725 to $63,859. All of these differences (except median total sanctions) are statistically significant to the 95 per cent confidence level.

The fact that mean fines and total sanctions are several times their respective medians illustrates the skewed distribution of sanctions — especially those in the past few years. Although the bulk of cases (nearly 60 per cent) involve relatively small fines of $10,000 to $50,000, there are now a significant number of large fines over $500,000.

CRIMINAL NEGLIGENCE, STRICT AND VICARIOUS LIABILITY AND *EX POST* CORPORATE CONDUCT

There has been considerable concern by many in the business community about vicarious liability for corporations under federal criminal laws.[17] It is difficult to test empirically whether or not judges take this concern into account when sentencing organizations, as the issue of corporate involvement and top–level knowledge is often in dispute. However, a close reading of recent cases finds several instances where sentences clearly reflected both corporate criminal "intent" and the immediate corporate response to the incident.

One case of particular note was a hazardous–waste dumping by an environmental engineer working for Eagle Picher. The dumping was against company policy and the firm removed the barrels immediately upon learning of the violation. After pleading guilty to a CERCLA violation for failure to notify, the judge fined the company $3,500 (US Environmental Protection Agency 1990b, 39).[18]

A more recent example is the case of Ashland Oil involving an accidental discharge of more than 500,000 gallons of oil in the Monongahila River near Pittsburgh. The spill reportedly cost Ashland Oil $60 million or more in direct cleanup costs and government and private settlements.[19] Ashland originally pleaded not guilty, and protested their indictment for a spill that was not intentional and "in light of Ashland's efforts to mitigate the spill's impact and the fact that the company quickly accepted responsibility for the incident".[20] However, they later changed the plea to *nolo contendere,* which the judge accepted after a six–hour hearing.[21]

Under provisions of the Alternative Fine Act, the prosecution requested a criminal fine of $12 million. They claimed documented damages of at least $6 million, with the law allowing for double the pecuniary loss. Instead, the judge imposed a fine of $2.25 million and apparently noted that "if Ashland had not acted so responsibly after the spill, he would have imposed the maximum fine".[22]

Finally, some evidence suggests that judges are reluctant to impose jail sentences on individuals who are held liable for criminal offenses that are charged under theories of strict liability or negligence. For example, Pennwalt and its plant manager in Tacoma, Washington, were charged with the negligent discharge of a hazardous substance and failure to notify the Coast Guard immediately of a discharge of a hazardous substance. According to the prosecutor, "although a call was made the evening of the tank rupture to the local office of the US Coast Guard...there was no mention of the fact that the material contained sodium dichromate, which was required by law to be reported".[23] Although the plant manager faced up to nine years in jail and a fine of $650,000 (Abramson, 1989), the judge fined him $5,000 and sentenced him to two years probation (US Environmental Protection Agency, 1990b, 84).

NONMONETARY SANCTIONS FOR CONVICTED ORGANIZATIONS

This section will briefly review the empirical evidence on the totality of sanctions for corporations convicted of environmental crimes — not just those imposed directly by the sentencing judge against corporations. Since data are unavailable for many types of sanctions, much of this section relies on preliminary empirical and/or anecdotal observations.

Corporate probation has proven to be one of the most controversial issues confronting government policymakers.[24] Discussion has centered both on the *frequency* with which probation should be imposed (i.e. how egregious must the violation be; should it be imposed only when there is top–level management or a repeat violation, etc.), and on the *terms* of probation (i.e. how involved should the court be in overseeing the firm's future compliance).

About 20–30 per cent of convicted corporations are placed on probation. However, most of these companies are placed on probation for the noncontroversial purposes of either collecting a fine over time or as a method of reinstating a suspended sentence in the case of a repeat criminal violation. Actual supervised probation is only occasionally imposed — generally in less than 10 per cent of the cases. Whether supervised probation ever involves active participation in the company's affairs is not known. Other forms of nonmonetary sanctions such as community service or public apologies are rarely used. Although firms convicted of crimes may be debarred or suspended from federal contracting, these sanctions do not appear to be prevalent in the case of environmental offenses.[25] Nevertheless, EPA apparently intends to pursue such actions against firms convicted of environmental crimes in the future.[26]

Although recent cases do not seem to involve instances of actively supervised probation, judges have frequently employed "nontraditional" sanctions in recent environmental cases. Judges oftentimes suspend a significant portion of a fine, contingent upon completion of a probationary period in which the firm does not violate environmental laws. Although I understand EPA and Justice attempt to include environmental audits as part of the terms of probation, I have no evidence on the incidence of this provision.

In several instances, firms were ordered to give money to various state, local or community environmental programs. For example, Transit Mix Concrete Company, Inc. pleaded guilty to knowingly discharging pollutants into a tributary of the Arkansas River without a permit. The judge suspended all but $50,000 of the $500,000 fine and ordered the firm to spend $55,000 on a community service project, with the "suggestion" that the money be spent on improving hiking trails near the river (US Environmental Protection Agency, 1990b, 100). Sellen Construction Company, Inc. pleaded guilty to negligently discharging pollutants without a permit. The firm's $100,000 fine was suspended in lieu of a payment of $50,000 to be made to "an Environmental Trust Fund, which the Seattle YMCA is the trustee" for expansion of community hazardous waste collection facilities (U.S. Environmental Protection Agency 1990 p. 112).

In at least two recent cases of note, firms were ordered to place advertisements in local newspapers to apologize for their actions. In one case, Valmont Industries and two of its managers pleaded guilty to tampering with a water quality monitoring device. The firm received a $450,000 fine, with all but $150,000 suspended contingent on no future violations. The judge also ordered the firm to publish a public apology in a local newspaper.[27]

One unique sanction was the widely publicized requirement by the judge in the Pennwalt case that the chief executive officer of the corporation personally appear in court to enter a guilty plea on behalf of the company — even though there was no personal involvement by the executive. According to a Justice Department memo, "This action forced an admittance of personal responsibility for the corporation's adherence to the environment..."[28]

Another sanction that has rarely been used is forfeiture of assets. Although forfeiture is commonplace in RICO convictions, to date there has only been one case involving RICO convictions for environmental crimes. At the time of writing, the defendants in that case have not been sentenced.[29] However, at least one state prosecutor has reportedly used forfeiture statutes to confiscate property such as garbage trucks and bulldozers used in illegal waste–disposal operations.[30]

Finally, although the ultimate sanction of "capital punishment" is rarely used, at least one company was essentially shut down by a judge after pleading guilty to a hazardous–waste violation. Chemical Commodities, Inc. of Olathe, Kansas, was "engaged in the business of chemical brokering. In December 1988, a truck containing hazardous waste caught fire, triggering the evacuation of residents from a Kansas City neighborhood." The firm was fined $500,000 plus $5,760 for the cost of probation. That sentence was suspended on condition that the firm shut down operations with the assistance of a qualified contractor/consultant selected by EPA, within one year of sentencing. All costs of liquidation, cleanup, and disposal " were to be paid by the firm" (US Environmental Protection Agency, 1990b, 120).

In addition to government–imposed sanctions, firms convicted of crimes may suffer a loss in reputation and future business. There is growing evidence that the marketplace does indeed penalize firms for fraudulent activity.[31] This reputation loss is expected to be more prevalent where the victims of the crime were customers (e.g. private or government fraud) than in cases of regulatory violations such as pollution. However, it is possible that certain types of environmental offenses will result in a marketplace penalty. For example, a firm convicted of falsifying documents might be viewed by customers as being untrustworthy. Likewise, a firm convicted of negligently discharging hazardous wastes due to improper safety precautions may be viewed with some concern by customers who are in need of a high–quality, safe product. "Green investing" may also give way to reduced demand for a firm's stock, as investment funds specializing in "socially responsible" companies refuse to buy stock in firms convicted of environmental crimes (Holcomb, 1991). There is even a possibility of consumer boycotts of companies with a bad environmental record.[32]

SANCTIONS AGAINST INDIVIDUALS AND THEIR FIRMS

As shown in Table 4.3, about one–half of all corporate convictions for environmental crimes involve an individual codefendant. During the post–1984 Fine Act period, 48 out of the 83 sentenced firms (57 per cent) had individual codefendants. However, since many companies had multiple individual codefendants, there were 74 individuals convicted along with their companies. About 30 per cent of convicted individuals (22 out of 74) received actual jail time, for an average length of about 7 months. Although the incarceration rate does not vary considerably from the earlier pre–1984 Fine Act cases, the average jail term for those who are sent to jail did increase from 3.5 months to 6.75 months.[33]

These incarceration rates and average jail sentences are probably lower than the average rate for all individuals convicted of environmental crimes. A tabulation of individuals convicted *without* a codefendant organization during the same time period (and listed in EPA's most recent criminal prosecution summary) reveals that 54.5 per cent of these individuals received jail time — for an average of 18 months (US Environmental Protection Agency, 1990b). Without a thorough analysis of the type of crime committed, it is not possible to determine the reasons for this difference. However, it is possible that pure negligence crimes are more likely to involve corporations and hence less likely to receive jail time.

It is clear from reading many of the cases involving both corporations and their individual codefendants that judges do not consider each party in isolation. The following examples illustrate some of the tradeoffs that appear to be prevalent.

Fines versus Jail for Owners of Closely Held Businesses

There is some evidence that judges are willing to trade off monetary sanctions against the firm for jail time for the owner when the offender is a small, closely held company. Two environmental cases illustrate this point. A chemical company in Georgia (Spartan Trading Co., Inc.) was convicted of storing, transporting and disposing of hazardous wastes without a permit. EPA reportedly spent $138,265 cleaning up one of the illegal dump sites. Although the firm was ordered to pay restitution to EPA, it was only fined $10,000 — an amount equal to about 7 per cent of the cleanup cost. However, the firm's owner was sentenced to one year in jail in addition to being liable for additional restitution to EPA for costs incurred beyond the estimated cleanup costs (US Environmental Protection Agency, 1990b, 82–3).

The second case involved Welco Plating, Inc., a firm in Woodville, Alabama, that pleaded guilty to various hazardous–waste violations. The firm was ordered to pay cleanup costs estimated at $1.3 million but was not fined beyond that amount. However, "J.C. Collins, Jr...president, stockholder and in charge of operations...was sentenced to pay a $200,000 fine, serve 18 months imprisonment, five years probation, 300 hours community service...[and]...pay $14,472.20 restitution to the State of Alabama Department of Environmental Management (US Environmental Protection Agency, 1990b, 79).

Corporate Officer Liability to Investors

Shareholders may sue corporate officers or directors to recover loss in share values or recoup fines and other costs related to criminal prosecutions. A recent ruling in the US District Court for Southern New York refused to dismiss a class action securities fraud and RICO suit against the board of directors of Par Pharmaceuticals — a generic drug manufacturer that pleaded guilty to falsifying test results and bribing FDA officials to obtain early approval for new drugs.[34] The firm was suspended from dealings with the federal government for three years. "After the bribes ceased, the rate of approvals slowed, earnings and sales declined, and the market price of Par securities fell sharply."[35]   The plaintiffs are seeking treble damages for loss in share value in this case under the theory that investors were first misled about the firm's special expertise in obtaining speedy FDA approval of new drug applications and later misled about the FDA investigation and the firm's role in bribing FDA officials. Several similar suits are apparently pending in the *Exxon Valdez* case.[36]

In some cases, courts have apparently shifted monetary sanctions to responsible individuals so as to lessen the impact on innocent shareholders — and hence avoid an expensive derivative lawsuit. For example, Rice Aircraft and its President, Bruce Rice, pleaded guilty to several counts of fraud and bribery, and admitted paying $155,000 in kickbacks and falsifying documents designed to certify product quality.[37] The firm was fined $50,000 and might also share some of the cost of restitution. However, Bruce Rice was fined $750,000, given a four–year prison term, and was ordered to pay court costs and restitution. According to the US Attorney in this case, Bruce Rice requested that the bulk of the fine be imposed on him personally, as he was in the process of being sued by minority shareholders.[38]

PRIVATE TORT SETTLEMENTS

It is extremely difficult to obtain reliable information on the frequency and magnitude of private tort cases related to corporate criminal offenses. In the few cases involving actual physical injury to victims, it is likely that these sanctions will far exceed any criminal penalty imposed by the sentencing court. In my earlier study of 288 cases from 1984–7, I found two instances of victim deaths — both resulting in minimal fines but substantial (and unreported) private settlements to victims (Cohen, 1989, 627). Similar results were reported for more recent cases.

The only environmental crime I know of that resulted in actual physical harm to individuals was the case against Orkin. The pesticide manufacturer was found guilty of violating FIFRA, following two deaths that resulted from the misuse of a pesticide. Orkin was fined $350,000 and ordered to perform 2,000 hours of community service. However, a significant private settlement was reportedly paid to the victims' family.[39] In addition, two employees earlier pleaded guilty in state court to unlawful use of a pesticide. They were each sentenced to two years probation, $1,000 fine and 200 hours community service.

EMPIRICAL ANALYSIS OF CURRENT SENTENCING PRACTICE

Most of the above discussion has been based on broad summary statistics and anecdotal evidence. Due to the nature of the sample size, this is often the best that can be done. However, this section will examine some of these issues in more detail and with somewhat more rigor. Table 4.4 reports on several regression equations where the dependant variable is either the criminal fine imposed on the organization or the total monetary sanction (converted to constant dollars and expressed in natural logs).[40] As shown in the first four equations, fines and total sanctions have increased over time and/or following passage of the higher statutory fine levels, although the coefficients on these variables are not overwhelmingly significant.[41] It should be noted that both of these variables were highly significant when fines and sanctions were expressed in current dollars. Thus, judges have increased fines and sanctions over time at a slightly faster rate than inflation.

Table 4.4 provides some insight into how judges currently sentence corporations convicted of environmental crimes. The level of monetary harm has been the most consistent and significant explanatory variable in earlier analyses of corporate sanctions in general (Cohen, 1991a). However, unlike pure monetary crimes such as tax evasion or fraud, harm is not always easy to quantify in environmental cases. In the context of environmental crimes, harm is generally the sum of cleanup costs and any residual environmental damage. It may also be expressed in terms of added risk of future injuries or illness. However, monetary valuations of these harms are seldom available.

For purposes of the regressions reported in Table 4.4, a zero–one dummy was constructed to account for crimes that caused significant monetary losses — usually in the form of required cleanup costs. This variable was coded one when there was an apparent loss in excess of $1 million, and zero otherwise. The "large loss" variable was highly significant and positive, as expected. Although a continuous monetary loss variable would be preferable, I only had actual data on monetary loss for about 20 cases.

The type of pollutant also had an important effect on sanctions, with hazardous–waste violations resulting in the largest fines. Toxic substances and Clean Water Act violations generally resulted in higher fines than in the case of pesticide violations, those involving false statements, testing violations or the Clean Air Act.

Although a variable labeled "vicarious liability" was included in the regression equations in Table 4.4, it was not significant. This is partly due to the fact that only six firms out of 116 could clearly be identified as being subject to this legal standard. Two of these six firms (Texaco and Helmerich & Payne) received relatively large fines

Table 4.4   *Regression analysis of fines and total sanctions, environmental offenses, 1984–90*

	Ln (Fine)	Ln (Total sanction)	Ln (Fine)	Ln (Total sanction)
Constant	8.82 (0.54) *	9.08 (16.39)	–9.35 (8.51)	–8.00 (8.88)
Pre–1984 Fine Act	–0.55 (0.37)	–0.42 (0.38)	——	——
Year of sentence	——	——	0.21 (0.10) *	0.19 (0.10) *
Large monetary loss	2.12 (0.98) *	3.47 (0.88) *	1.98 (0.97) *	1.62 (0.42) *
Hazardous waste	1.53 (0.53) *	1.62 (0.56) *	1.41 (0.53) *	1.50 (0.56) *
Toxic substances	1.08 (0.77)	1.44 (0.81)	1.23 (0.77)	1.60 (0.80) *
Clean Water Act	1.03 (0.56)	1.08 (0.59)	0.94 (0.56	0.96 (0.58)
Pesticides	0.76 (0.73)	0.44 (0.77)	0.71 (0.72)	0.42 (0.76)
Individual convicted	0.68 (0.32) *	0.59 (0.33)	0.67 (0.32) *	0.57 (0.33)
Vicarious liability	–0.36 (0.47)	0.04 (0.80)	–0.40 (0.75)	0.03 (0.78)

Table 4.4   Continued.

	Ln (Fine)	Ln (Total sanctions)	Ln (Fine)	Ln (Total sanction)
Testing violation	0.94 (0.74	0.57 (0.78)	0.74 (0.75)	0.34 (0.79)
False statement	−0.43 (0.62)	−0.34 (0.65)	−0/18 (0.63	−0.10 (0.66)
Not guilty plea (trial)	−0.24 (0.51)	0.01 (0.54)	−0.27 (0.51)	−0.02 (0.53)
Large firm	1.52 (0.41) *	1.63 (0.42) *	1.50 (0.40) *	1.62 (0.42) *
Adjusted R^2	0.22	0.29	0.23	0.31
Number of firms	109	113	109	113

Standard errors in parentheses.
* Difference is statistically significant at $p < 0.05$
NOTE: Since the fine and total sanction equations were estimated as log–linear models, cases where the fine or total sanction was zero were excluded from this analysis. However, in most cases, it appears that no fine was given due to special circumstances such as bankruptcy of the firm.

for a violation involving an employee who falsified safety test reports on an oil drilling platform. However, the other firms received relatively small fines.

Finally, we turn to the issue of individual versus corporate penalties. Segerson and Tietenberg (this volume) suggest that individual criminal liability and jail should be used primarily in instances where the firm cannot provide adequate incentives to employees, or when firm assets are inadequate to pay the "optimal" fine. Unfortunately, these explanatory variables are not easy to measure. Instead, a few less direct tests of this hypothesis will be attempted below.

Although information on firm size and financial ability was not available for all convicted companies, I was able to determine when firms are relatively large. Thus, a zero–one dummy variable was constructed to indicate when the organization is "large" — generally one with more than one establishment, and more than 500 employees or $50 million in sales. This variable proved to be highly significant and positive. The fact that monetary sanctions increase with firm size is somewhat troubling, especially if it is simply the case of judges or juries charging more to "deep pockets". If anything, the "optimal penalty" model might suggest just the opposite, as large firms are likely to suffer other nonmonetary losses such as loss in reputation or increased scrutiny of their other facilities (e.g. environmental audits).

One possible explanation for the larger penalty for larger firms is that individuals who are convicted in large firms are *less* likely to be sentenced to jail.[42] This would be consistent with the "optimal penalty" model summarized in Segerson and Tietenberg, suggesting that jail is generally required when the firm cannot afford the optimal penalty. Indeed, in a study of all corporate crimes (of which environmental crime is only one small part), I find that firms that *cannot* afford to compensate for the harm they imposed are *more* likely to have individual codefendants convicted of the same underlying crime (Cohen, 1991b, Tables 4 and 5). However, the latter study did not have data on the frequency of jail sentences — only individual convictions themselves.

Since individual and corporate penalties are supposed to be substitutes, several attempts were made to include variables on individual penalties in the regression equations explaining the corporate fine. Although not reported here, these equations generally found individual and corporate liability and penalties to be *complements*, not substitutes for each other (Cohen, 1991b, Table 6). However, it is possible that this reflects some unobservable measure of the severity of the offense.

It is possible that individual and corporate fines are considered to be complements for large organizations but substitutes for closely held firms. For an individual firm owner, it makes little difference if the fine is paid by the company or him/herself — it is ultimately the same pocket. However, for a large corporate entity, sanctions on employees and owners may serve very different purposes. Table 4.5 reports on two regression equations that isolate 40 companies known to be small and closely held. Although the evidence is not overwhelming, it appears that corporate fines and total sanctions are *negatively* related to a jail sentence for the owner of such companies. This *is* consistent with the Segerson–Tietenberg model, as jail and fines are seen as substitutes.

Table 4.5   Jail versus fines for 40 closely held companies

	Ln (Corporate fine)	Ln (Total monetary sanction)
Constant	9.90 (0.98)**	9.62 (0.82)**
Hazardous waste	0.19 (1.22)	1.14 (1.03)
Large monetary harm	–2.41 (2.78)	4.68 (2.35)**
Jail for owner (0–1 dummy)	–2.38 (1.30)*	–1.61 (1.10)
Sample size	40	40
Adjusted R–squared	0.04	0.13

NOTE: standard errors shown in parentheses.
* $p < 0.10$
** $p < 0.05$

IMPACT OF SENTENCING GUIDELINES ON ENVIRONMENTAL SANCTIONS

When Congress passed the Crime Control Act of 1984, it established the US Sentencing Commission ("Commission") as an independent regulatory body to write guidelines for sentencing federal offenders. The Commission published its first set of guidelines in November 1987. Since the law's basic purpose was to reduce judicial disparity, judges are essentially bound to apply the guideline sentence range for crimes committed after that date. Any departures from the guideline range must be explained in writing and are subject to appeal by either the government or the defendant.

Following a Congressional mandate to increase sentences for white–collar offenders, the Commission specifically set jail terms for individuals convicted of many white–collar offenses (including environmental crimes) at levels above current practice. In particular, the Commission significantly increased both the probability of going to jail and the length of the sentence for most white–collar offenses.

Under the sentencing guidelines, the mandatory jail term for a person convicted of an "ongoing, continuous, or repetitive discharge, release or emission of a pollutant into the environment...without a permit or in violation of a permit" is 21–27 months. If the pollutant is hazardous, toxic or a pesticide, this minimum is increased to 27–33 months. Further, if substantial cleanup expenditures are required, another 12–18 months is added to this range.[43] Not only do the new guidelines significantly increase the incarceration rate, but they will likely result in a substantial increase in the average length of jail time, shown to be 3 to 7 months in Table 4.3.

These higher incarceration rates and lengthy jail sentences have become extremely controversial. To see why, consider the case of John Pozsgai, who "was charged with 41 counts of systematically filling a 14–acre tract of land despite repeated warnings by inspectors of the Corps of Engineers that such activity required a permit under the Clean Water Act". Following the sentencing guidelines, the judge sentenced him to 27 months in jail with no parole. According to one critic of this sentence, although Mr Pozsgai did not obtain a permit despite repeated warnings, his offense was probably beneficial from an environmental standpoint. "The government does not dispute that the tiny stream adjacent to the property actually runs clearer due to Mr Pozsgai's cleanup efforts." Further, "before the guidelines were promulgated, no person ever was imprisoned for discharging nontoxic, non–hazardous pollutants" (Kamenar, 1990).

Aside from the philosophical/moral question of whether such sentences are "just", the prospect of overdeterrence is a real concern. This is of particular concern in light of the Justice Department's interest in attaching criminal liability to "responsible corporate officials" whenever they fail to prevent a violation.[44] Under this theory, corporate officials at Exxon could have received jail sentences of about $2\frac{1}{2}$ years for failing to prevent the *Valdez* oil spill.

More recently, the Commission adopted guidelines for the

sentencing of organizations. These guidelines, which go into effect for crimes committed after 1 November 1991, require full restitution and base the monetary fine on a multiple of the loss or gain resulting from the offense. The resulting fine levels are likely to involve substantial increases over current practice — perhaps as much as 10 to 20 times current levels. They also allow for the increased use of corporate probation and court–ordered apologies to be paid for by the defendant and published in appropriate media (US Sentencing Commission, 1991 8D1.3: Conditions of Probation).

The new corporate guidelines call for fines that are partially based on "culpability" scores, which contain strong financial incentives for firms to enact compliance programs in order to prevent crimes. These "culpability" scores apparently require a higher standard of care for large organizations. It remains to be seen how judges will interpret these factors and whether or not they will prove to be a burden to firms that are already showing a good–faith effort to comply.

Although environmental crimes are included in most of the organizational guideline provisions, the Commission did *not* include environmental crimes in the section dealing with monetary fines. Thus, at the time of writing, judges still have complete discretion in setting the monetary fine. However, the Commission expressed its desire to include fine provisions for environmental crimes in the near future. As discussed below, the impact of any new fine provisions will depend crucially on how "loss" or "harm" is defined. Given fine "multiples" of up to four times the loss, and the prosecution of strict–liability offenses, the potential exists for enormous increases in corporate criminal sanctions for environmental offenders.

CONCLUDING REMARKS

The criminal sanction can be a powerful vehicle for bringing about positive social change. However, it also has the potential to cause significant social harm. Unlike traditional street crime that serves no socially useful purpose, many types of white–collar and corporate crimes are outgrowths of legitimate business activities. Moreover, many of these crimes are strict liability (or vicarious liability to the firm whose employee commits the crime), or are subject to uncertain legal standards. For these crimes, society might wish to discourage but not entirely prohibit their occurrence. For example, eliminating all oil spills would require outlawing the transportation of oil itself.

Uncertain legal standards or strict liability for employee actions, coupled with the principal–agent relationship inherent in any large organization increase the possibility that legitimate firms acting in good faith to comply with existing regulations will find themselves on the wrong side of the criminal law. If criminal sanctions are too onerous, these legitimate "good actors" will undertake excessive and socially costly preventive activities to ensure they are never charged with a crime. Whether this form of overdeterrence is a real or merely a theoretical concern is an empirical issue.

This concluding section will explore several policy implications based on the empirical evidence reported on in this paper. It will conclude with a few suggestions for future research.

Are We "Overcriminalizing" Environmental Law?

This is one of the most important (and yet most difficult) issues that needs to be addressed before one can seriously begin to implement a rational criminal enforcement program. Some corporate crimes are committed by owners of closely held companies — essentially for their own personal gain. Other crimes are committed by employees and/or management in furtherance of company policy to break the law through regulatory noncompliance. Finally, some crimes are committed by companies and/or their employees through negligence, strict or vicarious liability.

There is growing concern about this last category — firms and/or corporate officers who are held criminally liable for incidents that are not intentional or not controllable by the party being held liable. Although few would argue against holding firms strictly liable for reasonable cleanup costs and third–party damages, punitive criminal sanctions in such cases are another matter. The data suggest that judges currently view these crimes differently, as they are reluctant to impose fines as punitive as would be necessary in cases of intentional conduct, gross negligence, or lack of appropriate or timely management follow–up.

Prior to the advent of sentencing guidelines, prosecutors who brought "bad" cases would be "punished" by judges with low fines and no jail sentences. Thus, Eagle Picher was given a slap on the wrist and fined $3,500 after being charged with a crime for an act of one of its employees that was clearly against company policy. The plant manager at Pennwalt who immediately notified the Coast Guard upon learning of an accidental spill (but unknowingly underreported the size and severity of the spill to the Coast Guard) and was later charged with "failure to notify the Coast Guard", was given a suspended sentence and $5,000 fine by the sentencing judge. Presumably, these sentences give important signals to prosecutors about which cases they should pursue in the future. However, under the current sentencing guidelines, the Pennwalt manager was likely to have been sentenced to a term of about two years in jail!

Sentencing guidelines that do not explicitly account for vicarious and strict liability increase the risk of future prosecutions of this sort *and* very punitive sanctions on these type of "offenders". If the judicial hand is tied without a comparable guideline for prosecutors, overdeterrence becomes inevitable.

Criminal Sanctions Should Be Based on Harm

Although the theory behind writing guidelines is laudable, in practice, one must take care not to impose more harm than good. The current guidelines for calculating criminal fines for organizations base their fine on a multiple of either "loss" or "gain". Economists have long argued that fines should not be based on a multiple of gain to the offender, since this may deter socially useful activities that are technically illegal. Thus, a harm–based guideline is likely to be preferable. Basing fines primarily on harm also has the advantage of forcing prosecutors to eschew prosecution of crimes that impose little social harm in favor of more significant crimes.

As mentioned earlier, the Commission did not include environmental offenses in the fine provisions of the organizational sanctions guideline. The main problem with including environmental crimes in these guidelines is the difficulty of quantifying harm. Particularly in the environmental area, concern has been expressed that requiring the government to prove monetary harm will burden the sentencing process (Coffee, 1989). The extent to which this is true will depend on the standards of proof required. There is no doubt that basing fines on harm will be a boon to environmental economists who will be called upon to monetize a whole host of environmental hazards. In at least one recent case, prosecutors brought in an expert economist to place a monetary value on birds that were killed by an offender.[45] Although this may not be necessary in many cases, permitting such testimony should be seen as a positive step towards making the punishment fit the social harm caused by the crime.

A potentially more important problem is that estimates of monetary loss can vary widely depending on how one defines the term "loss". For example, in the case of Ashland Oil, the prosecution claimed documented losses of $6 million and requested a $12 million fine (under provisions of the Criminal Fine Enforcement Act of 1984). However, note that if all cleanup costs and private settlements for losses to residents are inciuued in the loss calculation, the monetary loss in this case could easily exceed $55 million. A sentencing guideline that imposed a fine of two to four times the loss would require a $110 to $220 million fine in this case — far in excess of what either the prosecutors or the sentencing judge thought appropriate. Thus, a sentencing guideline that specifies a fine "multiple", without clearly defining the base to which it should be applied, could result in enormous disparity as well as fines that are far in excess of their intended levels.

Perhaps even more troubling, however, is the fact that a guideline based on a multiple of losses might hinder cleanup and victim– compensation efforts. If Ashland Oil or Exxon knew they would be fined a multiple of losses, the firms might have been much less inclined either to clean up as much of their spills as they did, or to settle private claims for monetary losses.

Admittedly, some crimes involve harms that are not amenable to monetary estimation. Examples include falsified test or monitoring results, obstruction of justice, and cases of significant risk to the national security or the public confidence in institutions. However, these cases are the exception rather than the rule and can be handled with separate guideline provisions not tied to monetary losses.

Criminal Sanctions Are Only One Part of the Total Picture

A million–dollar fine has the same effect on a firm as a million–dollar private settlement to victims or a comparable loss in reputational capital (after appropriate adjustments for the tax consequences of these various payments). There is some evidence that judges currently consider civil sanctions and private settlements to victims in determining an appropriate criminal sanction. At a minimum, sentencing guidelines should allow the judge to consider other direct monetary costs incurred by the firm, including private settlements made to victims, cleanup costs, and remedial action to ensure future compliance. If the goal is to ensure that firms have incentives to take the optimal level of care to prevent accidental spills, monitor their employees, etc., then one must be concerned about the overall effect of sanctions on the firm.

Future Research Issues

Although we know more about corporate crime and punishment than we did a few years ago, there is still a lot we do not know. We still do not fully understand the motives and complex interrelationships among the various actors in the criminal justice arena. Are judges an effective or a misguided check on prosecutorial behavior? We need a better understanding of the relationship between civil and criminal sanctions — why are some cases pursued through administrative remedies while others end up in criminal court?[46] Why do judges send some environmental offenders to jail while others receive little more than probation or a few thousand dollar fine?

In addition to studying current sentencing practice, more research is needed on the ultimate effect of sanctions on corporate behavior. Which sanctions are effective at deterring unlawful behavior while not stifling innovative and productive business behavior? What are the costs and benefits of imposing environmental audits as a condition of probation? Do reputational losses apply to environmental and/or small closely held firms? What effect does adverse publicity and court–ordered public apologies have on firm sales and profitability? What effect has the increased likelihood of jail sentences for environmental offenders had on corporate compliance? Although many commentators believe the overdeterrence issue is a red herring, there is sufficient historical evidence that law abiding corporations take socially costly actions when confronted with uncertain legal standards and high penalties.[47] We need to study this issue further before dismissing overdeterrence as a figment of the economist's imagination. This is particularly important in the light of current trends towards the prosecution of regulatory offenses and strict liability crimes.

NOTES

1. Rivers and Harbors Appropriation Act of 1899, 33 U.S.C. 407 (commonly referred to as the Refuse Act of 1899).
2. The most recent case against Exxon for the Valdez oil spill is an excellent example of this phenomenon. See, for example, Stephen Labaton, "Does an Assault on Nature Make Exxon a Criminal?", *New York Times* 23 April 1989.
3. There are many law review articles on criminal liability for environmental offenses. See for example, "Individual Liability..." (1989), Riesel (1985) and Carter (1980). For a comprehensive legal treatise on corporate and executive criminal liability in general, see Brickey (1984). It is important to note that the following discussion refers primarily to federal law. Although many state laws are patterned after federal laws, differences do exist.
4. However, recent changes in federal law have increased the compensation aspect of criminal enforcement, as judges are advised to award restitution whenever possible. See 18 U.S.C. 3663–3664.
5. The case is *U.S.* v. *Hoflin*, 880 F2d 1033 (9th Cir. 1989); cert denied, 110 S. Ct. 1143 (1990), as cited and discussed in Arkin (1990).
6. Corporate Crime Reporter, 14 August 1989, p. 16 (interview with David Vance Marshall).
7. Of course, since certain payments may be tax deductible, one would first have to compute the after–tax cost of each alternative before comparing them.
8. One preliminary and limited attempt to test for a differential effect between criminal and civil sanctions found no difference between the two. See Block (1991).
9. For example, executives in Pennsylvania have reportedly been sent to jail for terms as high as 5 to 12 years for hazardous waste violations. See M. A. Verespej, "The Newest Environmental Risk: Jail", Industry Week. 22 January 1990, p. 47.
10. It appears that the typical firm convicted of an environmental offense is larger than for other offenses. During the 1984–8 time period, only about 15–20% of these companies were large enough to be listed in the Standard and Poor's Register, which generally lists firms with at least $1 million in annual sales or more than 50 employees, while only about 3–5% had publicly traded stock (Cohen, 1991a).
11. According to 1988 Sentencing Commission data, corporations indicted for other crimes have a similar individual codefendant rate — 70%.
12. Monetary fines reported throughout this paper are based on the amount actually imposed by the court — excluding any suspended portion. If a portion of the fine was suspended, that suspended portion was not included in the fine calculation. Further, we do not know if the fine was actually collected, or if the suspended fine was eventually reinstated due to probation violations.

13. As of November 1989, Ashland reported spending $30 million on costs other than the criminal fine; including $14 million to settle more than 5,000 third–party claims; $11 million in direct cleanup costs; and $5.25 million in legal and administrative fees to handle the class action suits. "Ashland to Pay $4.7 Million in Spill", *Los Angeles Times*, 23 Nov. 1989, p. D1. More recently, the firm settled a class action lawsuit filed by nearby residents for $30 million. See "In Brief", *Corporate Crime Reporter*, 12 March 1990, p. 14.

14. Matthew Brelis, "Guilty Pleas in Oil Spill; Agreement Means $500,000 for R.I.", *Boston Globe*, 33 17 August 1989.

15. Ibid.

16. The Criminal Fine Enforcement Act of 1984, P.L. 98–596, 98 Stat. 3134, which took effect for crimes committed after 1 January 1985, increased the statutory maximum penalty for corporate offenders to $100,000 per misdemeanor count and $500,000 per felony count (or misdemeanors resulting in death), with a total fine no more than twice the most serious count for counts arising out of the same course of conduct. As an alternative, the court can impose a fine of up to twice the pecuniary loss or twice the pecuniary gain. In most cases, these changes represented significant increases in statutory maximum fines — often set at $5,000 to $10,000.

17. See for example, "Preliminary Comments of General Electric Company on the United States Sentencing Commission's Proposed Organizational Sanctions", 11 (September 1989) (on file with US Sentencing Commission).

18. Additional information on this incident is contained in Eagle Picher's 10–K filing for 1985.

19. See *supra*, note 13.

20. "Ashland Oil is Indicted in Pennsylvania Oil Spill", *Washington Post* 16 Sept 1988, p. A4.

21. "Ashland Pleads No Contest in Oil Spill", *United Press International*, 8 Feb 1989.

22. *Corporate Crime Reporter*, 3 April 1989, p. 15.

23. *Corporate Crime Reporter*, 14 August 1989, p. 14 (interview with David Vance Marshall).

24. For two differing views on corporate probation, see Toensing (1990) and Coffee (1990). See also Coffee, Gruner and Stone (1988).

25. Suspensions and debarments are imposed in at least 25% of government procurement cases, and 20% of government program fraud cases (Cohen, 1989, 615 – Table 4).

26. See "EPA Enforcement Officials Outline Plans to Bolster against Corporate Polluters", *20 Environment Reporter*, 2012 27 April 1990.

27. *Corporate Crime Reporter*, 7 August 1989, p. 16. Note that the recently adopted US Sentencing Commission guidelines for organizational sanctions include a provision for this type of sanction as a condition of probation (US Sentencing Commission, 1991, 8D1.3(c) — "Conditions of Probation").

28. *Corporate Crime Reporter*, 13 November 1989, p. 17.

29. A & A Land Development and 7 codefendants were convicted of RICO and conspiracy charges in connection with illegal waste disposal operations (US Environmental Protection Agency, 1990b, 115).

30. "EPA Enforcement Officials Outline Plans to Bolster against Corporate Polluters", *20 Environment Reporter*, 2012, citing John Kaye, prosecutor for Monmouth County, N.J.

31. Garbade, Silber and White (1982) analysed 34 companies named in either price–fixing or monopolization antitrust suits and found an average drop of 6% in share value within four trading days of the filing of a suit. Similar results have been found in more recent studies by Straachan, Smith and Beedles (1983) and Cloninger, Skantz and Strickland (1988), who find a 17% cumulative stock price drop. More recently, Karpoff and Lott (1990) examined 71 firms who had been engaged in fraudulent activity, and found a 3.5% loss in market share in 30 days following public announcements of investigations or prosecutions. However, the largest losses were suffered by firms who

reported fraudulent financial statements. Losses for government and consumer fraud were smaller — although still significant.

32. According to an article in *Fortune* (12 February 1990, p. 44), "Not long after the March accident in Valdez (Exxon), Alaska, 41% of Americans were angry enough to say they'd seriously consider boycotting the company." The recent boycott of tuna (due to concern for the safety of dolphins) suggests that this is a real possibility in the future.

33. As far as I know, only four of the individuals in Table 4.3 had sentences imposed under the Sentencing Guidelines. One received a 15–month jail sentence, and the other three (all of whom are partial owners of Finishing Corp. of America) received no jail time. In the second case, the prosecutor appealed the sentence on the basis that the Guidelines required imposition of jail time. This case was won by the government on appeal, and was sent back to the district court for resentencing (*U.S.* v. *John W. Rutana*, 1991 U.S. App. LEXIS 8968, 8 May 1991). Since the Sentencing Guidelines substantially increased the likelihood of a jail sentence, current sanctions against individual offenders are likely to be more punitive than they were in the past.

34. "Fraud Suit Based on Bribery Scheme Largely Withstands Dismissal Motion", 22 Securities Regulation and Law Report 551 (13 April 1990). (See, In re Par Pharmaceutical Inc. Securities Litigation, 88 Civ. 8154 (RPP), DC SNY, 3/16/90.)

35. Ibid.

36. "Getting Ready for Exxon vs. Practically Everybody", *Business Week*, 25 September 1989, p. 190.

37. "Aerospace Exec Given Four–Year Prison Term", *Seattle Times*, 10 March 1990, p. B8.

38. Phone conversation with Assistant US Attorney Bruce Carter, 15 June 1990.

39. "Pest Control Company Fined $500,000 in Death of Couple", *New York Times*, 18 November 1988, B7.

40. Although both linear and log–linear models were tested, the log linear specification is clearly a better fit and is reported here.

41. Since the sentence year was highly correlated with the zero–one dummy used to represent cases subject to the post–1984 Fine Act, it was not possible to include them both in one equation. Sentence year had more explanatory power than the Fine Act, suggesting that environmental sanctions have increased over time.

42. Of the 116 firms, 23 are classified as being "large". The individual conviction rate is about 50% in both small and large firms. However, only about 9% of large firms involve individuals sent to jail, compared to 25% for small firms. Of those individuals convicted, the chance of going to jail is 18% in a large firm and 43% in a small firm.

43. US Sentencing Commission (1990), 2Q1.2 and 2Q1.3. Other aggravating factors (such as prior criminal history) may also increase the sentence. In addition, it is possible to reduce the sentence by about 6 months if the defendant "clearly demonstrates a recognition and affirmative acceptance of personal responsibility for his criminal conduct" (3E1.1 – Acceptance of Responsibility). It is also possible to obtain a reduction of 6 months to 1 year if the person is only a minor or minimal participant in a larger group committing the criminal offense (3B1.2 – Mitigating Role). Finally, judges are permitted to depart from the guidelines if they desire, for cases "involving negligent conduct" as opposed to "knowing conduct" (2Q1.2, comment, note. 4). See also, Starr and Kelly (1990).

44. See Beth Olanoff and John S. Summers, "Polluting is now More of a Crime than Ever Before", unpublished manuscript. The authors argue that Justice Department officials are looking to pursue cases of this nature in the future.

45. See "Goldfish Farmer's Sentencing Delayed Three Weeks", *United Press International*, 19 March 1990, and "Bird Killings Draw 13–Month Sentence", *Los Angeles Times*, 1 May 1990, p. A20.

46. To date, EPA has not coordinated their civil and criminal enforcement programs. More surprisingly, it is still virtually impossible for EPA to determine the overall

compliance record of a company. For example, the air office does not know the compliance history of the firm with the water office. Both of these shortcoming are being addressed by the current EPA Administrator, and future enforcement actions are likely to be more targeted.

47. For example, a study of Fortune 500 companies found that a majority of those surveyed had instituted antitrust compliance programs that included provisions to avoid legal activity that might prompt a government antitrust investigation. For example, many firms require that price discounts be approved by several management levels and that they never fall below fully allocated costs even if geographic competition is intense. Other policies include the frequent rotation of sales personnel and prohibiting employee membership in trade associations. See Beckenstein, Gabel and Roberts, 1983.

5. Private Enforcement

Wendy Naysnerski & Tom Tietenberg[1]

INTRODUCTION

The Issue

The degree to which environmental quality is improved by public policy depends not only on the wisdom inherent in policy design but also on the effectiveness of policy enforcement. Policies which initially seem to offer promise may, in the glare of hindsight, prove unsuitable if enforcement is difficult or lax.

The economics literature on enforcement has focused on a number of topics, including the role of enforcement considerations in policy instrument choice,[2] the effectiveness of current enforcement techniques,[3] and suggestions for improving the enforcement process.[4] One theme that emerges from these works is that a considerable amount of noncompliance is occurring.[5] Furthermore, limited public enforcement budgets and judicial limits on public enforcement powers[6] suggest that traditional enforcement agencies are not likely to mount a completely adequate response to the environmental degradation resulting from noncompliance.

One possible means of dealing with inadequate compliance is to complement public enforcement with private enforcement. In principle, private groups could perform many of the functions performed by public enforcement agencies, thereby circumventing some of the public resource and staff constraints. But how would such an alternative work out in practice?

Fortunately, some recent experimentation with private enforcement in the United States allows us to begin to assess how this approach works out in practice.[7] Private groups can now use the courts to pursue better environmental quality in three main ways: (i) by suing polluters to recover monetary damages caused by the pollution, (ii)

109

by suing public officials entrusted with responsibility for implementing the laws to force compliance with Congressional or Constitutional requirements, and (iii) by suing polluters for the purpose of bringing them into compliance with the law.

The third of these channels, the focus of our analysis, is the most recently authorized. Prior to 1970, state and federal agencies held exclusive enforcement responsibility. However, in 1970, while amending the Clean Air Act, Congress authorized private citizens to seek injunctions (and in some cases financial penalties) against firms violating the terms of their operating permits; environmental enforcement was no longer purely the exclusive responsibility of the government. Since that time a number of other federal statutes have incorporated citizen suit provisions.

Overview

Although citizen suits are becoming a widely used method of enforcing environmental statutes, economists know little about how they fit into the fabric of environmental policy.[8] What determines the amount of litigation activity? What are the consequences of these suits? Where do they fit in the overall fabric of environmental policy? The remainder of this chapter will begin the process of filling the void.

EXPLAINING PRIVATE LITIGATION ACTIVITY

Profit–maximizing choices do not necessarily maximize social net benefits. Environmental problems represent one well–known example of this type of inefficient behavior. In the absence of some kind of external restraint a polluting firm will typically not only produce too much pollution, but can also make inefficient decisions with respect to its choice of inputs, the location of its production facilities and its scale of operations, to name a few.

The Demand for Private Litigation

In the past, the government has been expected to be the sole means of correcting such externalities by enacting rules, standards, penalties or subsidies. An appropriate application of these instruments changes producer incentives and forces a recognition of the external costs.

However, political solutions are not always efficient solutions. Self–interest in politics can create political failure, just as it can create market failure in economics. When an inefficiently low level of environmental quality results from the political process, an unsatisfied demand for better environmental quality exists. This unsatisfied demand provides an economic basis for the establishment of environmental organizations.[9]

Why do non–profit groups develop? The theory pursued in this research, a variant of a model originally developed by Weisbrod (1988), suggests that nonprofit groups arise to provide higher levels of public goods which are incompletely supplied by the government. If the government does not supply the efficient amount of public goods, an unsatisfied demand for higher levels of provision exists. Although the theory of public goods is quite clear that it would be unrealistic to expect private, nonprofit organizations to make up all of the deficient supply, they can and do satisfy some of this unsatisfied demand.[10]

One such public good is environmental quality. When the government is unable to produce the efficient amount of environmental quality, non–profit environmental groups work to bring about higher levels. This would be expected whenever the increased benefits of environmental improvement to the membership exceed the cost of securing that improvement. Once organized to increase the amount of environmental protection, environmental groups maintain themselves through membership fees, contributions, grants, etc.

Privately Optimal Litigation Activity

One process by which non–profit environmental groups pursue higher environmental quality, the specific process providing the focus for our analysis, is by initiating private enforcement actions, known popularly as citizen suits. Environmental groups undertaking citizen suits must first determine which suits to pursue, taking into account their budget constraint. In our model individual groups are presumed to maximize their individual net benefits (the excess of benefits over costs) from their litigation activity.

Imagine that the environmental organization's strategists have made up a list of potential litigation targets. Each potential target is characterized by both the expected benefits and the expected cost from pursuing a citizen suit. The resulting array of targets is then sequenced; those potential targets with the highest net benefits would appear earlier in the array. As the organization moves further down its list of litigation targets the marginal net benefit (the expected net benefits from undertaking another suit) decreases, since cases with a lower net benefit to the citizen organization would be considered after those offering higher net benefits.

To maximize total expected net benefits environmental groups will take on additional suits until the marginal expected net benefit associated with the last chosen case would be equal to zero.[11] Pursuing addition targets would be nonoptimal because the costs of enforcement action would exceed the benefits.

To implement this model it is necessary to be quite specific about the nature of the expected net benefits from litigation. Expected net benefit is the product of three variables: the probability that the suit will result in an environmental improvement, the value of the resulting improvement to the members, and the cost to the organization of securing this improvement.

The Benefits from Litigation
The increase in environmental quality which results either directly or indirectly from successful enforcement is the prime benefit to the organization. Members, foundations and other donors respond to concrete evidence of successful action. The value of the improvement that could be expected from targeting any particular pollution situation would depend on such factors as the toxicity of the substance, amount of the substance involved and the amount of exposure to the substance by humans or other species in the ecological system and the amount of damage posed by this particular risk.

Litigation benefits can extend well beyond those achieved in the immediate case. Since the courts pay a great deal of attention to the precedents established by earlier decisions in reaching subsequent verdicts, establishing a favorable precedent can convey significant subsequent benefits to private enforcers. When a successful suit has precedent value to the private enforcer (meaning that it facilitates successful subsequent enforcement actions), it conveys more net benefits, all other things being equal. Suits with precedent value could therefore be expected to be higher in the ranking of litigation targets than otherwise comparable suits with no precedent value.

Litigation Costs
The cost of litigation includes all time and money spent by the environmental organization in pursuit of litigation (net of any reimbursement award by the court). Discovery, investigation, lawyer fees, court costs, and support staff are all expenses that have to be covered.

Public/Private Enforcement Interactions

Though simple, the model does have a number of interesting implications, including the relationship between public and private enforcement. Private enforcement does not operate in a vacuum. Since public and private enforcement are partial substitutes, the demand for private enforcement should be related to the level of public enforcement.

Complete Public Enforcement
One interesting implication of this model can be derived immediately by examining a rather special, limiting case. If government enforcement were complete, all polluters would be in compliance with their legal requirements. Since a successful citizen suit action depends upon proving a violation of these requirements, the probability of successful litigation activity would be zero. With a zero probability of success the expected net benefits for all cases would be zero. Citizen suits would not develop if government enforcement were complete because no marginal net benefit would be derived from taking any private enforcement action.

Lax Public Enforcement
Another implication, this one testable in principle, follows immediately. Low levels of public enforcement could be expected to

increase the private benefits from private litigation activity. Violations could be expected to be more frequent and more serious in periods of lax enforcement. It follows that the optimal level of private enforcement is inversely related to the amount of public enforcement. All other things being equal, we would expect more citizen enforcement activity in periods with diminished government enforcement activity.

The evidence seems to support this hypothesis.[12] A slowdown in federal environmental enforcement, especially under the Clean Water Act, did occur in 1981 and 1982. The number of suits filed fell from 184 in 1979 to 118 in 1981 and 47 in 1982 (Miller, 1984a, 10424).

Declines in the EPA budget mirror the declines in environmental programs and enforcement during the early 1980s. EPA's total budget, which was $1.4 billion in 1981, fell to $1.16 billion in 1982. A further reduction to approximately $975 million occurred in 1983. These budget decreases caused a resulting fall in the number of EPA staff enforcement attorneys from 200 to 30 during 1983 (Feller, 1983, 554).

Our model would lead us to expect an increase in private enforcement activity during this period. Our database confirms that this is exactly what happened.[13] Although citizen suits were first instituted in 1970, fewer than 25 suits were filed between 1970 and 1978. It wasn't until 1983 that they became a significant factor in environmental enforcement. During the period from 1982 through 1986 the number of citizen actions jumped from 41 to 266.[14] While federal enforcement was decreasing in the early 1980s, private enforcement was picking up the slack. Once the staffs were hired, a track record established, and donors located, the private enforcement process became self-sustaining.

Patterns of Litigation Activity

One of the intriguing puzzles one encounters when closely examining the data on citizen suits is the patterns of activity that have emerged. Not only have some statutes spawned many more citizen actions than others, but the pattern of private litigation activity is quite different than the pattern of public enforcement activity.[15] The Clean Water Act and the Resource Conservation and Recovery Act triggered the lion's share of the suits. Interestingly, the Clean Air Act, the forerunner of the entire process, was responsible for fewer suits than later Acts, so clearly chronology is not an adequate explanation. To examine the sources of this particular evolutionary pattern it is necessary to imbed the characteristics of the different statutes into our model.

The Availability of Penalty Remedies

While most statutes provide for an injunctive remedy, some have provided for penalties to be awarded in addition to an injunction. While the criteria for deciding when additional penalties may be possible has been hotly contested in recent court decisions,[16] the impact of the various decisions on private litigation can be explored with our litigation model.

The ability to impose penalties, as well as injunctions, on polluters increases the benefits from private litigation activity even when all penalties go directly into the general treasury. An action which results in penalties as well as an injunction is perceived by the organizations and members to have a higher deterrence value.[17] More effective deterrence ultimately translates into a higher probability that environmental improvement would result from a successful suit.

Since any firm sued for an injunction and penalties faces a higher cost of noncompliance, it is presumed more likely to comply with regulations. The implication is clear; according to our model, statutes which allow penalty actions would be expected to induce a higher level of private enforcement litigation activity than those which allow only injunctions.

Once again, despite our inability to control for intervening influences, the evidence seems to support this implication. The database focuses on six statutes, three of which offered penalty remedies during the period covered by our analysis. Of the 1414 statute citations in the 1205 actions, 1373 were to the penalty statutes.[18] Statutes which allow penalties represent only 50 per cent of the statutes in the database, but were responsible for over 97 per cent of the citations.

The Disposition of Penalties

Our litigation model implies that the amount and type of litigation activity is affected not only by whether a penalty remedy is available, but also by the disposition of the penalty. When penalties go to the general treasury, the marginal benefit received on behalf of the environmental group is limited to increased compliance. However, penalties earmarked for environmental improvement ensure a larger improvement in environmental quality in the specific area covered by the suit than is achieved by general revenue penalties. By bringing suit the environmental group reveals an interest in the environment, an interest which is threatened by noncompliance. If the citizen group did not care about this particular environmental problem, they presumably would not have brought suit. Therefore, penalties earmarked for improvements in environmental quality would provide yet another increase in benefits to the environmental groups. The expected benefits from litigation would be higher for those potential targets offering the possibility of earmarked penalties than for those where earmarked penalties were not possible.[19]

The availability of earmarked penalties could be expected to change not only the level of litigation activity, but it would also change the litigation priorities for the citizen group. All other things being equal, suits offering the possibility of earmarked penalties have higher net benefits and could therefore be expected to appear higher in the priority list of potential targets. Once the firm reordered its litigation priorities to reflect this difference, one would expect a rise in the percentage of suits with targeted penalties.

The proposition that targeted–penalties suits could be expected to comprise a larger portion of litigation activity as earmarking becomes more common is also supported by our data. Although the database does not contain settlement information on all 1205 cases, it does show that earmarking occurred as early as 1982 but didn't become widespread until the mid– to late– 1980s. The data reveal that, as expected, once earmarking became possible, earmarked penalties tend to dominate penalty remedies. Over the period from 1983 to 1986, 80 per cent of the cases involving penalties dedicated the money to an environmental fund rather than to the US Treasury.

Another attractive feature of earmarked penalties for environmental groups is the fact that larger penalties are frequently possible with earmarking. According to our database, the average earmarked penalty is larger than the average penalty dedicated to general revenue.[20] Larger earmarked penalties are possible in part because the polluter sees them as less onerous. Penalties earmarked to an environmental fund, for example, are perceived to produce a better public image. Also, in some cases, earmarked "contributions to environmental improvement" are tax deductible while civil penalties are not.

Attorney Fee Reimbursement

Attorney fee reimbursement is yet another factor which can be expected to influence the pattern of litigation activity. Most federal statutes allow citizen groups to be reimbursed for all the court costs including lawyer fees. If the citizen action is deemed to be "appropriate", the environmental group will be reimbursed for attorney fees in addition to other costs. Since only successful or partially successful claims are reimbursed, any incentives to initiate nuisance or harassment suits are diminished.

Since reimbursement only occurs for successful suits, the likelihood that a suit will be successful is one major determinant of the expected cost of undertaking any suit where attorney reimbursement is an issue. What is the likelihood of success? Of the 507 settlements recorded in our database only four involved a decision for the defendant. Obviously private enforcement actions tend to have a very high likelihood of success; the probability of reimbursement is high.

With attorney fee reimbursement, the net benefits (after reimbursement) placed on environmental groups increase. Our model would suggest that this increase in net benefits would encourage more litigation activity and a rearrangement of resources toward those claims which offer the possibility of attorney fee reimbursement.

One way to examine this implication is to examine the relative amount of private enforcement activity under federal and state statutes. Because attorney fees were not usually provided for in state statutes during the period covered by our data, all other things being equal, more citizen suits could be expected under federal statutes than under state statutes. Once again the data seem compatible with the implications of our model. Of the total sample of 1205 citizen suits in the period from 1978 to 1987 only 55 were brought under state statutes. Attorney fee reimbursement appears to have been a major stimulant to private enforcement activity.

Burden of Proof

Under the Clean Water Act the National Pollutant Discharge Elimination System (NPDES) requires polluters to file with EPA discharge monitoring reports (DMRs) which list discharge levels and method of discharge. By reducing the costs of monitoring and validation of suspect emission levels, this system of reports has become a very important component of private enforcement of water pollution violations. Citizens have access to the discharge monitoring reports, and the courts have generally accepted the information contained in them as proof of violations.[21] By allowing citizens to use them as the basis for their claims, monitoring reports significantly reduce the cost of private enforcement litigation.

Although the monitoring reports under the NPDES program of the Clean Water Act are the most consistently useful to citizen groups, reports which share some of these characteristics are available under other statutes as well. While these statutes require some monitoring and provide some citizen access, the usefulness of the resulting information is more limited than that available under the Clean Water Act. First of all, determining whether a violation has occurred under these two acts is more complex and the reports on their face do not stipulate whether the firm is or isn't in compliance. Therefore the private enforcer must be intimately familiar with the exact guidelines of the statute and the information in the reports must be sufficient in order to determine whether compliance is occurring. Secondly, while CWA reports are available to the public without condition, reports under other statutes may be deemed confidential and citizen access forbidden (Fadil, 1985, 68–9). While these less–specific reports can serve as a basis for proving a violation, they do not reduce the cost of taking a private enforcement action as greatly as the straightforward discharge monitoring reports under the Clean Water Act. The burden of proof is heavier. The relatively light burden of proof citizen suits face under the Clean Water Act is certainly a major contributing factor in the dominance of this Act in attracting private litigation activity. Apparently Congress has now extended the discharge monitoring report system to the Clean Air Act.[22]

Reliance on EPA reports is crucial to the private enforcement process because private investigators do not have the same investigatory powers as the government. Private parties will normally be denied entrance to the property of the polluter, making it difficult to prove many kinds of violations.[23]

The Geographic Distribution of Private Enforcement Activity

Another pattern emerging from the data is the uneven distribution of private enforcement actions among the states. Suits were much more likely to be filed in some states than others. The ten states with the largest shares of suits filed is presented in Table 5.1.

The list strongly suggests the importance of the scale of industrial production in motivating private enforcement actions. States with larger scales of production appear to receive more private litigation activity.

Settling Out of Court

The previous discussion has assumed that litigation activity involves a full examination of the issues in a courtroom, culminating in a court–imposed decision. But that is not the only possible outcome. Environmental groups have the choice of settling out of court either formally, by signing a consent agreement, or informally through a negotiated settlement. Under what conditions would they do so?

Our first expectation would be that, in general, consent decrees would be preferred to court decisions by both parties because they are so much cheaper. Both defendants and plaintiffs can cut their legal expenses by settling out of court, a powerful incentive to both sides.

The one classic case when a full court process is desirable is when one of the litigants is using the case to establish a precedent. Since negotiated settlements do not carry the precedent value of court decisions, litigants may pursue a case purely to establish a favorable precedent. Once the favorable precedent is in place, future favorable outcomes would be easier to achieve.

One empirical question of some importance is whether or not settling out of court produces a quantitatively or qualitatively

Table 5.1   *The geographic distribution of private enforcement*
actions

Top 10 states	Percentage of total private suits filed
Pennsylvania	13.53%
New York	10.33%
New Jersey	6.35%
Connecticut	5.98%
Indiana	4.98%
Texas	4.73%
Massachusetts	4.65%
Michigan	4.07%
Louisiana	3.98%
California	3.57%

SOURCE : Compiled by the authors from citizen suit database.

different outcome than proceeding through the entire court process. While the data are not sufficient to reach a strong conclusion on this point, some interesting information is available.

Our expectation that out of court settlements would normally be preferred is borne out by the data. More cases are settled out of court than in. However, the average penalties assessed do differ. Although only 20 in–court settlements involved penalty assessments, three of the assessed penalties were $15 million, 8 million and 5 million. The average penalty assessment for out–of–court settlements was $89,214, while the average penalty for in–court settlements was $1,928,745; the difference is large, but the sample size is too small to make much of it.

ENFORCEMENT AND COMPLIANCE INCENTIVES

The effectiveness of private enforcement depends not only on the behavior of citizen groups but also on how the targets of the suits, the polluters, respond. According to our model of compliance behavior, their response depends on several characteristics of the private litigation process. These characteristics vary considerably among the various statutes authorizing citizen suits. We will initially assume that the firm faces administrative or civil public enforcement; this becomes the benchmark case. We will then add the effect of private enforcement to derive the resulting effect on the degree of compliance.

The Benchmark: Public Enforcement Only

Suppose the polluting firm is presumed is to be a cost–minimizer. One of the choices it faces in minimizing costs is the degree of compliance with environmental regulations it will pursue. Cost–minimization for the firm would be achieved at that degree of compliance where the sum of the costs of compliance and the expected costs of noncompliance were minimized.

The costs of achieving compliance involve the capital, material and labor costs associated with greater control of emissions, while the expected costs associated with noncompliance include the likelihood that any noncompliance would be discovered, the likelihood that any discovered noncompliance would be successfully prosecuted, and the noncompliance sanctions imposed by the administrative agency or the court. The expected costs associated with any degree of non–compliance are the probability of a successful enforcement action multiplied by the expected penalty.

The expected penalty curve is assumed to decline with the degree of compliance due to the lower probability that any penalty would be imposed and the smaller size of any imposed penalty. At complete compliance the appropriate emission standard would be met so the expected penalty would be zero for all levels of emission reduction at least as great as required by the standard.

The cost of compliance is assumed to increase with the degree of compliance. Greater emissions control is expensive and the costs typically rise more than proportionately with the amount controlled.

The Effect of Citizen Suits

With the initiation of citizen suits, the expected penalty to the firm would increase for all noncomplying firms. Adding the likelihood of a private enforcement action to that of public enforcement implies a higher probability of a successful enforcement action against the firm; this increased likelihood of enforcement increases the expected penalty for noncompliance. Any firms not in compliance with the standards under public enforcement would be expected to take higher levels of precaution when confronted with citizen suits. Firms in compliance would not change their behavior in response to private enforcement because their expected penalty would be zero both before and after the onset of citizen suits.

Although increased compliance is in principle a testable hypothesis, in practice no systematic compliance data are publicly available. However, interviews with officials at EPA and the Conservation Law Foundation, two organizations with first–hand knowledge of the private enforcement process from two different perspectives, reveal a shared belief that citizen suits have indeed led to greater compliance.[24] This view is apparently shared by at least some business executives.[25]

Remedies and Compliance Behavior

The degree of compliance can be expected to be affected by the available remedies as well as by the existence of private enforcement activity. As discussed above, different statutes make different remedies available to citizen groups.

A firm confronted by noncompliance sanctions which include both penalties and injunctions faces higher costs of noncompliance than a firm faced only with an injunction. Not only would an enforcement action require noncomplying firms to come into compliance with the standard as soon as possible (the traditional costs associated with an injunction), but paying the imposed penalties would add to the financial burden. (Higher penalties would have no effect on precaution for complying firms.)

A second, less–obvious reason why greater compliance would be expected from statutes authorizing penalties involves the greater incentives for citizen groups to undertake these suits, a point covered in earlier sections. This greater likelihood of a suit translates into yet another rightward shift in the marginal expected penalty curve. Firms facing suit under statutes authorizing penalties are more likely to be in compliance than firms facing suit under the other statutes because of the greater likelihood of private enforcement.

Attorney Fee Reimbursement

Under federal statutes a polluting firm which loses a least a portion of a private enforcement action must reimburse that portion of attorney fees, court costs, etc. of the private enforcer who brought the suit. At least for the period covered by our database state statutes typically did not include this provision.

Attorney fee reimbursement has two separate effects on the cost–minimizing degree of compliance. On the one hand it raises the expected penalty for violations. Not only does the firm have to bear the costs of coming into compliance and paying any imposed penalties, it also has to pay court costs (including attorney fees) of the other side. This should trigger an increase in the cost–minimizing degree of compliance. In addition as we suggested above, the likelihood of any polluter being subject to private enforcement is higher when attorney fees are reimbursed, since the optimal amount of litigation activity for citizen groups increases when their fees are reimbursed. Increased private enforcement would cause the marginal expected penalty curve to shift out as well, since the likelihood of being the subject of an enforcement action would have increased.

The Substitutability of Public and Private Enforcement

We have already discussed above how public and private enforcement can be substitutes on the demand side. Enhanced public enforcement can diminish the demand for private enforcement and lax public enforcement can increase it. How about on the supply side? Are public and private enforcement perfect substitutes in terms of their effects on firm behavior?

They are not. One area where private enforcement may have the edge is in pursuing public polluters. Despite the fact that public facilities represent a substantial proportion of the pollution problem,[26] enforcement of pollution control laws presents special problems for public enforcers. The evidence seems very clear that public enforcement of violations by public polluters has been quite ineffective and the problem is not the inadequate availability of remedies, but rather a reluctance to use the available remedies.[27]

Bringing public polluters into compliance represents an ideal application of private enforcement, because private enforcers do not harbor the same reluctance. They are able to take full advantage of the existing penalty structure to increase compliance by this important class of previously under–regulated polluters.

Another supply side difference between public and private enforcers involves remedies. Public and private enforcers do not draw from the same menu of remedies. Citizen groups cannot impose criminal penalties. To the extent that criminal penalties are appropriate, citizen groups would be less effective enforcers in those circumstances where criminal penalties are appropriate.

Public and private enforcement can also complement each other. EPA currently has several enforcement initiatives designed to focus its resources on specific high–priority environmental problems.[28] Focusing enforcement activity in this way makes a great deal of sense because of ease of transferring information and expertise from one case to another. If enforcement were the exclusive responsibility of the public sector, however, focusing on priority areas could open the possibility for polluters operating in nontargeted areas to respond to a perceived decline in the expected penalty by reducing compliance. Since private enforcers are not operating on the same set of priorities, the likelihood of private enforcement is not diminished. With a continuing threat from private enforcers polluters have a continuing reason for compliance even when the public sector has its focus elsewhere. The very existence of the private enforcement alternative allows more flexibility to the public sector in targeting its resources, a flexibility which offers the opportunity to use those resource more efficiently.

Some specific statutes grant citizen enforcers even greater powers than their public counterparts. Sovereign immunity usually protects the federal government, including federal polluters, from suit. However, several pollution control laws specifically waive sovereign immunity specifically for citizen suits. Because a similar waiver was not extended to state governments, citizen groups can now bring suit against federal facilities in some circumstances even when state governments cannot.[29]

ENFORCEMENT EFFICIENCY AND COST–EFFECTIVENESS

The overarching question, of course, is not why and how private enforcement is taking place, but rather how well it serves social objectives. More effective enforcement does not always lead to greater efficiency. Does private enforcement promote either greater efficiency or greater cost–effectiveness?[30] Or are the outcomes efficient or cost–effective only under particular circumstances? Can we create a more efficient or cost–effective overall enforcement mechanism which combines public and private actions? In this section we shall examine the degree to which private enforcement, as currently structured, is compatible with efficient pollution control and, subsequently, with cost–effective pollution control. We shall also examine the ways in which this role could be improved.

Efficient Compliance

Do private enforcement efforts increase the efficiency of environmental policy? One way to seek an answer to this question, the one we have chosen, is to examine the incentives of private enforcers to establish whether or not they are compatible with efficient litigation choices.

Equal private and social costs and equal private and social benefits would be sufficient conditions for the incentives of private enforcers to be efficient. Are the costs and benefits faced by private enforcers the same as those which go into calculating the efficient choice?

They are not. Environmental improvement is a public good which typically accrues nonexclusively to a large group of people. It would be pure coincidence if the membership of the environmental group and the set of beneficiaries from the environmental improvement were the same. In general the magnitude of the benefits accruing to the environmental organization would be smaller than the benefits accruing to society as a whole. While all organization members are also members of society, the converse is not normally true. Public and private benefits are rarely the same.

Private and social costs differ as well. The polluter's cost of complying with the regulation would be included in the social cost, but not in the private enforcer's cost. Private enforcers would be quite willing to enforce inefficiently stringent regulations. Since both private enforcement benefits and costs diverge from their social counterparts, we cannot presume that complementing public enforcement with private enforcement is necessarily more efficient.

Efficiency, however, is a tough criterion, especially in an enforcement context. How does private enforcement stack up when measured against the somewhat weaker criterion of cost–effectiveness?

Complete Compliance and the Pursuit of Cost–Effectiveness

Cost–Effective Emission Reduction

A cost–effective allocation of the responsibility for achieving a given aggregate emission reduction target is achieved when the marginal costs of emission reduction are equalized across all discharge points for that pollutant.[31] While the discharge standards imposed by the regulatory authority may or may not be cost–effective, normally they are not. Complete compliance with any set of standards which did not result in equal marginal costs would not be cost–effective. High marginal cost firms would be controlling relatively too much and low marginal cost firms relatively too little.

Necessary Conditions for Cost–Effective Compliance

Under what conditions would compliance be cost–effective? Two conditions are necessary: the control responsibilities have to be allocated among the firms in a cost–effective manner and compliance has to be complete.

To show that these are necessary conditions we must examine what would happen in their absence. Suppose the control responsibility were not allocated cost–effectively. Could any allocation of enforcement activity result in cost–effectiveness? Restoring cost–effectiveness would necessarily require encouraging some firms (the ones with low marginal costs) to take on more than their legal responsibility while encouraging the others to take on less. While it would certainly be possible to use enforcement policy to encourage firms to take on less than their legal responsibility, it is not possible to use strict enforcement to get them to take on more. Since the expected penalty falls to zero once the regulated standard has been achieved, greater enforcement would not induce any firm to do more than it is legally required to do.[32] Anything less than complete compliance is cost–ineffective for the simple reason that only complete compliance will result in sufficient emission reductions to meet the target.

Discharge Standards in Practice

According to the necessary conditions, private enforcement can create a movement towards cost–effectiveness providing that the discharge standards themselves are cost–effective. Are they?

The majority of citizen suit cases have involved claims under the Clean Water Act. The discharge standards in the Clean Water Act are based on specific pollution control technologies identified by the control authorities. Technology–based standards have traditionally placed too much emphasis on the type of equipment used and not enough on the amount of emissions reduction to be achieved and the relative costs of achieving that reduction among the various discharge points. A number of empirical studies have found that the implementation of the Clean Water Act provisions has not been cost–effective.[33]

Due to the fact that the EPA water discharge standards do not provide for cost–effective pollution control, it is not possible to guarantee that the addition of citizen suits to the enforcement arena has lead to greater cost–effectiveness in environmental policy. Although noncomplying firms will perceive a higher threat of enforcement and are likely to increase their degree of compliance, the improved environmental quality will generally not be obtained at minimum cost.

Unfortunately, the problem is even more serious than that. According to our model the firms most likely to be in less–than–complete compliance are those facing the highest marginal cost of emission reduction. In other words, the process is in all probability targeting further environmental improvement on the firms for which further improvements are the most expensive. Whenever the discharge standards are not cost–effective, citizen suits secure environmental improvements from precisely the wrong firms.

Blending Instrument Choice and Enforcement

The fact that citizen suits target the most expensive sources of environmental improvement is not a fatal flaw. Combining citizen suits with appropriately designed policy instruments could produce a better outcome than either component of the policy package could achieve by itself.

It is well–known that appropriately designed emissions trading systems can in principle produce cost–effective outcomes.[34] An initial allocation of control responsibility which is cost–ineffective can be rectified by trading emissions–reduction credits. Once these trades have been consummated the allocation of control responsibility should be cost–effective or at least more cost–effective.

An immediate implication becomes apparent when the effects of private enforcement are contrasted depending upon whether the emissions standards being enforced are complemented by emissions trading or not. The ability of private enforcement to enhance cost–effectiveness is higher, probably substantially higher, when emissions trading can be used to comply with the standards being enforced. Furthermore the existence of private enforcement should encourage high marginal cost firms to trade, making for a more active market.

Citizen suits are currently targeted precisely at the environmental law where the problem of cost–ineffective standards is most acute, the Clean Water Act. In air pollution, on the other hand, where emissions trading has taken hold, citizen suit activity has been at a very low level. This is the reverse of what should happen into order to ensure cost–effective environmental improvement. Fortunately, the recent amendments to the Clean Air Act should encourage more private litigation activity on air pollution where the likelihood that it will increase cost–effectiveness is high. [35]

PROCEDURAL EFFECTIVENESS

As we enquire as to the appropriate role for citizen suits in the totality of environmental policy it is appropriate to examine the rules under which this institutional innovation operates. The political compromises which paved the way for citizen suits were responsible for adoption of a number of restrictions on their powers. Do these restrictions encourage or discourage the effective use of private enforcement?

The 60–Day Notice

A 60–day notice of intent to sue is required to be filed with the government and with the defendants. The apparent purposes of this notice requirement are: (i) to allow the government to take over enforcement if it so desires, or (ii) to allow the violator to come into compliance and therefore avoid going to court. Is the 60–day notice requirement consistent with efficient enforcement?

The main reason for the notice is to goad the government into action by letting them know that the citizens intend to take action if the government does not. If the government agency has superior knowledge and resources in a particular case, it would be more efficient for them to take over the enforcement action. On the other hand, if the citizen organization has superior knowledge and resources they should be able to continue with enforcement action. Thus, a 60–day notice period allows the federal government to weigh the costs and benefits of taking over a suit and to do so if they are the best–suited enforcer.

Other, less–noble motivations may prevail, however. If political pressure causes the government to drag its feet after taking over the case, public enforcement could turn out to be a poor substitute. Fortunately the courts have anticipated this possibility and have held that if the government does not demonstrate diligent enforcement, the citizen suit may be allowed to proceed. Therefore, in order for efficiency to prevail, the party who can litigate at the lowest cost and who has the best knowledge and resources must be allowed to do so. While the 60–day notice requirement provides an opportunity for this assessment to be made, it does not guarantee that it will be made correctly.

The 60–day notice to defendants is a separate issue. In most cases due to the Supreme Court decision in *Gwaltney of Smithfield* v. *Chesapeake Bay Fdn Inc.*, citizens are only allowed to sue for ongoing or intermittent violations. If this ruling were strictly construed, the citizen group could be barred from initiating an enforcement action whenever the firm was able to achieve compliance within the 60–day period.

On the one hand, this seems to bring about an efficient solution because the desired result, compliance, is achieved without lengthy and expensive court proceedings. On the other hand in this case no penalty would be assessed; the firm would gain the benefits of delay and would have an insufficient incentive to comply. Any firm that could come into compliance rather quickly could exploit this restriction on citizen suits.[36] A more efficient solution would allow for the 60–day notice to defendants but stipulate an administrative penalty for damages continuing after the date the complaint is filed. This would create a higher degree of compliance and lead to greater efficiency overall.[37]

The Preemption Provision

Another restriction bars citizen suits when federal judicial action or an administrative proceeding has been initiated. Although all judicial actions bar citizen suits, the conditions under which actions are barred by administrative proceedings varies by statute. Some statutes specifically specify that citizen suits are barred only if administrative penalty assessment proceedings have been initiated, while others bar citizen suits if any administrative action is taking place.[38]

Is it efficient to allow government administrative action to bar citizen suits? If citizen suits are allowed to proceed even though the government has initiated administrative action, the resulting duplication of enforcement efforts would be inefficient. If the government is reaching the desired result through administrative action, it is more efficient for the citizen organizations to spend their time and resources investigating other violations rather than acting on the same violations as the government. Also, if industry perceives that administrative actions do not bar citizen suits, they may be hesitant to cooperate with the government in administrative proceedings (Garrètt, 1986, 10162).

Since allowing citizen suits could cause overcrowding in the courts and high litigation costs, it is important to avoid court proceedings when enforcement objectives can be met in less costly ways. In many cases important objectives can be achieved at a lower cost through settling out of court or through administrative action. Administrative action also reduces the problem of excessive litigation. The government in most cases prefers to proceed administratively because it is a cheaper method of enforcement. Thus, it would seem efficient for administrative action by government to preclude citizen suits. The main goal of the suits is to bring a violating industry into compliance, and if the government can do so at a lower cost in an administrative forum, then it is efficient for citizens to let them.

POLICY IMPLICATIONS

Though private enforcement is now being used in the US and the European Economic Community, it is not a common component of environmental policies around the world. Should it be? What can be learned from the US experience?

Governments are not universally able to assure compliance with environmental laws. In many countries apparently tough environmental laws may be accompanied by little or no enforcement. The appearance of concern over the environment diverges sharply from the reality of indifferent enforcement. Recognizing the ineffective (and in some cases counterproductive) role of their governments, environmentally aware citizens have become discouraged and pessimistic about the future. Improving environmental policy seems a rather hopeless venture in the face of an uncooperative, corrupt or merely underfunded government. Effective enforcement is the foundation upon which successful environmental policy is built.

Private enforcement provides two specific sources of hope. If the government monopoly on enforcement can be challenged, private enforcers could complement public enforcers, producing greater compliance and, quite possibly, a more responsible public sector. Since the value of private enforcement is greatest when public enforcement is not very effective, the significant challenge to regulatory policy posed by ineffective public enforcement can be turned into an opportunity. Furthermore if private enforcers were entitled to attorney fee reimbursement, the financial burden of enforcement could be transferred to those who create the need for it.

Limited public resources need not be a barrier to effective enforcement.[39]

Private enforcement does not flourish in all environments, however. If it is to fulfill this promise, certain preconditions must be satisfied. The most important of these involve establishing a reasonable burden of proof and allowing for the reimbursement of legal fees, including justifiable attorney fees.

Private enforcement will necessarily play a very limited role unless attorney fees are routinely reimbursed for successful suits. The improved environmental quality these groups seek though litigation is a public good. The economics literature makes it very clear that private interests will undersupply public goods and private enforcement would not be an exception. Subsidizing private enforcement by the reimbursement of legal fees provides an offset to this tendency for too little litigation activity.

Similarly, for private enforcement to be effective, proof of violation must be easy to establish. Fuzzy regulations and inadequate monitoring would raise the private burden of proof sufficient to preclude an effective private enforcement process. Lacking the government's power to conduct on–site inspections citizen groups are heavily dependent on the self–monitoring reports filed by those subject to the regulations. If the effectiveness of citizen suits under the US Clean Water Act is to be replicated elsewhere, similar monitoring reports must be required and the information must be available for public scrutiny. Furthermore, the penalties for falsification of the reports must be sufficiently severe as to encourage veracity.

The very existence of private enforcement allows the public sector greater flexibility in targeting its limited enforcement resources. This flexibility offers the opportunity to use public enforcement resources more efficiently, without creating new incentives for noncompliance in the process. Without private enforcement the government would be forced to spread its limited resources much more thinly over the vast territory regulated by environmental policy.

Citizen suits may offer a distinctly superior form of enforcement whenever public enforcement agencies seem reluctant to enforce pollution violations committed by public facilities. Private enforcers have no such lack of will to pursue public polluters and therefore would presumably be able to produce compliance faster for this important class of polluters.

Adding private to public enforcement would represent an unambiguous move toward cost–effectiveness only if the emission standards were cost–effective. Private enforcement should probably not be introduced when the emission standards being enforced distribute the control responsibility in a very cost–ineffective way. When some individual firms face unrealistically stringent standards, the private enforcement process would in all probability target further environmental improvement on precisely those firms.

While it is unrealistic to expect a bureaucracy to establish cost–effective emission standards because of the prohibitively high information burden that presupposes, it is not unrealistic to expect that outcome from a suitably designed emissions trading system. Blending private enforcement with emissions trading would not only encourage compliance with the standards, but it would provide an additional inducement for high marginal cost firms to trade, making for a more active market.

The experience in the United States points up one other remediable way in which the process is currently much less efficient than it should be. US environmental policy has been crafted in a piecemeal fashion over time, usually motivated by some highly publicized environmental crises. This piecemeal approach to environmental policy has created some striking nonuniformities in approach. Relatively similar pollution problems may be treated rather differently, depending upon the governing statute and the latest year that statute was amended.

The private enforcement process in the United States reflects this nonuniformity and to a certain extent has been undermined by it. The amount of mandated monitoring and publicly available information varies considerably among the various statutes, creating very different burdens of proof for the plaintiffs. Some statutes authorize penalty remedies; others don't. Some allow earmarked penalties; others don't. Some governmental units authorize attorney reimbursement; others don't.

This difference in how citizen suits are treated by the various statutes has created an uneven playing field which undermines the degree to which private enforcement priorities mirror the public interest. Private litigation priorities are established on the basis of private costs and benefits, not social costs and benefits. Nonuniformity of treatment of private enforcement means that bringing claims under some statutes is much more attractive than bringing claims under other statutes. Serious pollution problems under a statute which treats citizen suits less favorably may be ignored in favor of suits under statutes with a more generous penalty of reimbursement provisions, creating a bias in favor of permissive statutes. This bias drives a wedge between the interests of public and private enforcers; suits which offer the highest net benefits to the private enforcer are not necessarily the suits which offer the highest net benefits to society as a whole.

Recognizing the problem points immediately to a solution. To harmonize public and private litigation priorities it will be necessary to develop more uniformity in how citizen suits are treated among the federal statutes and among state and federal governments. Only with more uniform treatment will public and private litigation priorities be determined by the seriousness of the problems rather than the generosity of the statute. Since the analysis in this project suggests that private litigation is indeed quite sensitive to these differences, removing these biases would appear to be an important next step.

NOTES

1. This paper is based upon our earlier, more technical paper (Naysnerski and Tietenberg, forthcoming). Readers interested in more details about the data and methods involved in the analysis which underlies our conclusions should consult that paper.
2. See, for example, Harford (1978), Viscusi and Zeckhauser (1979), Storey and McCabe (1980), Lee (1984), and Martin (1984).
3. See, for example, Downing and Kimball (1974), Beavis and Walker (1983), Cohen (1987), and Magat and Viscusi (1990).
4. See, for example, Russell, Harrington and Vaughan (1986), Harrington (1988) and Russell (1990a).
5. Russell (1990b, 243), for example, states: "Efforts to monitor regulated behavior appear to have been inadequate to the task–a very difficult task in many instances– and typical enforcement practices appear to have been insufficiently rigorous. Together these inadequacies seem to have encouraged widespread violations of environmental regulations."
6. The nature of these limits as well as some suggestions for how to mitigate their effects are discussed in Russell, Harrington and Vaughan (1986) and Harrington (1988).
7. Private enforcement is also being used in Europe to enforce environmental standards under the 1957 treaty creating the European Economic Community. According to Sand (1991, 272) the number of public and private environmental complaints filed rose from

about 10 in 1982 to 460 in 1989. More than half of these have been filed by private individuals or organizations. Our paper will focus on the US experience, leaving the analysis of the European experience to others more familiar with it.

8.   The only paper we could locate in the economics literature which focused on private environmental enforcement was Cohen and Rubin (1985). That article proposed a radically different form of private enforcement in which private enforcers would replace public enforcers, receiving fees from polluters based upon their level of emissions.

9.   The extent to which private demands for environmental improvement coincide with efficient environmental improvement will be addressed below.

10.   Enforcement is, of course, not the only channel for private efforts to produce more environmental quality. Environmental organizations also attempt to influence legislation directly through lobbying or indirectly through increasing public awareness. Some organizations, such as the Nature Conservancy, directly acquire unique ecological assets to preserve and protect them.

11.   With a binding budget constraint the environmental organization may have to terminate litigation activity at a point where the marginal net benefit was greater than zero as long as the reimbursement of expenses was less than complete.

12.   It is possible, of course, that diminished enforcement during the Reagan Administration was merely a response to increased compliance. While a sudden increase in compliance could not be ruled out by our data, we have yet to find a shred of evidence in support of that possibility.

13.   Our data base consists of a compilation of citizen suits published in Jorgenson and Kimmel (1988, 113–65). The Bureau of National Affairs retrieved the data from filings with EPA headquarters and the data on settlement activity was based on discussions with attorneys, individuals and environmental groups.

14.   Much of this increase occurred specifically under the Clean Water Act. We shall explain the predominant position of the Clean Water Act below.

15.   The pattern of public enforcement activities can be found in USEPA (1991, Table 2)

16.   In *Hamker* v. *Diamond Shamrock Chemical Co.* the 5th Circuit allowed penalties to be assessed only for ongoing violations. However, in *Chesapeake Bay Fdn* v. *Gwaltney of Smithfield* the 4th Circuit ruled that penalties can be assessed even if based solely on past violations. The Supreme Court made a final ruling in *Gwaltney of Smithfield* v. *Chesapeake Bay Fdn Inc.* when it decided that a penalty assessment will be permitted only when the request for penalties is accompanied with a reasonable request for injunctive relief.

17.   This point is explained in more detail in a subsequent section of this chapter.

18.   A single action may involve claims citing more than one statute.

19.   While federal statutes have not typically authorized direct payment of financial penalties to private enforcers, under its Proposition 65 "bounty hunter" provision, California allows such direct payment. (Roberts, 1989, 306). Due to our focus on enforcement of federal law we have not examined the effect of this provision, but it is an interesting avenue for future research.

20.   The average earmarked penalty was $223,527, while the average non–earmarked penalty was $72,543.

21.   See *Student Public Interest Research Group* v. *Fritzsch, Dodge & Olcott, Inc.* 579 F. Supp at 1538.

22.   Sections 503 and 504 of the 1990 Amendments to the Clean Air Act require facilities to certify that they are in compliance with all applicable regulations and permit conditions, similar to the discharge monitoring reports required under the Clean Water Act, subject to sanctions for false or improper certification. 104 Stat 2641–2.

23.   See *In re Investigation Pursuant to the Clean Air Act*, 20 ELR 21068.

24.   Stephanie Pollack, Conservation Law Foundation, Boston Massachusetts, 1 February 1990 and Mark Stein, Water Enforcement, Environmental Protection Agency — Region I, Boston, Massachusetts, 6 December 1989. Interviews by Wendy Naysnerski.

25.   See Strelow (1990). Roger Strelow is a Vice President at General Electric.

26. Witness for example the 1983 headline "Toxic Waste Laws: U. S. May Be Biggest Violator", *Washington Post,* 17 August 1983: A1, A6.
27. See the detailed evidence on this point in Gelpe (1989, 69–146).
28. These include pretreatment issues in the Clean Water Act and asbestos removal in the Clean Air Act. See Arbuckle *et al.*(1989, 70). See also Strock (1990b, 10327–10332).
29. See *Ohio* v. *United States Department of Energy,* 20 ELR 20953. The federal government's sovereign immunity from civil penalties is waived through the Resource Conservation and Recovery Act's (RCRA) citizen suit provision, but not its sovereign immunity provision. States were not completely denied access to RCRA civil penalties by this decision, however, because the court also ruled that they could bring suit under the citizen suit provision.
30. We follow here the standard convention that efficiency involves maximizing net benefits, while cost–effectiveness involves meeting a predefined environmental standard (which may or may not be efficient) at minimum cost.
31. The original proof of this proposition can be found in Baumol and Oates (1971, 42–54).
32. Note that even though it may be possible to use selective enforcement to equate the marginal costs, the resulting equilibrium would not be cost–effective. Easing up on enforcement against the firms with the higher marginal costs could encourage them to choose a lower degree of compliance, an action that could reduce their marginal costs until they were equal to the lower marginal costs of the other firms. But this would not achieve the target aggregate emission reduction; too little reduction would have been achieved. Since only allocations which achieve the desired target at minimum cost are cost–effective, failure to achieve the desired target means that the resulting allocation would not be cost–effective. Selective enforcement would minimize the cost of meeting a weaker standard.
33. For a discussion of the sources of cost–ineffectiveness see Freeman (1990, 97–149). For a survey of the existing empirical studies see Tietenberg (1988, 410–15).
34. See Baumol and Oates (1971). For a description of how these programs are working out in practice see Hahn and Hester (1989, 361–406) and Tietenberg (1990, 17–33).
35. See the description of the changes in note 22.
36. Examples of behavior which could exploit this weakness are not hard to find. A firm could use a cheaper, but more polluting, substitute fuel on occasion, knowing full well that if it is caught it could simply switch back on short notice.
37. Apparently at least one Circuit Court of Appeals agrees with our model. On 5 April 1990 the 11th Circuit allowed plaintiffs in a citizen suit to seek penalty remedies as long as the defendant was in violation on or after the date the complaint was filed. See *Atlantic States Legal Foundation, Inc.* v. *Tyson Foods, Inc.*, 897 F. 2d 1128.
38. See Miller (1984a, 10072–3).
39. It has been suggested to us by some economists from developing countries that this argument may have particular relevance in the developing country context, since public agencies in those countries are frequently characterized as having neither the administrative apparatus, nor the financial resources, to pursue effective environmental enforcement. Even corrupt enforcement is undermined by the private enforcement process.

PART II
Environmental Liability Law

6. Tort Law and the Deterrence of Environmental Pollution[1]

Donald Dewees

INTRODUCTION

During the last two decades those interested in environmental improvement have focused on regulatory agencies, particularly the federal Environmental Protection Agency, as the principal instrument for achieving their ends. But long before the creation of the federal EPA or the many state EPAs, before the principal pollution control statutes were enacted, the common law of tort provided a seemingly powerful set of rights for pollution victims. A person was entitled to the enjoyment of his property free from unreasonable interference from pollution, and riparian property owners were entitled to the flow of water undiminished in quantity and quality. In other fields, such as product liability and medical malpractice, an explosion in tort litigation has occurred in the last two decades. This explosion is defended on the grounds that private litigation is a necessary supplement to government regulation that is often ineffective or inefficient or both. This paper considers whether the focus on government regulation by the public and by economists has ignored an important and effective private tool for improving environmental management, and what role tort might play in the future.

The "environmental" problems considered here include injuries to persons, property or the environment caused by the discharge of air and water pollution and by the discharge and disposal of solid and liquid wastes. I exclude lawsuits arising out of workplace exposures and product–liability actions that do not include environmental (outdoor) exposure. Thus while asbestos is often regarded as an environmental problem, most of the litigation in the United States has arisen from workplace exposures (see Brodeur, 1985) and is clearly a matter of occupational not environmental health, with the lawsuits taking the form of product liability claims. The Agent Orange case (see Schuck, 1986) is also a product–liability case.

The classic environmental tort actions are based on private nuisance, trespass, public nuisance, riparian rights, negligence and on Rylands and Fletcher. This paper will focus on the first five causes of action, since the last has limited applicability. It will also consider civil actions based on liability created by statutes such as actions for compensation under the Comprehensive Environmental Response Compensation and Liability Act, CERCLA.[2] Such actions represent a rapidly growing area of environmental civil litigation that is distinct from common law tort.

THE EVALUATIVE FRAMEWORK

What criteria should be used in evaluating the efficacy of the tort system? Law and economics scholars, drawing on concepts of economic efficiency, stress the deterrent objectives of the tort system and evaluate legal doctrine in terms of whether appropriate incentives are created to induce the parties to minimize the sum of accident and avoidance costs by taking cost–justified precautions (see Shavell, 1987b; Polinsky, 1989; Cooter and Ulen, 1988, Ch. 8; Landes and Posner, 1987). Other scholars argue that the tort system should be evaluated against its capacity to spread risk and to compensate accident victims (Sugarman., 1985; Abel, 1987), or against its ability to impose on a wrongdoer the duty to fully compensate the victim (Weinrib, 1989). This paper will focus on the deterrence objective.

In theory, the performance of the system could be evaluated by measuring pollution abatement and performing a statistical analysis of the effect of the tort system and the regulatory system on pollution discharge. However the data required to extract convincing results from such a study are daunting. For that reason, this paper places primary emphasis on an analysis of the inputs to the tort litigation process. The analysis of inputs determines the theoretical assumptions that are required for the tort system to provide optimal deterrence, and examines whether those assumptions are satisfied by legal doctrines and empirical facts. This is followed by an analysis of outputs which examines actual performance itself, attempting to identify the changes in behaviour that the tort system has induced, and then examining whether these changes are consistent with optimal deterrence.

INPUT EVALUATION

Market Failure and Optimal Remedies

Coase (1960) noted that if the law was clear, the number of parties small, and transactions costs low, then polluters and pollutees could negotiate to an efficient level of pollution control. Strikingly, the outcome would be optimal regardless of whether the law imposed liability for pollution damage or not. In these situations, the parties should be able to resolve the problem efficiently. Unfortunately, few environmental problems arise between a single polluter and a single pollutee. The overwhelming preponderance of pollution problems arise with multiple victims, often with multiple sources, and often with great uncertainty relating to discharge, dispersion and harm. Here the negotiations postulated by Coase will not take place, as he recognizes in his high transactions costs case. Thus we require careful examination of tort doctrine to determine whether an efficient solution will be reached or not.

Consider a single polluter and a number of victims where the efficient outcome may involve joint precautions by both polluters and pollutees. The economic literature on the efficient solution to this problem is clear: the polluter must pay for the actual social damage resulting from his pollution discharge, and victims should not be compensated, to avoid excess activity and entry (Baumol and Oates 1988, Ch. 4). The general prescription for this problem is a Pigovian tax on pollution discharge. Because the victims are not in a market relationship with the polluter, payment by the polluter will arise only if the tort system compels it, or if a government agency imposes liability. The first half of the prescription, that the polluter pay for all harm caused, should be obvious as a means of inducing optimal deterrence. The second half, that victims should not be compensated, is less obvious. The rationale is that if victims are fully compensated for all harm that they suffer, then there is theoretically nothing to deter sensitive victims from moving close to a source of pollution, because they will be made whole for any losses that they suffer. Neither is there an incentive for victims to mitigate their damages by engaging in less rather than more sensitive activities. A complete absence of compensation for victims will generate incentives for optimal levels of precaution by those victims.

The law and economics literature on efficiency in nuisance law is roughly consistent with this economics literature. It is recognized that efficiency requires that the parties on both sides face the social costs of their actions; that the polluter must at the margin pay for the incremental harm that he causes, and that victims must not be compensated for excess harm that they could have avoided at a lesser cost. Landes and Posner conclude that courts in the United States approximate the results required by economic efficiency. In nuisance law, for instance, the requirement that there be substantial harm and unreasonable use before an injunction will be awarded recognizes the two–sided nature of pollution problems and that, generally, polluters should not be required to stop polluting unless the damage caused exceeds the cost of abatement (Posner, 1986, 56; Landes and Posner, 1987, 44).

Are Liability Rules Efficient?

Common Law Rules
The doctrine of private nuisance protects interests in land, and the doctrine of public nuisance protects other interests. In Canada, common law private nuisance actions protect an owner or tenant from unreasonable interference with the use and enjoyment of land. Pollution that causes physical damage including physical injury to health is actionable but it is unsettled whether injury to health alone will support a claim in nuisance. If the interference causes only a reduction in enjoyment, not physical damage, then the test applied is whether an ordinary person would be offended; the extraordinarily sensitive landowner or his property is not protected from invasion. This is equivalent to a "reasonable victim" rule. Defenses may also

arise if the neighbourhood is one in which the pollution complained of is to be expected because of the industrial character of the neighbourhood. Courts may award injunctive relief or damages but the injunction will be awarded only if the injury is substantial and continuing. (Linden, 1988, 500–19).

In the United States, an action in private nuisance can be supported when there is damage that is "substantial and unreasonable". The defendant's action must be intentional in the sense that a condition is created or continued with knowledge that the interference is or is likely to harm the plaintiff's interests. Substantial and unreasonable harm can include physical harm to land or property, and physical discomfort or annoyance. Injunctive relief is rare, requiring unreasonable conduct on the part of the defendant as well as substantial and unreasonable harm to the plaintiff's interests. Unreasonable conduct is determined by "balancing the equities" which allows the court to consider, among other things, the social utility of the polluting activity. The onus is on the plaintiff to show that the gravity of the harm outweighs the utility of the conduct. Theoretically, damages are awarded when there is no determination of unreasonable conduct. It is unclear whether or not courts also consider the nature of the defendant's conduct when determining unreasonable interference. An injunction will not be awarded simply on the basis of the inadequacy of damages. (Keeton, *et al.*, 1984, 624–34.)

The "coming to the nuisance" defence often bars actions by plaintiffs arriving after the discharge was established. While this will discourage excessive entry by victims, it fails to impose on the polluter the cost of the harm he causes. As in Canada there are defenses based on the reasonableness of the victim and on the character of the neighbourhood. Again, those suffering modest invasion are likely to be left with no recourse in private nuisance.

In both countries the liability rules for private nuisance seem to exclude recovery for harm that is insubstantial or reasonable, or which results from the plaintiff's special sensitivity, yet such cases may represent a substantial proportion of pollution discharge. If the nuisance is "unintentional" the conduct required to sustain an action must be negligent, reckless, or ultrahazardous with respect to the plaintiff's interest.

Trespass protects interests in real property from tangible invasion. Originally intended to protect against others coming on to or using one's land, the doctrine has been extended to include the settling of dusts and vapors on the property, and even small invasions are actionable, including smells and vapors. (Grad, 1985, 2–36–2–39, 2–47–2–52.) Unlike private nuisance, no defense is associated with the reasonable conduct of the defendant, or with the plaintiff's having arrived after the defendant. Thus trespass may be available in some cases when private nuisance is not.

The law of public nuisance may be used to address violations of a general interest in environmental quality through an action brought by the government rather than by a private individual. (Keeton, *et al.*, 1984, 90 643–48.) Actions may be brought by individuals if they can demonstrate that their losses differ in kind, not quality, from those of the rest of the community. Public nuisance is broader than private nuisance and can be applied to interference with public health, public comfort, and public convenience. The harm must be widespread and substantial. It would appear that major discharges of toxic substances could probably qualify as a public nuisance. (Environmental Law Institute, 1980, 480). However, private individuals can rarely sue, and governments rarely do, so this doctrine is of little effect. Public nuisance was similarly ineffective in Great Britain in the nineteenth century, for the same reasons (Brenner, 1974).

The doctrine of riparian rights, applicable in most Canadian provinces and the eastern United States, entitles owners of riparian land along a body of water to the flow of water undiminished in quality and quantity (the natural flow doctrine), or subject to reasonable use. In Canada the natural flow doctrine, which tests reasonableness against the natural quality of the water, has been applied and has included a right to an injunction whenever the water quality is diminished in law, if not in fact. This doctrine in Canada has provided powerful protection for riparian owners against water pollution, although in several cases where small riparian owners secured an injunction against a large pollution source, the government legislatively suspended the injunction, leaving the victim with a remedy of damages only.[3] The doctrine does not give any right to compensation for injury to fishing or fish, nor is it clear that it would give a right of action for the smell arising from pollution of a river.

In the eastern United States the reasonable use system allows riparian owners to maintain an action for a substantial and unreasonable impairment of water quality or quantity (Gindler, 1967, 53; Grad, 1985, 2.02). "Unreasonable" is usually defined in accordance with the beneficial use to which the plaintiff puts the water. The application of the former rule implies that riparian rights will only serve to protect water from declining below a standard required by the last down–stream owner and that there will be no cause of action for smaller injuries. Nonriparian owners have no cause of action under riparian rights but riparian owners can recover for nonriparian injury caused by interference with water. Injunctive relief is available but not common. As with nuisance actions, the court will determine unreasonableness through a consideration of all of the circumstances.

Water rights in the western states are defined by the appropriation doctrine and irrigation law (which completely separates land and water rights). Under the appropriation doctrine the first in time is the first in right (Gindler, 1967, 212). A subsequent appropriator may not diminish the quality or quantity of water used by a prior appropriator for a beneficial use. To sustain an action there must be substantial harm to the prior appropriator's beneficial use. Harm *per se* is irrelevant. The discharges captured by this system depend upon the beneficial use to which the superior rights holder puts the water. A large portion of discharges are thus exempt from liability.

Certain lands under navigable waters belong to the state, and the public trust doctrine has traditionally required the state to administer these lands in accordance with the public interest. Originally the public trust doctrine protected navigation and fishing interests. Recently, it has been extended to the protection of recreational and environmental quality interests in these waters, and jurisdiction has been extended to tidal wetlands that would be navigable only by a "toothpick sailboat" (Austin, 1989). This doctrine is proving useful for preventing water pollution damage and wetlands destruction in some situations where private property is not directly affected.

Negligence actions may be applied regardless of proprietary interest. Environmental actions will require the standard four elements: a duty protecting others from unreasonable risk, a breach of that duty, legal cause, and actual damages (Keeton, *et al.*, 1984,

164). Defenses lie in assumption of risk and contributory negligence
(Gaskins, 1989, 39–40). Unreasonable risk may occur where the cost
of taking precautionary measures would have been less than the
probability and gravity of the accident. Negligence *per se* may arise
when a party violates a statute designed for protection from injury,
and when there is a causal connection between the violation and an
injury. The statute must have the purpose of protecting a class from a
particular hazard and the plaintiffs must fall within that class (Keeton,
et al., 1984, 224).

While relatively little environmental litigation has relied upon
negligence doctrine, some commentators fear that courts could begin
to expand from negligence to strict liability and beyond in the
environmental field as they have in product liability (Abraham, 1988,
974). In the field of product liability, the courts have imposed
liability for past conduct that was not wrongful when the defendant
acted, and in fact could not have been discovered to have been
harmful at that time, a form of retroactive strict liability.[4] The
Superfund legislation imposes retroactive strict liability with joint and
several liability for the tortfeasors, and some worry that the courts
may begin to apply similar principles to common law environmental
tort claims, a development that could vastly expand the scope of
liability for environmental pollution (Abraham, 1988, 925). While
these developments have not occurred, the fear that they might has
affected current perceptions of the crisis in environmental litigation.

Product liability actions have recently been used to attack mass
environmental exposures, the Agent Orange case being the most
notorious example (see Schuck, 1986). Since the plaintiffs were
exposed to the herbicide in Vietnam, they could not rely on a
property–based lawsuit, and instead alleged that the product was
defective and harmful. This case brought together the problems of
low exposure for large numbers of victims, multiple plaintiffs (2.4
million veterans), multiple defendants (seven), unknown individual
exposures, and a substance proven toxic in animal tests, but not
proven to have harmed any plaintiff. The court approved a
settlement of $180 million, the largest personal–injury award for
environmental exposure, after concluding that causation was not
proven. This case displays the enormous difficulties of litigating mass
torts and the potential liability of firms selling products for which

there is some evidence of harmful effects, at least in large doses. Significant concerns about environmental liability are rooted in the fear that lawsuits similar to Agent Orange may succeed in the future.

In summary, the Canadian rules appear to impose on the polluter the full cost of substantial pollution discharges that affect property owners which are found unreasonable in the circumstances and of some discharges that are not unreasonable. They may over–deter discharges causing physical harm, since the victim is entitled to an injunction and, where there are large numbers of victims, Coasian bargaining cannot take place. Widely dispersed pollution discharge will be under–deterred because small amounts of harm suffered by a large number of victims will not support an action in private nuisance. The US rules provide less complete deterrence, since the requirement to balance the reasonableness of the conduct of the plaintiff and that of the defendant will fail to impose costs on polluters in a large number of cases. While this would be efficient if the test for "reasonable" were a cost–benefit test, it is unlikely that the courts can perform this calculation accurately, given the difficulty of determining abatement costs and damage costs for large numbers of victims. The evidence that victims are often undercompensated, discussed below, also supports the conclusion that benefits will be understated, leading to underdeterrence. Furthermore, the defense of coming to the nuisance relieves many US polluters of liability. Most important, however, is the fact that injuries not associated with private property are generally not well protected by the doctrines discussed here. The assertion by Landes and Posner that these doctrines are efficient seems overstated.

Statutory Liability
Responding in part to the great difficulty that environmental plaintiffs face, the US Congress, and many states, have passed laws giving explicit rights to compensation to some pollution victims. These laws explicitly remove some common–law barriers to suit. The principal US legislation providing civil liability for environmental harm is the Comprehensive Environmental Response, Compensation, and Liability Act of 1980 (CERCLA or Superfund) which was intended to facilitate the cleaning up of hazardous–waste sites and, where possible, to impose liability for cleanup on responsible parties.

Section 104[5] authorizes the EPA to arrange for the cleanup of designated hazardous waste sites and then to seek reimbursement from "responsible" parties. Liability is triggered by a release or a threatened release of a hazardous substance into the environment which causes the plaintiff to incur expenses from cleaning up the hazardous waste site.[6] Superfund cleanup at a site may lead to a lawsuit to recover the costs from responsible parties who then sue each other to apportion liability. The facts revealed in the cleanup provide the basis for lawsuits for property damage and personal injury by those owning property or living in the vicinity of the site. Section 107(a)(4)(B) allows private citizens to bring suit under CERCLA, but because expenses must be incurred prior to filing suit, the government is almost exclusively the plaintiff in CERCLA actions (Glass, 1988, 392). CERCLA does not compensate for personal injuries. Responsible parties may be: present owners or operators of the waste facility, any past owners or operators during whose tenure the offending substances were deposited, generators who arranged to have their wastes deposited, and any party transporting the offending wastes for treatment or disposal. The courts have imposed: strict liability, retroactive liability holding parties responsible for actions that preceded the 1980 enactment, and joint and several liability (impliedly reinforced by section 113 (b) of the 1986 Superfund Amendments Reauthorization Act (SARA)[7]) which allows parties held liable to sue other potentially responsible parties for contribution (Garber, 1987, note 12).

From a deterrence standpoint these rules diverge considerably from what is required for optimal economic efficiency ("Developments...", 1986, 1513). Enormous liabilities may be imposed under CERCLA, easily exceeding the value that the property would have in the absence of the contamination. Liability may be imposed on parties not causing damage. Some parties may be faced with far more than the full social cost of their activities, while others pay little or nothing of their costs. The pursuit of parties able to pay, believed necessary to fund essential cleanups, is entirely inconsistent with efficient deterrence. Retroactive liability provides no deterrent effect at all except to induce parties to avoid becoming financially associated with others who may be retroactively liable.

The transaction costs of dealing with CERCLA liability are not small. With many parties potentially responsible for a contaminated site, many insurers of each responsible party, enormous potential costs, and a widespread belief by many responsible parties that they are blameless since the disposal actions were legal at the time and not expected to result in environmental risks, horrendous litigation often attends the attempt to devise a cleanup strategy or to assign liability to individual actors. It has been estimated that these transactions costs may amount to between 24 per cent and 44 per cent of total cleanup expenditures (Butler, 1985). This is a high price to pay for very limited deterrence.

A number of states have enacted laws dealing with toxic substances that provide for civil liability to fund clean up costs and third–party damages, incorporating provisions similar to those in CERCLA, including joint and several liability of all waste generators, transporters and disposers associated with a dump site (Huber, 1988a, 140). In Canada, Ontario's Environmental Protection Act incorporates a "spills" section that imposes civil liability for cleanup costs and economic loss on the owner or person having control of a substance involved in an "abnormal" discharge.[8] Some other provinces have similar legislation.

CERCLA was not the first law to supplement tort liability with statutory civil liability. The 1977 Clean Water Act[9] provided in section 311 that persons responsible for oil spills in the marine environment may be liable to the government for any natural resource damages that result, including the cost or expense of restoring or replacing the natural resources. The Natural Resource Damage Assessment (NRDA) regulations promulgated in 1986 specified how damages under CERCLA and CWA were to be assessed. Still, much of the damage caused by marine oil spills could not be reached by individual lawsuits, and liability under the available statutes was sometimes limited in practice to the value of the vessel, which after the accident tends to fall short of the damage. In response to this problem, Congress enacted the Oil Pollution Act of 1990,[10] which regulates the transportation of oil and provides for liability in the event of spills. The OPA requires double hulls in many oil tankers and imposes a number of other requirements designed to reduce the likelihood of an accident and to limit the amount of oil spilled if an accident occurs. A comprehensive victim compensation scheme provides compensation for natural resource damage, injury to property, lost revenues, profits, or subsistence use from natural resources, and the net cost of providing public services during cleanup. This compensation is financed by liability of responsible parties, up to specified limits, and by a fund financed by a five cent per barrel tax on oil. Dunford, in chapter 7 of this volume, concludes that section 311 of the CWA substantially increased the liability of businesses responsible for oil spills, and that the OPA has further increased that liability, although the liability limits and the fund may mean that the actual net liability of some responsible parties has been reduced by the OPA. He also concludes that this liability has had an effect on responsible parties, including actions to reduce the risk of spills, and actions to limit liability in the event of a spill. It seems likely that during this decade additional statutes will provide for civil recovery of cleanup costs and other damages from those responsible for environmental harms, particularly the discharge into the soil or water of hazardous substances.

Do Damage Rules Correspond to Theoretical Norms?

Plaintiffs under the common law doctrines discussed above can recover actual damages including economic loss (other than pure economic loss), costs of restoration, and damages for pain and suffering. Courts have been reluctant to grant relief for claims of emotional stress, aesthetic or recreational loss, or increased risk of injury in the absence of actual proof of injury.[11] For this reason some portion of the social costs of pollution may go uncompensated by polluters. Those who suffer injuries such as aesthetic or recreational loss and inconvenience may recover only a fraction of the true value to them of that loss, on the grounds that it is difficult to value or too remote to allow recovery (Environmental Law Institute, 1980, 518). In this respect, damages will be inadequate, and deterrence will be insufficient.

There is also the problem of ecosystem harm that may be most serious at some time in the future, or that may affect more than individual property owners. Courts may not accept claims for future harm where that harm is subject to considerable scientific uncertainty. It seems likely that there would be a set of harms that are not adequately compensated by current damage rules, either because they are not specific to an individual, or because they are extremely difficult to value.

Claims Initiation: Do Lawsuits Actually Impose Full Costs?

Significant barriers to claims initiation arise in common law environmental cases from problems in proving causation, statutes of limitation, and costs. The result of these barriers is that legal action is rarely taken and when taken is often unsuccessful, so that polluters are not faced with the full social costs of their activities.

Causation

A major barrier to success in claims for air and water pollution problems is the difficulty of proving causation. A successful plaintiff must prove that he has suffered actual harm, that the harm arose from a specific pollutant, that the pollutant is of a type discharged by the defendant, and that this pollutant arose from the defendant and not from some other polluter ("Developments...," 1986, 1617–30). In the case of an isolated factory discharging a concentrated waste that causes a unique form of harm, these burdens may all be surmounted (Brennan, 1990, 157). It is more difficult, but still possible, to trace pollution discharged into a stream back to the pollution source, and some river pollution cases have been successful (Grad, 1985, 3.02). Still, if there are multiple polluters, it may be very expensive to determine who is responsible for what portion of the contamination in the river and then to ascertain the effect of that contamination on the aquatic ecosystem. The difficulty of proving causation at one or more of the four stages is a crippling barrier to traditional tort lawsuits for the vast majority of pollution problems experienced in North America. The situations where causation is not an important barrier are likely to involve a large isolated pollution source causing a characteristic form of damage, and these are precisely the sources most likely to have attracted the attention and control of regulatory authorities. Even in such circumstances, causation may raise problems (Dewees, 1990b).

Some developments have served to lessen the burden of causation in situations typical of environmental injury. Joint and several liability has been applied when a single defendant cannot be identified, and when the harm is "indivisible" (Brennan, 1986, 112). While this approach is obviously beneficial for plaintiffs, it may confront some defendants with far more than the full social costs of their activities, leaving others cost–free. Other emerging types of joint liability include market share liability and enterprise liability ("Developments...," 1986, 1624–30).

Lack of knowledge about exposure to a hazardous substance is a barrier to suit that has been considerably reduced in the last five years. Under OSHA regulations, manufacturers of hazardous materials must inform users of the presence of the material and its characteristics,[12] which should inform workers about hazards in the workplace. Title III of the Superfund Amendment and Reauthorization Act[13] provides for community right–to–know, which requires sources to notify local, state, and federal public officials of the presence and release of any of a number of potentially hazardous chemicals. Information about such releases or even the presence of the chemicals in the community will facilitate the proof of causation for some victims, probably increasing litigation.

Traditionally, liability could be imposed only when it could be shown that it is more likely than not that this defendant caused this plaintiff's harm. A modern version of this rule would find causation when the attributable risk or the probability of causation exceeds 50 per cent. Yet only a horrific exposure to the most potent carcinogens would raise to 50 per cent the probability that a common cancer, such as lung cancer, was caused by that chemical, so only rarely could cancer victims succeed in recovering from dischargers of known carcinogens. Even if a given pollution discharge were proven to have raised the lung cancer rate in a population by one–third, *no* lung cancer victim could recover. And in the rare cases where exposure to a pollutant gave rise to a 50 per cent cancer risk, if there were multiple sources, no individual source may be found liable.

In the product liability area this problem has been addressed with market share liability, but this concept is not widespread for environmental injury. While some courts have moved to accept statistical evidence of causation ("Developments...", 1986, 1619), Brennan (1988) has advocated the use of science panels to assist courts in fact–finding, and Shavell has recommended liability proportional to the probability of causation (proportionate liability), these are still not widely accepted.

As courts have struggled to find relief for plaintiffs with serious health problems, Huber (1988a, 153) has suggested that they have found causation where none existed at all. Previous problems of inadequate deterrence may be joined by problems of deterrence without proven causation, not obviously a step toward efficient deterrence.

Unfortunately, reliable epidemiological data are available for very few toxic substances, and since epidemiological studies require large numbers of victims to be reliable, the number of substances for which the dose–response function is well–understood may grow very slowly. In this circumstance, even the likely underdeterrence identified above does not incline me to advocate substantial easing of the burden of proving causation. While proportionate liability and science panels are theoretically attractive, inviting US courts to find *some* liability for diseases suffered by large numbers of injured people runs the risk of opening yet another giant legal lottery in which the uncertainties of fact–finding leave little likelihood that justice, or efficient deterrence, will be done. The high cost of the legal system ensures that considerable resources would be consumed. While the present system quite likely achieves substantial underdeterrence, more tort is not clearly a solution.

Statutes of Limitation

The traditional rule that lawsuits may not be filed more than two or three years from the time of injury or from the time of the tortious act is a barrier to plaintiffs suffering from latent illness or who are not immediately aware of their injury and also to owners of property contaminated by toxic materials first discharged or deposited long ago ("Developments...", 1980, 1605). The recent "discovery" rule, adopted by most states, which dictates that limitation periods run from the time injury is or ought reasonably to have been discovered, preserves the right of victims of latent injuries to take legal action and thereby better serves the deterrence objective. Still, the risk of a lawsuit decades after the pollution is discharged may not act as an effective deterrent to all but the most foresighted firms (Dewees, 1986).

Costs

The vast majority of air and water pollution discharges impose small costs on large numbers of people. It is rarely worthwhile for individuals to litigate these matters because individual damages will fall significantly short of the legal costs required for maintaining an action. This is particularly true in Canada where costs follow the event so that any substantial risk of losing a lawsuit means a substantial risk of being responsible for one's own legal fees and for the legal fees of the other side. It is especially true in Ontario where contingent fees have been prohibited.

One solution to this problem, of course, is the aggregation of claims, most commonly achieved in the United States through the class action lawsuit, which was facilitated by amendments to the Federal Rules of Civil Procedure in 1966.[14] The solution is not perfect, however, since environmental exposure cases will not always lend themselves to class actions, for example when injuries to different members of the class arise at different times and are of widely varying severity. Furthermore, there are substantial costs associated with identifying and certifying the class, and then with distributing the proceeds if the action is successful (Schuck, 1986).

Furthermore, costs represent a significant drain on compensation eventually paid. A 1985 study estimated that, considering all tort cases, plaintiffs retain 46 per cent of total litigation expenditures as compensation (Kakalik and Pace, 1986). A 1983 Rand study of asbestos litigation found that of the $661 million in total expenditures by defendants and their insurers on asbestos cases that had been closed by 1982, the plaintiffs received only 37 per cent of that total, while 63 per cent was consumed in litigation (Kakalik, *et al.*, 1983, vi). Environmental litigation may be even more expensive than asbestos litigation because of the problems discussed above and because even less is usually known about the harmful effects of the substance than about asbestos.

Standing

The common law of private nuisance is excessively limited in granting standing only to owners (or tenants) of real property, when in fact the general public may have a legitimate interest in many pollution problems, yet governments rarely launch public nuisance actions. A number of states have passed statutes expanding standing, but the volume of litigation is still small.

One example of the public interest not being protected is the failure in Ontario of the Crown to press claims for damage to public lands that were devastated by the sulfur oxide emissions from the nickel smelters in Sudbury in the first half of this century. This represents both a failure of the tort system, although it is not clear how those damages could have been assessed, and of the political system, since the Crown not only made no attempt to recover compensation, but when it released public land for settlement, it retained an easement for smoke pollution, preventing subsequent owners from launching private nuisance actions (Dewees, forthcoming).

Claims Resolution

Existing environmental litigation provides some evidence on whether courts actually award appropriate damages in environmental cases. The 1980 ELI study of toxic pollution attempted to assess the extent to which victims are compensated for injuries in environmental exposure cases (Environmental Law Institute, 1980). The study concluded that compensation in environmental exposure cases is significantly inadequate. The obstacles cited include legal remoteness of damages, valuation of damages, and the exclusion from compensation of latent medical effects and barriers to claims initiation. Since that study was conducted compensation awards have increased significantly (Huber, 1988a, 136). It is difficult to establish how these recent awards compare to the totality of damage caused in each case. Furthermore, with respect to suits for the contamination of property by toxic or hazardous waste, where the cost of restoration may be enormous, the responsible party may often not have assets sufficient to satisfy a judgment obtained by a successful plaintiff. This problem, which is generally acknowledged to be serious, is discussed by Segerson and Tietenberg in Chapter 3 of this volume.

Volume of Litigation

The overall effect of the input factors should be reflected in the volume of environmental tort litigation that has occurred. I have found no aggregate data on the number of such claims filed and settled. There is no suggestion, however, that pollution–related lawsuits formed a significant fraction of tort litigation prior to 1970. During the 1970s, the flood of asbestos litigation arose in the United States, but these are product–liability lawsuits based on workplace exposures, and not environmental pollution cases. Hensler (1987, 481) reports that total tort filings in the United States grew by only 3 per cent per year during the early 1980s, while product liability cases grew much more rapidly, and other personal injury filings grew somewhat more rapidly. Explosive growth was noted and expected to continue in mass toxic torts, but these are generally product liability cases such as those involving asbestos, the Dalkon shield, and DES, none of which arise from environmental pollution. Huber reports a "torrent" of lawsuits involving hazardous–waste sites following the Love Canal suit, but he cites only 14 such cases between 1983 and 1986. The total of awards and settlements in these cases exceeds $375 million, but if the Agent Orange settlement is omitted on the grounds that causation was not proven, the remainder is only $195 million, of which most was for property damage, and less than $50 million for personal injury (Brennan 1990, 152). Much current environmental litigation involves disputes over who will pay for toxic waste cleanup, rather than whether an injured individual will be compensated for his injuries. The level of environmental litigation thus appears to be consistent with the barriers to suit discussed above.

OUTPUT EVALUATION

The deterrent effects of tort liability may appear in various forms: reductions in environmental damage, reduced pollution discharge, reduced activity in polluting industries, or the introduction of environmental factors into the decision–making process of polluting organizations. Substantial liability could cause increased costs. But environmental protection is a response not only to tort liability but also to an amalgam of laws and regulations promulgated by virtually all levels of government in the wake of growing scientific awareness and public concern for environmental issues, and to a desire to maintain a favorable public image.

The review of inputs leads me to expect little deterrent effect from tort prior to 1980. Since 1980, the expansion of liability for hazardous–waste sites should have led to increased care in the disposal of hazardous–wastes and some reduction in the volume and toxicity of those wastes. As scientific capabilities for tracing pollutants to their source has improved, and as we have developed information about the harm caused by some pollutants, we might expect to find some reduced pollution emissions arising from an increased risk of tort lawsuits, where the harm is predictably large, and where the pollution may be traced easily, as in the case of soil or ground–water contamination.

Pollution Control Expenditures

Between 1972 and 1988, real business spending on pollution abate–ment and control increased by about 70 per cent, from about $28 billion to $48 billion in 1982 dollars (Bratton and Rutledge, 1990, 33). Of this spending, the capital investment portion was relatively constant, while operating costs nearly doubled; both experienced a small decline in the early years of the Reagan administration. This increase is consistent with increasing regulatory demands during this period, and does not reveal a burst of spending in the 1980s that could be attributed to tort litigation. Indeed, if one looks at the pollution abatement share of total business expenditures on new plant and equipment, that share rose from 3.5 per cent in 1972 to more than 4 per cent in 1975, then fell steadily to about 2 per cent in 1988 (Rutledge and Stergioulas, 1988, 27). This pattern is consistent with a boost in spending in response to the legislation of the early 1970s, followed by a decline as abatement investment outpaced increases in the stringency of regulation. There is no evidence of a response to massive environmental liability in the 1980s. Personal spending on pollution abatement and control, representing the cost of motor vehicle emission controls, tripled during the same period, a direct response to regulation, not to litigation. These statistics do not reveal a response to what has been described as growing environmental liability; they are consistent with the view that tort law has not caused a significant increase in pollution control since the mid–1970s.

Pollution Emissions

Data on annual emission rates for the criteria air pollutants from 1970 to 1988 reveal considerable reductions in the emissions of most pollutants, particularly when the growth in population and economic activity are taken into account (Dewees and Trebilcock, 1991, Table 3). Might these reductions be attributed to the tort liability system? That seems unlikely because there is no evidence of such litigation regarding these pollutants and because government regulation easily explains these reductions. The barriers to tort litigation discussed above are directly applicable to these pollutants which are emitted from many sources and which do not cause specific diseases. It would be virtually impossible for an individual in a major metropolitan area to prove that a single source of these pollutants had caused his injury, or even that his injury arose from air pollution at all. There is no evidence of litigation that could have caused these reductions.

Regulation, on the other hand, provides a clear explanation for the reductions. Motor vehicle regulations have greatly reduced the emissions of hydrocarbons (VOCs) and carbon monoxide, and reduced by about half the emissions per mile of oxides of nitrogen. The emission control systems resulting from those regulations have required unleaded gasoline for many vehicles, and EPA regulations have further limited the amount of lead in gasoline. These regulations together account for most of the reduction in emissions of lead, nitrogen oxides and carbon monoxide and much of the VOC reduction. If these data demonstrate success in the fight against air pollution, the credit must go to regulation, not to the tort system.

Corporate Decision–Making

The Rand Corporation studied corporate responses to, and the economic consequences of, expanded civil liability in all areas (Reuter, 1988). The study is based on a series of interviews with senior corporate officials from the chemical industry, the pharmaceutical industry, the semi–conductor industry, and small firms. Of all the varieties of liability, the expansion of environmental liability, including that arising from CERCLA, is identified along with product and wrongful–dismissal liability as having the most significant influence on corporate behaviour. The responses indicate that environmental liability has had its greatest effect with respect to land contamination by toxic wastes, where liability is governed by CERCLA, and do not indicate any significant effect on traditional air and water pollution discharge.

Another source of information is statements by industry executives regarding the effect of tort liability on care and activity levels. In a representative article, the vice president of environmental programs at General Electric stated that while during the 1970s, corporations tried to avoid fines for noncompliance with statutes and regulations, today the principal concerns are large remedial liabilities and large tort liability verdicts such as the $16 million recently awarded against Monsanto for a dioxin spill (Strelow and Claussen, 1988). This statement reflects a significant corporate concern about compliance with pollution regulations and about tort liability, but the focus of the tort concern is on land and water contamination by toxic chemicals spilled, dumped, or leaked by the defendant and the associated clean–up costs. Little concern about traditional tort liability for air and water pollution is revealed.

The Chemical Manufacturers Association has surveyed its members' hazardous–waste management practices annually since 1981. Between 1981 and 1985 the value of chemical shipments in the US rose from $180.5 billion to $214 billion. At the same time, waste generation decreased by 51.8 per cent.[15] Between 1981 and 1987 the use of landfills for disposal decreased by 64 per cent and incineration use increased. No reasons are given for these changes but the desire to avoid cleanup liability by minimizing disposal activity may very well have been a factor along with increased costs of disposal resulting from greater care by disposal sites attributable to both more extensive regulation and tort liability.

Case Studies

A review of studies of industries or regions with significant pollution problems reveals little evidence that tort lawsuits cause pollution abatement. Several case studies provide some insights.

Descriptions of the smoke problem and smoke abatement in heavily industrialized Unites States cities in the early 1900s emphasize activism and regulation. Little credit is given to the operation of the tort system. One historian, in his analysis of the smoke abatement in post–Civil War America discusses specifically the role played by tort actions. Grinder (1980, 92) alleges that nuisance law became ineffectual against the smoke problem because during the 1800s courts in the United States, as in Great Britain, developed a predisposition in favor of industrialization and began to weigh the utility of the polluting activity against the rights of the offended property owners.[16] A further obstacle was the problem of pursuing a nuisance action against one polluter in a city full of polluters. For some time it was virtually impossible to win a lawsuit against polluters, but after the turn of the century the courts became somewhat more sympathetic to plaintiffs. Grinder does not elaborate on the role of nuisance litigation in the smoke abatement process, but implies that it was modest. In a history of the progress of smoke abatement in Pittsburgh, a city of legendary air pollution prior to World War II, T.O. Thackery (1967, 139) ignores common law actions, attributing success in smoke abatement to activism, public discontent, and regulation. In 1941 Pittsburgh followed St Louis in adopting a municipal ordinance banning the burning of smoky fuels, especially soft coal, except in equipment that could control smoke. In 1947 the state legislature imposed the same requirement over the surrounding Allegheny County, and in a few years the air over Pittsburgh was dramatically transformed as particulates were reduced to a fraction their previous levels (Lorant, 1964, Ch. 10). Similarly, in a study of urban noise abatement in America, Smilor (1980, 135) indicates that the common law had little impact and that noise was better dealt with by municipal ordinance.

This evidence suggests that common law tort actions are an ineffective deterrent to multisource, widespread pollution problems.

This result is consistent with nuisance liability rules and problems of proving causation discussed above under Input Evaluation.

Two case studies of abatement in Canadian industry discuss specifically the deterrent role played by tort liability (Dewees, 1990a). In 1969 mercury from fifteen chlor–alkali plants was determined to be contaminating Canadian rivers. In the span of only three years the discharge of this pollutant was reduced by 99 per cent. Three public nuisance actions were filed, and while none of these cases resulted in a judgment, the study suggests that the possibility of substantial liability, far in excess of any fines that could have been imposed, induced the firms to accelerate the abatement process beyond what could have been achieved by regulation alone.

In contrast, the abatement of sulfur oxide emissions from the world's largest source, in Sudbury, Ontario, has been slow. Modest abatement occurred between 1915 and 1930 in response to claims by farmers for crop damage (Dewees, 1990b). Since the first regulations in 1970, sulphur emissions have fallen slowly. No tort action has been taken against the major producers of sulfur oxide since 1970 because of problems of proving causation and the existence of four defenses: prescription, considering the neighbourhood, statutory authority, and easements created by the Crown that ran with the land. There was far less consensus that sulfur oxides were causing serious harm than that mercury had that effect, so proof of causation would have been more difficult.

Traditional tort liability, Superfund liability, and the environmental insurance crisis all converge upon the chemical industry. An evaluation of behavior and performance in the chemical industry, therefore, can serve as a yardstick by which to measure the combined effects of these three elements of the purported environmental liability crisis on American industry.

The economic performance of the industry as a whole does not suggest a crippling liability burden. After–tax profits for the US chemical industry rose steadily from slightly over $5 billion in 1985 to $18.4 billion in 1988, setting records in 1987 and 1988.[17] The industry has grown faster than the general economy.

Allegations that increased liability is damaging international competitiveness are not borne out for the chemical industry. Since at least 1985, and in the face of a general trade deficit, the industry has held a significant trade surplus.[18] In 1988 chemicals ran a surplus, after six to eight years of growth, of $11.8 billion.[19]

Since we do not know how the chemical industry would fare in the absence of the threat of environmental liability, we cannot draw firm conclusions from this evidence. Still, it suggests that although the threat of environmental liability is prompting some caution, it has not crippled the chemical industry.

CONCLUSIONS

The characteristics of tort doctrines for redressing environmental harms that operated a century ago continue to exclude recovery for many environmental harms. Equally important, it is often impossible to prove that a given defendant caused the plaintiff's harm, rendering even favorable doctrines useless. The cost of the tort system pre-cludes its use except for major harms, and with plaintiffs receiving as little as one–third of the total cost of the tort system it is a terribly inefficient means of compensating victims or deterring polluters. These input limitations are reflected in outputs — the performance of the tort system itself. Most studies of pollution abatement have attributed such successes as have occurred primarily to government regulation rather than to civil litigation. There is no substantial evidence that civil litigation has caused substantial control of air and water pollution. The principal exception is in the field of toxic waste disposal, but here CERCLA has created new civil actions, and extensive regulations compel careful handling of toxics. A leading environmental law casebook devotes less than 10 per cent of its pages to civil litigation (Grad, 1985). These considerations suggest that tort is most effective for local pollution problems involving a single polluter and very substantial damage, and is of little significance for pollutants dispersed in low concentrations over a large area, or discharged in a developed area with many other pollution sources, including most air and water pollution problems. Indeed, it appears that much of the expansion of environmental tort litigation in the last decade has involved property damage, where it was relatively easy to prove that the presence of the toxic waste had reduced property values or required costly remedial measures.

In contrast, it is clear that government regulation has substantially reduced some pollution emissions. Automotive emissions have been greatly reduced in total, despite considerable growth in motor vehicle usage. Emissions of particulates have fallen dramatically during the last half century in part because of the abandonment of coal for railroads and for home heating, but at least equally because of local, state and federal regulation of particulate emissions. Emissions of sulfur dioxide have declined somewhat, again because of the regulation of major sources such as smelters and power plants. Improvements in water pollution discharge have been more modest, in part because major classes of sources, such as nonpoint sources, have barely been regulated. Improvements in toxic–waste disposal have arisen from a combination of regulation and fear of civil liability under CERCLA, or of common law tort liability.

To some extent regulation has succeeded where tort has failed, as in the case of motor vehicle emission regulation and the control of particulate and sulfur oxide emissions from stationary sources. In other cases both have failed for similar reasons. If we are uncertain about the harm caused by a pollutant it is no easier to promulgate a regulation than to win a lawsuit. If thousands of small sources discharge a pollutant, the cost of monitoring that discharge may be large relative to the benefits of controlling it, whether the control is motivated by civil litigation or by government regulation. And with thousands of pollutants to be regulated, the process of setting technology–based emission standards is enormously time–consuming and costly, so that years or decades will be required to promulgate regulations covering the list of substances that we *currently* worry about.

Despite the serious limitations of tort law and the clear imperfections of the regulatory system, I am not persuaded that a general expansion of the tort system is warranted. Many of the barriers to suit arise from genuine uncertainty about cause and effect relationships which cannot be resolved by changes in the law. Tort litigation is enormously costly, highly uncertain in its outcome, and may deal with only one source at a time. The wise course may be to continue to allow tort to do what it does best — resolve disputes between a victim and his injurer when the individual harm is great and the causal relationship can be clearly established, and leave to the regulatory authorities the control of pollutants of questionable harm to large numbers of persons and to the general environment. There may also be a useful role for statutory civil liability to supplement or replace tort for environmental problems in which the harm is largely private and can be valued easily, although the CERCLA experience reveals that legislation may create new problems as well as solving existing ones. The deterrent effect of tort and of legislation may be augmented by expanding the authority of private citizens to enforce environmental laws and regulations, particularly substantive regulations, as a means of allowing victims to ferret out violations of the law and cause enforcement to be more responsive to local concerns than is possible with a government monopoly on prosecution.

NOTES

1. This paper draws heavily on a much larger study entitled "The Efficacy of the Tort System" undertaken for the American Law Institute. Funding has also been provided by the Social Sciences and Humanities Research Council of Canada.
2. Pub.L.No. 96–510, 94 STAT. 2767, 42 U.S.C. 9601–9675 (1982 & Supp IV. 1986).
3. *McKie et al.* v *The K.V.P. Co. Ltd.* [1948] O.R. 398 (H.C.), [1948] 3 D.L.R. 201, aff'd. 1 D.L.R. 39 (C.A.), aff'd S.C.R. 698. and the resulting *K.V.P. Company Limited. Act,* 1950, S.O. 1950, c.33. See McLaren (1972).
4. *Beshada* v. *Johns–Manville Products Corp.,* 90 N.J. 191, 447 A.2d 539 (1982).
5. Pub.L.No. 96–510, 94 STAT. 2767, 42 U.S.C. 9601–9675 (1982 & Supp IV. 1986), at 9611.
6. Ibid. 9607.
7. Pub.L. No. 99–499, 100 STAT. 1613, 42 U.S.C. 9613(f).
8. R.S.O. 1980, c. 141, Part IX.
9. Pub. L. 95–217, 91 Stat. 1566, 33 U.S.C. 1251 *et seq.*
10. Pub. L. 101–380, Title I, Aug. 18, 1990, 33 U.S.C. 2701–2761.
11. Recent decisions have allowed recovery for creating the fear of contracting cancer, and for creating the need for medical monitoring, but it is still not possible to collect damages for increased risk of future disease (Abraham, 1988, 972; Huber, 1988a, 145).
12. Hazard Communication Standard, 29 C.F.R. 1910.1200 (1987).
13. 42 U.S.C. 11001–11050 (Supp. IV 1986).
14. Fed. Rules Civ. Proc. Rule 23, 28 U.S.C.A.
15. *Environmental Science and Technology,* Sept. 1988 (vol. 22) p. 1003 It is not clear whether the value of total shipments is in constant dollars.
16. For a chilling review of the ineffectiveness of tort law with respect to deterrence in Great Britain in the nineteenth century see Brenner (1974).
17. *Chemical Week,* 4 Jan. 1989 (vol. 144) p. 34.
18. Ibid., p. 36.
19. *Chemical Week,* 1 March 1989 (vol. 144) p. 8.

7. Natural Resource Damages from Oil Spills

Richard Dunford[1]

Under the Clean Water Act, businesses that spill oil in the marine environment are liable for the resulting natural resource damages. In 1986 the US Department of the Interior (DOI) promulgated regulations implementing the natural resource damage provisions of the Clean Water Act. A 1989 Court of Appeals ruling upheld portions of the DOI regulations, while overturning or remanding other portions of those regulations. The Oil Pollution Act of 1990 requires additional changes in the determination of natural resource damages from oil spills. This chapter examines the liability implications of the DOI regulations and subsequent changes in the procedures for measuring the natural resource damages for oil spills in US waters.

The first three sections of this chapter describe the evolution of natural resource damage liability for oil spills. Specifically, the first section summarizes the natural resource damage provisions of the DOI regulations. The second section describes the changes in these provisions resulting from the 1989 Court of Appeals ruling. The third section presents the natural resource damage provisions of the Oil Pollution Act of 1990. The fourth section examines the liability implications of the evolution of the natural resource damage provisions. The final section briefly summarizes the findings.

DOI REGULATIONS[2]

In 1977 the Clean Water Act (33 USC 1251 *et seq*.) authorized certain government agencies to recover compensatory damages for injuries to natural resources resulting from oil spills. Specifically, Section 311(f)(4) provides that clean–up costs "shall include any costs or expenses incurred by [authorized governmental agencies] in the restoration or replacement of natural resources damaged or destroyed as a result of [such spills]". The authorized governmental agencies "shall act on behalf of the public as trustee of the natural resources to cover the costs of replacing or restoring such resources" (Section 311(f)(5)).

In 1980 Section 107(a)(4)(C) of the Comprehensive Environmental Response, Compensation, and Liability Act (CERCLA—42 USC 9601 *et seq.*) extended the liability of the businesses responsible for releases of hazardous substances to "damages for injury to, destruction of, or loss of natural resources, including the reasonable costs of assessing such injury, destruction, or loss resulting from such release". CERCLA (also known as the Superfund Act) required the promulgation of regulations for Natural Resource Damage Assessments (NRDA) for both oil spills (under the Clean Water Act) and hazardous substance releases.

In 1981 President Reagan delegated the responsibility to develop the NRDA regulations to the US Department of the Interior (DOI). Under court–imposed deadlines, the DOI promulgated the NRDA regulations in August of 1986 (see 43 *CFR* Part 11). These regulations apply to natural resources "belonging to, managed by, held in trust by, appertaining to, or otherwise controlled by the United States ... any state or local government, any foreign government, any Indian tribe" (43 *CFR* Section 11.14(z)) or members of Indian tribes under certain conditions. Eligible trustees include federal natural resource management agencies, designated state agencies, and Indian tribes (43 *CFR* Section 11.14(rr)).

As required by CERCLA, the DOI regulations delineate two types of natural resource damage assessments: Type A assessments and Type B assessments. Type A assessments apply to small, short–duration, one–time releases of oil or hazardous substances in coastal and marine environments. Type A assessments use a computer model to estimate damages. Type B assessments apply to all other releases in coastal and marine environments, and releases in all other environments. We focus on Type B assessments in the remainder of this paper since trustees have used some variant of a Type B assessment for almost all major oil spills.

Damage Assessment Steps

Type B assessment consists of three steps:
*   Injury determination,
*   Quantification of effects, and
*   Damage determination.

We briefly describe each of these steps below.

The Injury Determination step ensures that injuries are well–documented and linked to the release. The detailed definitions of injury in the NRDA regulations are based on measurable adverse changes in the physical and/or chemical quality of five major types of natural resources:
*   surface water,
*   groundwater,
*   air,
*   geologic, and
*   biologic.

The Quantification of Effects step determines the reduction in natural resource services resulting from the injuries attributable to a release. A natural resource service is defined in the NRDA regulations as a function one resource performs for another resource or for humans, including:
*   recreation,
*   provision of habitat, food, and other needs of biological resources,
*   flood control, and
*   waste assimilation (Section 11.70(e)).

This step begins with the determination of the level of services that the resource would have provided if the release had not occurred (i.e. baseline services level). Natural changes (e.g. ecological succession) and cyclical changes in the resources must be taken into account when estimating baseline service levels. The service reduction attributable to the release is the difference between the with–injury service level and the baseline service level.

Natural resources may provide two types of services: use services and nonuse services. Use services involve some physical or visual contact between people and the natural resources. Examples of use services include recreation activities such as fishing, boating, bird–

watching, hunting, hiking, and camping. Forgone recreational activities are the most common use services giving rise to natural resource damages from oil spills.

Nonuse services include services that resources provide for other resources and services that resources provide for people that do not require physical or visual contact between people and the resources. The services that some natural resources provide for other natural resources are mainly limited to the provision of food, nesting habitat, protection from predators, and similar biotic support services. A marsh providing nesting habitat for migratory waterfowl is an example of this type of service to other natural resources (i.e. migratory waterfowl). Nonuse services can also arise from natural resources that provide wellbeing to some people through their mere existence, even though these people have no plans ever to use the resources. Examples of natural resources that may provide such existence services include unique geologic resources (such as the Grand Canyon) and rare, threatened, or endangered biologic resources (such as bald eagles).

The third NRDA step is the Damage Determination step. The DOI regulations specify that damages are: the *lesser of* restoration costs (i.e. the cost of restoring, rehabilitating, replacing, or acquiring the equivalent of the injured natural resources, plus the diminution of use values between the date of the release and the date natural resource services are restored) *or* the diminution of use values resulting from the release, *plus* the costs of assessing natural resource damages. Regardless of whether natural resource damages are based on restoration costs or the diminution of use values, the recovered monies must be used for the restoration, rehabilitation, replacement, or the acquisition of the equivalent of the injured resources.[3]

The DOI regulations identify three components of use values:
*   the value to the public of recreational or other public uses of resources, as measured by changes in consumer surplus;
*   any fees or other payments collectable by the government for a private party's use of the natural resources (i.e. user fees); and
*   any economic rent accruing to a private party because the government does not charge a fee or price for the use of the resource (43 *CFR* Section 11.83).

Use values can also include all the net income lost by government agencies that are the sole or majority owner of an economic activity adversely affected by a release. In conclusion, the DOI claims that the diminution of use values reflects the "loss to the public" in general as a result of the release.[4]

In contrast, natural resource damages under the DOI regulations exclude:

* taxes forgone by government agencies;
* wages and other income lost by private individuals; and
* direct or indirect losses incurred by private commercial users of natural resources, other than economic rent (51 *Fed. Reg.* 27691 [1986]).

Furthermore, the DOI regulations exclude forgone existence values and option values in the diminution of use values unless there are no use values for the injured natural resources.[5] DOI gave two reasons for excluding existence and option values in natural resource damages: CERCLA only mentions use values, and "option and existence values are less well–defined and more uncertainty surrounds their measurement" (51 *Fed. Reg.* 27719 [1986]).

Valuation Methods

Figure 7.1 lists the seven possible methods specified in the DOI regulations for valuing forgone natural resource services. The first two methods directly measure changes in the market value of natural resource services. Specifically, the market price method uses the decrease in the market price of injured natural resources as the measure of the diminution of use values. Similarly, the appraisal method relies on an appraiser to estimate the decreased value of injured natural resources attributable to an oil spill.

The second group of valuation methods (i.e. the indirect methods) determine natural resource damages from changes in the market value of related goods or services. For example, the factor income method is appropriate when the services provided by a natural resource are an input in the production of another service or commodity that is traded in a market. Any change in the net income of the final product caused by a natural resource injury is used as a measure of the value of the reduced services. The hedonic method is appropriate when natural resource services are a characteristic of private property. Natural resource damages are measured as the change in property values

Figure 7.1. Methods for valuing natural resource damages

Direct	Market Price
	Appraisal
Indirect	Factor income
	Hedonic
	Travel cost
Expressed	Contingent valuation
Generic	Unit-day value

resulting from the natural resource injury, holding all other characteristics constant. Finally, the travel cost method is based on the notion that recreationists at a particular site pay an "implicit" price for using natural resources through their travel and time costs. Since recreationists come from diverse locations, we can use their "travel behavior" to analyse the demand (i.e. willingness to pay) for the natural resource's services. From a demand curve, we can estimate the consumer surplus that recreationists forgo when natural resource services are reduced.

The contingent valuation method directly elicits households' willingness to pay for natural resource services using a survey. By simulating market linkages between the natural resource services and household behavior in a survey questionnaire, this method measures expressed preferences for the natural resource services. In a natural resource damage setting, we ask people to value their natural resource service losses as result of the natural resource injuries from the release, within the context of the other goods and services they purchase.

Finally, the unit–day–value method provides generic values for natural resource services based on the results of studies of various areas using a variety of methods. For example, suppose that there have been a total of six salmon fishing studies (four using the travel cost method and two using the contingent valuation method) in Washington, Oregon, and Alaska over the last 12 years. The unit–day–value method would develop an "average" value for a salmon fishing day from the results of these six studies. Natural resource damages are determined by multiplying this average value by the number of salmon fishing days forgone as result of a particular release.

The DOI regulations establish a hierarchy for the use of the seven valuation methods. Specifically, trustees must use the market price method unless the market for the resource is not "reasonably competitive" (43 *CFR* Sec. 11.84(c)(1)). Under this circumstance, trustees must use the appraisal method "if sufficient information exists" (43 *CFR* Sec. 11.84(c)(2)). If neither the market price nor appraisal methods are appropriate, then trustees can use one of the nonmarket valuation methods.

Other Important Provisions

Two other provisions of the DOI regulations are particularly noteworthy from an economic perspective. First, willingness to pay to avoid the service losses experienced as a result of a release is the relevant valuation criterion for forgone use values, not willingness to accept. While acknowledging that "willingness to accept may be the criterion most germane to natural resource damages, since the public has the property right to the injured natural resource", DOI felt that "the application of the willingness–to–accept criterion can lead to more technical difficulties and uncertainties than the willingness–to–pay criterion" (51 *Fed. Reg.* 27721 [1986]).

Second, the DOI regulations specify a 10 per cent real discount for determining the present value of natural resource damages. While economists have not reached a consensus regarding the "correct" social discount rate, most economists would probably agree that a 10 per cent real discount rate is too high (Kopp, Portney, and Smith, 1990, 10130). Thus, this discount rate results in a lower present value of natural resource damages incurred in future years than would a lower discount rate. Alternatively, a "high" discount rate increases the present value of natural resource damages experienced in the past relative to a "low" discount rate.[6] The impact of the discount rate on the magnitude of natural resource damages when both past and future damages are present depends on the specific mix of these damages over time (see Desvousges, Dunford, and Domanico, 1989, 5–10, for an example).

1989 *OHIO* DECISION

Within three months of their promulgation, petitioners filed nine lawsuits contesting various aspects of the DOI regulations with the DC Circuit of the US Court of Appeals. The petitioners included six states, three nonprofit environmental organizations (led by the National Wildlife Federation), the Chemical Manufacturers Association, a public utility, and one manufacturing company (see Desvousges, Dunford, and Domanico, 1989, 1–11 — 1–14, for a summary of the major issues/provisions contested in the nine cases). At the judge's request the nine cases were combined into one case, known as the *Ohio* case. The DC Circuit ruled on the lawsuits in July of 1989 (880 *F. 2d.* 432–481 [1989]).

The 1989 *Ohio* decision upheld several important economic provisions of the NRDA regulations, including the use of:
* willingness–to–pay criterion for valuing forgone natural resource services;
* contingent valuation as a valid nonmarket valuation method; and
* 10 per cent real discount rate for aggregating past and future damages.

However, the *Ohio* decision overturned two important economic provisions in the DOI regulations: the "lesser–of" rule and restrictions on the inclusion of nonuse values in the diminution of natural resource service values.[7]

As explained previously, the "lesser–of" rule in the NRDA regulations based damages on the lesser of restoration costs and the diminution in use value of natural resource services. The Court of Appeals ruled that the legislative history of CERCLA clearly indicated that Congress had "a distinct preference for using restoration cost as the measure of damages" (880 *F. 2d.* 444 [1989]). However, the Court acknowledged two possible exceptions — namely, when restoration is infeasible or when restoration costs are "grossly disproportionate" to the value of the natural resource services forgone. In a footnote, the Court provided an example to illustrate the "grossly disproportionate" exception — if restoration costs are three times the diminution of value, then the latter could be the basis for natural resource damages (880 *F. 2d.* 443 [1989], note 7). In summary, the Court of Appeals rejected a benefit–cost approach for determining natural resource damages, arguing that restoration costs should be the basis for these damages in most cases.

As noted above, the NRDA regulations limit consideration of nonuse values to situations where use values cannot be determined. DOI gave two rationales for excluding nonuse values: CERCLA only mentioned use values and the measurement of nonuse values was more uncertain than the measurement of use values. The Court of Appeals ruled that CERCLA does not restrict damages to use values, even though only use values are mentioned in the statute (880 *F. 2d.* 464 [1989]). The Court acknowledged the difficulties in using contingent valuation to measure nonuse values (880 *F. 2d.* 476–480 [1989]), but apparently did not find those difficulties as troublesome as DOI. Clearly, the Court of Appeals expanded the scope of natural resource damages by putting nonuse values on an equal footing with use values in determining the diminution of value attributable to a natural resource injury.

In addition to the provisions overturned, the Court of Appeals remanded one NRDA provision to DOI for clarification — the distinction between public and private resources in the regulations. Specifically, the Court asked DOI to clarify the extent to which the NRDA regulations apply to resources that are not owned by a government agency, but are subject to "a substantial degree of government regulation, management, or other form of control" (54 *Fed. Reg.* 39018 [1989]). Since the NRDA regulations only apply to injured "public" resources, the distinction between public and private resources has important implications for the scope of natural resource damages.

In September 1989, DOI solicited public comments for implementing several aspects of the *Ohio* decision, including:
*   defining the term "grossly disproportionate";
*   criteria for selecting the most appropriate valuation
    methodology for particular releases;
*   ways of classifying resource uses to avoid double–counting
    forgone natural resource services; and
*   the degree of management, regulation, control, or property
    interest that would make natural resources subject to the NRDA
    regulations (54 *Fed. Reg.* 39017–39018 [1989]).

In late April 1991, DOI issued proposed revisions in the NRDA regulations pursuant to the *Ohio* decision (56 *Fed. Reg.* 19752 [1991]). The proposed NRDA revisions define natural resource damages as the sum of:

* restoration costs;
* forgone compensable value; and
* damage assessment costs.

The proposed regulations define compensable value as

> the amount of money required to compensate the public for the loss in services provided by the injured resources between the time of the discharge or release and the time the resources and the services those resources provided are fully restored to their baseline conditions. (56 *Fed. Reg.* 19772 [1991])

Forgone compensable value would includes losses of both use values and nonuse values, as required by the *Ohio* decision. The proposed regulations define use values as the value of direct, public uses of natural resources. Nonuse values are defined as the difference between compensable value and use value.

While the proposed regulations base natural resource damages on restoration costs, they do not mandate the two exceptions mentioned in the *Ohio* decision — namely, when restoration is infeasible or when restoration costs are "grossly disproportionate" to the value of the natural resource services forgone. As an alternative, the proposed regulations list ten factors that trustees should consider in selecting one or more restoration alternatives:

* technical feasibility;
* net benefits of the alternatives;
* cost–effectiveness of the alternatives;
* results of response actions;
* potential for additional injury resulting from the actions;
* natural recovery period;
* ability of the resource to recover with or without alternative actions;
* acquisition of equivalent land where restoration, rehabilitation, and/or other replacement of land is not possible;
* potential effects of the action on human health and safety; and
* consistency with applicable Federal and state laws. (56 *Fed. Reg.* 19770–19771 [1991])

The proposed regulations do not provide any guidance on the relative importance of these factors, nor are trustees required to meet any of them. So trustees could possibly select a technically infeasible restoration alternative or a restoration alternative having grossly disproportionate costs under the proposed regulations.

As required by the *Ohio* decision, the proposed regulations eliminate the hierarchy of valuation methods in the current regulations, but they rate the reliability of these methods. Specifically, the market (i.e. direct) methods are rated as more reliable for measuring use values than the nonmarket (i.e. indirect and expressed) methods, which are rated as more reliable than the expressed method (i.e. contingent valuation method) for measuring nonuse values (56 *Fed. Reg.* 19772 [1991]). Although the expressed method for valuing nonuse services is rated as the least reliable method, the preamble to the proposed regulations indicates that this is the only currently available method for valuing nonuse losses (56 *Fed. Reg.* 19759 [1991]).

As noted above, the Court of Appeals asked DOI to clarify its distinction between public and private resources in the NRDA regulations. Essentially, the preamble to the proposed regulations just restates DOI's perspective on this distinction from the current regulations (see 56 *Fed. Reg.* 19766 [1991] and 51 *Fed. Reg.* 27696 [1986]). However, the proposed regulations require the trustees to cite their authority for asserting trusteeship for affected natural resources (Section 11.31(a)(2)). This requirement should help clarify which trustees are seeking damages to what natural resources, as well as help reduce the possibility of more than one trustee seeking damages for injuries to the same natural resources.

OIL POLLUTION ACT OF 1990

Largely in response to the 1989 *Exxon Valdez* oil spill in Alaska, Congress passed comprehensive oil spill legislation in August 1990 — the Oil Pollution Act of 1990 (P.L. 101–380). The basic goal of the Oil Pollution Act (OPA) is to minimize the frequency and severity of oil spills by increasing:

* efforts to prevent oil spills (e.g. by requiring double hulls on tankers and by mandating improvements in tanker navigation systems);
* oil spill response capabilities involving containment, recovery, and cleanup actions; and
* oil spill liability as an incentive to avoid oil spills.

Section 1002 of OPA identifies six possible types of damages resulting from oil spills:

* natural resource damages;
* losses resulting from injuries to real or personal property;
* loss of subsistence use of natural resources;
* losses of government revenues (such as taxes, royalties, rents, and fees) resulting from injuries to real property, personal property, or natural resources;
* losses of profits resulting from injuries to real property, personal property, or natural resources; and
* net costs of providing increased or additional public services during or after removal activities.

Many of these damages are not specifically covered under the four federal laws that the OPA superseded (i.e. the Clean Water Act, the Deepwater Port Act [33 USC 1501–1524], Outer Continental Shelf Lands Act [43 USC 1331 *et seq.*], and Trans–Alaska Pipeline Authorization Act [43 USC 1651 *et seq.*]). However, most of these damages were previously recoverable under common law (e.g. losses of real or personal property). Nevertheless, OPA broadens the scope of recoverable damages, in general.

Under Sec. 1006(d) of OPA, natural resource damages are the cost of restoring, rehabilitating, replacing, or acquiring the equivalent of the damaged natural resources (restoration costs, for simplicity), *plus* the diminution in value of those natural resources pending restoration, *plus* the reasonable cost of assessing those damages. The Conference Report on OPA indicates that "diminution of value" refers to "the standard for measuring natural resource damages used in the 1989 DC Circuit Court decision" (US House of Representatives, 1990, 108). In effect, this means that forgone nonuse values should be included in the diminution of natural resource values prior to restoration. The Conference Report also incorporates the Court's "grossly disproportionate" exception with a slight, but important, twist.

Specifically, trustees must give priority to efforts to restore, rehabilitate, or replace injured resources.

> The alternative of acquiring equivalent resources should be chosen only when the other alternatives are not possible, or when the cost of these alternatives would, in the judgment of the trustee, be grossly disproportionate to the value of the resources involved. "Equivalent" resources are resources that the trustee determines are comparable to the injured resources. Equivalent resources should be acquired to enhance the recovery, productivity, and survival of the ecosystem affected by a discharge, preferably in proximity to the affected area (US House of Representatives, 1990, 108–9).

OPA contains several other provisions pertaining to natural resource damages. For example, section 1006(b) identifies four types of trustees:
* federal agencies;
* state agencies;
* Indian tribes; and
* foreign governments.

Each trustee is responsible for assessing damages and developing a restoration plan for natural resources under its trusteeship. However, federal agencies can assess natural resource damages for state agencies and Indian tribes, if requested. These other trustees must reimburse the federal agencies for the assessment costs. The *Conference Report* encourages trustees to coordinate their assessments and restoration plans, but "the Act does not preclude different trustees from conducting parallel assessments and developing individual plans" (US House of Representatives, 1990, 109). Unlike the Clean Water Act and CERCLA, OPA provides up–front money for damage assessment studies.[8]

Section 1006(e) of OPA directs the US Department of Commerce to develop new NRDA regulations pertaining to oil spills. The Conference Report states that these regulations, "not the regulations previously issued by the Department of the Interior, shall apply to all oil spill incidents occurring after the enactment of this Act" (US House of Representatives, 1990, 109).[9] Furthermore, these regulations "should be designed to simplify the trustees' task of assessing and recovering" (US House of Representatives, 1990, 109) natural resource damages. Clearly, the Congress does not support the NRDA process developed by the Interior Department. The implication is that different protocols will eventually be required for assessing damages to specific natural resources depending on whether those natural resources were injured by an oil spill (covered under OPA) or a hazardous–substance release (covered under CERCLA).

Although not directly related to natural resource damages, four other important provisions of OPA are noteworthy. First, section 1004(a) place limits on the liability of responsible parties for cleanup costs and damages in general. The liability limit for oil tankers can range from $10 million up to $135 million depending on their size. The liability limit for offshore facilities is removal costs plus $75 million. OPA has a $350 million liability limit on all onshore facilities and deepwater ports. These liability limits do not apply to spills proximately caused by gross negligence, willful misconduct, or a violation of federal safety, construction, or operating regulations. Additionally, liability is unlimited if the responsible party fails to report the spill, cooperate and assist in removal activities, or comply with certain federal orders.[10]

Section 311 of the Clean Water Act established a $35 million revolving fund to cover oil spill cleanup costs *incurred by the federal government*. This fund, financed by "appropriated monies, recovered costs, and fines, has never reached its authorized size ... and as of June 1989 had a balance of $7.3 million" (Jones, 1989, 10333–4). OPA specifies the possible uses of a new Oil Spill Trust Fund, which was created by the Budget Reconciliation Act of 1989 (P.L. 101–239). This Fund, which replaces the Clean Water Act fund and other federal funds,[11] is financed by a 5 cents per barrel tax on oil produced in or shipped into the United States. Section 1012 of OPA allows uses of the Fund for:

* cleanup costs by federal agencies;
* cleanup costs by state agencies up to $250,000 subject to federal approval;
* costs of assessing natural resource damages incurred by government agencies and Indian tribes;
* claims for uncompensated cleanup costs or damages; and
* federal costs to implement the Act subject to specified limits.

OPA places a $1 billion expenditure limit per incident on uses of the Fund. Additionally, OPA puts a $500 million expenditure limit per incident on uses of the Fund for natural resource damages. If needed, OPA allows the Fund to borrow up to $1 billion from the US Treasury.

One of the main controversies during the debate in Congress on the OPA, and similar, unsuccessful legislation in prior years, was the pre–emption of state oil spill liability laws by the new federal liability law (see Jones, 1989, for information on this controversy). Ultimately, the opponents of preemption won this debate. OPA states,

> [n]othing in this Act ... shall affect the authority of any State or political subdivision thereof from imposing any additional liability ... with respect to the discharge of oil or other pollution by oil within such State ...; or affect ... the liabilities of any person under ... State law, including common law. (Section 1018)

As of October 1990, all but two coastal states (Delaware and New York) have unlimited liability for cleanup costs and/or natural resource damages (Government Institutes Inc., 1991, 169–75). So most responsible businesses face unlimited liability for oil spills under state law — OPA only limits their liability under federal law.

Similarly, the OPA debate included discussions of the pros and cons of ratifying two 1984 international agreements on oil spill liability: the International Convention on Civil Liability for Oil Pollution Damage (CLC Convention) and the International Convention on the Establishment of an International Fund for Compensation for Oil Pollution Damage (Fund Convention). The CLC Convention places a $78 million limit on the liability of shipowners for cleanup costs, natural resource damages, and third–party claims. The Fund Convention, which is financed by oil–receiving nations, brings the total maximum compensation available to $175 million (Jones, 1989, 10336). By enacting OPA, Congress decided not to support the ratification of these conventions. OPA states that US interests would be best served by participating in an international oil pollution liability and compensation regime that is at least as effective as federal and state laws in preventing incidents and in guaranteeing full and prompt compensation for damages resulting from incidents (Section 3001).

IMPLICATIONS FOR NATURAL RESOURCE DAMAGE LIABILITY

In this section we evaluate the impact of the evolution of NRDA laws/regulations on the liability of businesses responsible for oil spills.[12] First we compare and contrast the NRDA liability specified in the DOI regulations, the *Ohio* decision, and the Oil Pollution Act of 1990. Then we examine the actual implementation of these NRDA laws/regulations in practice. The next subsection broadens the scope of our analysis to the *net* NRDA liability of businesses responsible for oil spills under OPA. Finally, we discuss *net* NRDA liability in practice under OPA.

NRDA Liability Under the Law

Prior to the Clean Water Act, natural resource damages resulting from oil spills were not recoverable by government agencies or any other parties.[13] Unquestionably, the natural resource damage provisions of the Clean Water Act, as reflected in the DOI regulations, substantially increased the liability of businesses responsible for oil spills in most cases. Maraziti has concluded that "recoveries for natural resource damage are likely to be very large and will, in some cases, far outweigh cleanup costs" (1987, 10036).

As discussed above, the DOI regulations measured natural resource damages as the lesser of restoration costs and the diminution of use values. This "lesser-of" approach is consistent with both the common-law measure of damages[14] and economic efficiency, if no losses of nonuse values result from an oil spill. As stated by Kopp, Portney, and Smith, "one would not want to restore a resource if the cost of doing so exceeded the value society placed on it" (1990, 10128). However, when nonuse services are affected by an oil spill, then the lesser-of approach in the DOI regulations undervalues damages.

The *Ohio* decision added the value of forgone nonuse services to the value of forgone use services in determining the diminution of value as a result of an oil spill. However, natural resource damages under the *Ohio* decision are based on the diminution of value only if restoration costs are much larger than this value (i.e. grossly disproportionate).[15] So the value of natural resource damages under the *Ohio* decision will significantly exceed the value of natural resource damages under the DOI regulations whenever substantial nonuse values are forgone and/or restoration costs significantly exceed forgone use values. By simultaneously putting nonuse values on an equal footing with use values and eliminating the lesser–of rule, the *Ohio* decision may significantly increase natural resource damages in some cases.

OPA further expands natural resource damage liability for oil spills by substantially changing the "grossly disproportionate" exception in the *Ohio* decision.[16] As noted above, OPA defines natural resource damages as the sum of restoration costs and the diminution of value prior to restoration (plus damage assessment costs), unless restoration costs are grossly disproportionate to the value (not the diminution in value of the resources involved). Unless an oil spill completely destroys natural resources for many years, the diminution in value will be less (and perhaps much less) than the full value of the natural resources prior to the spill. Therefore, the "grossly disproportionate" exception in the *Ohio* decision will be reached at a lower dollar value than the "grossly disproportionate" exception in OPA. Assuming that the cost of acquiring the equivalent natural resources is comparable to the pre-spill value of the injured natural resources, the value of natural resource damages under OPA may be much higher than the value of natural resource damages under the *Ohio* decision.

Under the DOI regulations, the *Ohio* decision, and OPA, restoration costs play a crucial role in the magnitude of natural resource damages. Table 7.1 provides an example that illustrates the importance of restoration costs. The top half of the table provides assumed values for:
* values forgone between the spill and the damage assessment;
* values forgone after the damage assessment under natural recovery;
* restoration costs;
* values forgone after the damage assessment under restoration;
* cost of acquiring the equivalent to the injured natural resources, and which we assume is comparible to the pre-spill value of the injured natural resources; and
* damage assessment costs.[17]

Note that the assumed values for each of these elements of natural resource damages are the same for all four scenarios (A, B, C, and D), except for restoration costs (i.e. only restoration costs vary across the scenarios).[18]

The bottom half of Table 7.1 shows the value of natural resource damages for each scenario under three liability schemes: DOI regulations, *Ohio* decision, and OPA. Under Scenario A, restoration costs plus the post–assessment value forgone under restoration is less than the post–assessment value forgone under natural recovery. Consequently, all three liability schemes yield the same amount of natural resource damages (i.e. $19 million) for Scenario A. This value is based on the sum of the pre–assessment value forgone, restoration costs, post–assessment value forgone under restoration, and damage assessment costs.

Table 7.1.   *Comparison of natural resource damages under three liability schemes for four hypothetical spill scenarios (million dollars)*

	Spill scenarios			
	A	B	C	D
Assumed values for:				
Pre–assessment value forgone	12	12	12	12
Post–assessment value forgone under natural recovery	8	8	8	8
Restoration costs	4	10	24	36
Post–assessment value forgone under restoration	2	2	2	2
Cost of acquiring equivalent natural resources	30	30	30	30
Damage assessment costs	1	1	1	1
Natural resource damages under:				
DOI regulations	19	21	21	21
Ohio decision	19	25	21	21
Oil Pollution Act	19	25	39	43 or 51

Under Scenario B, restoration costs slightly exceed the diminution of value under natural recovery. The DOI regulations result in the smallest amount of natural resource damages, because of the lesser–of rule. Alternatively, the *Ohio* decision and OPA base natural resource damages on restoration costs, plus the pre–assessment value forgone, the post–assessment value forgone under restoration, and damage assessment costs.

Under Scenario C, restoration costs are grossly disproportionately higher than the diminution of value, based on the "three–times" example given by the Court of Appeals. Consequently, the DOI regulations and the *Ohio* decision result in the same amount of natural resource damages. However, OPA yields a much larger amount of natural resource damages, because restoration costs must be included in natural resource damages under this scenario since restoration costs are not grossly disproportionately larger than the cost of acquiring the equivalent natural resources. (In fact, restoration costs are *less* than the cost of acquiring the equivalent natural resources in Scenario C.)

Under Scenario D, restoration costs exceed the cost of acquiring the equivalent natural resources, both of which are much larger than the diminution of value. As in Scenario C, the DOI regulations and *Ohio* decision result in the same amount of natural resource damages. OPA could result in two different amounts of natural resource damages, depending on whether the trustees consider restoration costs to be grossly disproportionately larger than the cost of acquiring the equivalent natural resources. OPA does not specify the alternate measure of damages when trustees determine that restoration costs are "grossly disproportionate" to the cost of acquiring the equivalent to the injured natural resources. This measure will not be known until NOAA promulgates its NRDA regulations for oil spills. For the purposes of this example, we assume that the alternate measure will be the sum of the cost of acquiring the equivalent natural resources, pre-assessment value forgone, and damage assessment costs. In any event, OPA results in a much larger amount of natural resource damages than either the DOI regulations or the *Ohio* decision in Scenario D.

In summary, the DOI regulations result in the smallest amount of natural resource damages in all four scenarios. The *Ohio* decision results in a larger amount of natural resource damages than the DOI regulations only in Scenario B, when restoration costs exceed the diminution of value, but not grossly disproportionately. OPA produces the same amount of natural resource damages as the *Ohio* decision under Scenarios A and B. However, OPA yields a much larger amount of natural resource damages than the *Ohio* decision and the DOI regulations in Scenarios C and D. Thus, OPA could substantially increase NRDA liability in some cases.

NRDA Liability in Practice

While NRDA liability under the law has increased substantially since the passage of the Clean Water Act in 1977, changes in NRDA liability in practice are not very clear for several reasons. First, the DOI regulations were not promulgated until almost nine years after the passage of the Clean Water Act (CWA), so no regulations operational-ized the CWA's natural resource damage provisions until 1986. Consequently, these provisions were basically ignored for oil spills.[19]

As noted above, several lawsuits contesting various provisions of the DOI regulations were filed about three months after promulgation of the regulations. It was 33 months later when the Court of Appeals ruled on those lawsuits in the *Ohio* decision. It then took DOI more than 21 months to issue *proposed* revisions in the NRDA regulations to implement the *Ohio* decision. (It is difficult to predict when DOI will issue the final revisions.) During this same period, OPA was enacted. OPA requires NOAA to develop new NRDA regulations applying to oil spills by August of 1992. (The DOI regulations are operative until the new NOAA regulations are promulgated.) At present it is very difficult to predict the specific provisions of these new NRDA regulations. In conclusion, significant uncertainty has surrounded NRDA liability in practice since the promulgation of the DOI regulations in 1986.

In addition to the uncertainty about NRDA provisions, trustees have not actually followed the DOI regulations for any oil spill since their promulgation in 1986 (Olson, 1989, 10552). Typically, the trustees have followed a "cafeteria" approach, using only selected provisions of the DOI regulations. This is especially significant since trustees' NRDA estimates are given a rebuttable presumption if they follow the DOI regulations. (This presumption means that the courts must assume that the trustees' damage estimates are correct if the DOI regulations were followed.) The trustees have given up the right to a rebuttable presumption in order to have more flexibility in estimating natural resource damages.

Although the NRDA rules are still evolving and trustees have not followed the DOI regulations for any oil spills, trustees have pursued natural resource damage claims for several oil spills in recent years. The Martinez oil spill was the first major oil spill in US waters after the promulgation of the DOI regulations where trustees sought natural resource damages. In late April 1988 a pipe connection broke in an oil holding tank at Shell Oil Company's manufacturing facility at Martinez, California. As a result, about 430,000 gallons of oil escaped through an open drainage valve into nearby sloughs, marshes and the eastern part of San Francisco Bay. In addition to adverse effects on wetlands and associated wildlife, the Martinez spill also disrupted fishing and boating activities in the area during the late spring and summer.

In late 1989 Shell and the trustees finalized a settlement for damages resulting from the spill. According to the Consent Decree (1989), the settlement totaled $19.75 million and was allocated as follows:

* $11.6 million for natural resource damages;
* $4.65 million for various penalties;
* $1.31 million for various oil spill studies;
* $0.75 million for the city of Martinez;
* $0.6 million for the city of Benicia;
* $0.5 million for reimbursement of costs incurred by federal and state agencies;
* $0.2 million for the East Bay Regional Park District; and
* $0.15 million for Solano County.

So over half of the Martinez settlement was designated as natural resource damages. However, some of the money allocated to specific trustees will also be used to restore or enhance natural resource services in the affected area. For example, $275,000 of the $600,000 received by the city of Benicia must be used to construct two marsh overlooks. The trustees have formed a committee consisting of representatives from six public agencies to determine how to spend the money recovered for natural resource damages.

While the details are still sketchy, trustees and Exxon have reached a settlement on the natural resource damage claim associated with the

Arthur Kill oil spill. This spill occurred on 1 January 1990, when an underwater pipeline connecting Exxon's Bayway Refinery and a nearby terminal ruptured, releasing over 500,000 gallons of refined oil into the Arthur Kill, a waterbody separating New Jersey and New York near Elizabeth, NJ. The spill affected several miles of shoreline and killed hundreds of birds in the area. The Arthur Kill settlement reportedly totals $15 million over a five–year period, including:

* $10 million for "environmental initiatives", including the purchase of additional wetlands and funding research projects in the area;

* $4.8 million for restitution to the governments of New York state, New Jersey, New York City, and the city of Elizabeth, NJ; and

* $0.2 million criminal fine.[20]

No further details on this settlement are currently available.

These two settlements clearly indicate that trustees are successfully obtaining natural resource damages from oil spills. Furthermore, OPA's provision of "up–front" money for trustees' damage assessment studies may accelerate the recent increase in natural resource damage claims. (In the past, trustees have sometimes had difficulty getting enough money for damage assessment studies, which can be expensive.) Nevertheless, the specific impact of the *Ohio* decision and OPA on NRDA liability is difficult to determine from the two settlements discussed above.

Net NRDA Liability under OPA

As explained above, OPA has substantially increased the *gross* NRDA liability of businesses responsible for some oil spills theoretically. However, OPA's liability limits in conjunction with the creation of the Oil Spill Trust Fund may actually *decrease* the *net* NRDA liability of responsible businesses in some cases. Table 7.2 illustrates this phenomenon, using some hypothetical costs and NRDA liability for oil spills releasing different amounts of oil.[21] This example assumes that the spiller has a $120 million maximum liability under OPA based on the size of the tanker that spilled the oil. For simplicity, we exclude fines, penalties, and other damages from the example.

Table 7.2. Hypothetical costs and liability for supertanker oil spills of various sizes under the Oil Pollution Act (million dollars)

	Size of spill (thousand gallons)		
	100	1,000	10,000
Pre–OPA			
Cleanup costs	5	50	500
NRDA liability	10	200	700
Total cost to responsible business	15	250	1,200
Post–OPA			
Cleanup costs	5	50	500
Gross NRDA liability	20	300	1,000
Gross total cost to responsible business	25	350	1,500
Costs paid by oil spill trust fund	0	230	1,000
Net total cost to responsible business	25	120	500
Net NRDA liability	20	70	500[a]

a. OPA has a $500–million limit on payments from the Oil Spill Trust Fund for natural resource damages. For the purposes of this example, we assume that the spiller is liable for the remaining natural resource damages under state law.

NOTE: Assumes a $120 million federal liability limit under OPA and unlimited state liability. Excludes fines, penalties, and other damages for simplicity.

The top half of Table 7.2 provides hypothetical information on cleanup costs, NRDA liability, and total cost to the responsible business for each oil spill prior to the passage of OPA. The bottom half of the table shows similar information for each oil spill after the passage of OPA. Consistent with our earlier conclusions, we assume that OPA will increase the gross NRDA liability for each oil spill. For simplicity, we refer to the 100,000–gallon, the 1,000,000–gallon, and the 10,000,000–gallon spills as the large, very large, and extremely large spills, respectively.

In our example, the total cost of the large spill does not exceed $120 million, so the Oil Spill Trust Fund (hereafter the Fund) does not pay for any of the cleanup costs or natural resource damages. Consequently, the gross NRDA liability and the net NRDA liability under OPA are the same, which exceed the pre–OPA NRDA liability. The very large spill has a gross total cost to the spiller of $350 million. The Fund pays for costs in excess of $120 million, which results in a net NRDA liability of $70 million, as compared to $200 million NRDA liability in the absence of OPA. In other words, the spiller actually pays a smaller amount of natural resource damages under OPA, even though the Act increases the spiller's gross NRDA liability. The extremely large spill produces a similar result. In the extremely large spill the Fund pays for all the cleanup costs and half the gross NRDA liability, since OPA limits natural resource damage payments to $500 million per incident and overall payments to $1 billion per incident. In our example, we assume the spiller is still liable for the remaining natural resource damages under state law.[22] Thus, the spillers net NRDA liability for the extremely large spill is $500 million, which is less than the spiller's pre–OPA NRDA liability.

In summary, even though OPA increases spillers' gross NRDA liability for many oil spills, the Fund may pay for a substantial portion of this liability. Consequently, OPA may actually reduce spillers' NRDA liability relative to their NRDA liability prior to the passage of OPA. In particular, this reduction in spillers' NRDA liability is most likely for very large or extremely large spills that result in costs exceeding the OPA liability limits.

This conclusion is subject to three important caveats. First, large oil spills (i.e. spills involving 100,000 gallons or more) constitute much less than 1 per cent of all US oil spills each year. Consequently, there will be few actual cases where the OPA Fund may reduce the spiller's NRDA liability. Second, as noted earlier, OPA eliminates liability limits for oil spills resulting from various types of misconduct (such as gross negligence, willful misconduct, and violations of federal regulations). In these cases the Fund will not pay for any cleanup costs or damages for the larger oil spills. Thus, spillers will incur the total cost for the larger oil spills resulting from "misconduct". While this depends on uncertain legal interpretations of "misconduct", most spills usually involve a violation of one or more federal safety or operating regulations. So OPA's liability limits may not apply to very many oil spills.

The example above excludes fines, penalties, and non–NRDA damages for simplicity. Even when the OPA liability limits apply, increases in the non–NRDA components of oil spill liability under OPA may offset some or all of the reduction in net NRDA liability for larger spills resulting from the Oil Spill Trust Fund. Thus, spillers' total liability for the larger spills could possibly increase even when the Fund pays for some of the liability. A complete analysis of the total liability of businesses responsible for oil spills before and after the passage of OPA is beyond the scope of this chapter.

Net NRDA Liability in Practice

Since it will be many months before NOAA's NRDA regulations are promulgated, it is too early to assess the actual impact of the OPA on oil spill liability in general, and NRDA liability in particular. However, insurance carriers recently added a per–voyage surcharge on tankers carrying oil to or from US ports "to reflect the additional exposure which can now be expected from oil pollution claims".[23] This surcharge is a fixed rate per gross registered ton (grt), which is a measure of a tanker's volume. So large tankers are paying a larger surcharge in absolute terms on each voyage to the United States than small tankers. Even though the Oil Spill Trust Fund will pay some of the costs/damages from the larger oil spills involving no "misconduct", insurers apparently believe either that the federal government will allege and/or US courts will rule that most spills are the result of "misconduct" or that OPA will increase the total liability for most oil spills in proportion to the amount of oil that could be spilled in spite of the Fund paying for some of the costs/damages.

Prior to the passage of OPA, the specter of unlimited state liability for oil spills in coastal states resulted in averting actions by some shippers. For example, some shippers started subdividing their tanker fleets into a series of single–ship companies having minimal assets (Sullivan, 1990). This effectively limits the firm's oil spill liability to the salvage value of the tanker involved in the spill, which would typically be below the OPA liability limits. Other shippers (including the Royal Dutch/Shell Group and A. P. Moeller, a big Danish shipping company) are avoiding unlimited liability risks by refusing to send their tankers into US ports.[24] This will provide more transportation opportunities for shipping companies lacking the resources to pay for cleanup costs and natural resource damages. Thus, OPA's increased liability for smaller spills and spills involving "misconduct" may not increase the costs/damages actually paid by spillers in practice.

SUMMARY OF FINDINGS

The Clean Water Act of 1977 expanded the liability of businesses responsible for oil spills by allowing governmental agencies to collect compensatory damages for resulting injuries to natural resources. Acting on behalf of the public as trustees for the injured natural resources, government agencies must use recovered damages to restore, rehabilitate, replace, or purchase the equivalent of the injured natural resources. Clearly, the natural resource damage provisions of the Clean Water Act, as implemented by US Department of the Interior (DOI) regulations substantially increased the liability of businesses responsible for oil spills in most cases. In 1989 the *Ohio* decision further expanded the natural resource damage liability for some oil spills by overturning two key provisions in the DOI regulations. Last year the Oil Pollution Act (OPA) made additional changes in natural resource damages, resulting in yet another increase in liability for some oil spills.

While the DOI regulations, the *Ohio* decision, and OPA have substantially increased natural resource damage liability in theory, the practical implications of these developments are not clear for several reasons. First, trustees have never followed the DOI regulations to measure natural resource damages; they have used some of the provisions of the regulations while ignoring other provisions. Second, DOI has still not issued final revisions in the NRDA regulations to implement the *Ohio* decision. Thus, trustees have no formal guidance for operationalizing the NRDA provisions overturned in the *Ohio* decision. Finally, OPA requires NOAA to promulgate new NRDA regulations for oil spills by August 1992. So the provisions of these regulations will not be known for many months.

Even though trustees have not followed the DOI regulations and despite uncertainties about specific provisions in these regulations, trustees have successfully obtained natural resource damages from businesses responsible for some recent oil spills, such as the Martinez and Arthur Kill oil spills. However, the specific impacts of the *Ohio* decision and OPA on NRDA liability are difficult to determine from the settlements for these spills.

Although increasing NRDA liability in theory, OPA also puts limits on the liability of responsible businesses for cleanup costs and damages in general. Furthermore, OPA operationalized an Oil Spill Trust Fund that will cover cleanup costs and damages in excess of these liability limits. So even though OPA increases spillers' gross NRDA liability for many oil spills, the Oil Spill Trust Fund may pay for a substantial portion of this liability. Consequently, OPA may actually *reduce* some spillers' NRDA liability relative to their NRDA liability prior to the passage of OPA. This reduction in spillers' NRDA liability is most likely for very large spills. However, very few of these spills occur each year, and OPA's liability limits do not apply to spills resulting from "misconduct", which may cause most oil spills. Even when OPA's liability limits are operative, increases in fines, penalties, and non–NRDA damages under OPA may offset some or all of the reduction in spillers' NRDA liability attributable to payments from the Fund.

NOTES

1. Jim Broadus and Carol Jones provided useful comments as discussants of an earlier draft of this chapter. Tayler Bingham also provided helpful written comments on an earlier draft. However, they are not responsible for any errors of omission or commission in this chapter.
2. Much of the description of the DOI regulations comes from Robilliard, Desvousges, and Dunford (1991).
3. This requirement can result in an interesting contradiction. Restoration activities are only supposed to restore natural resource services to their baseline (i.e., without–spill) level. If restoration cost is the basis for natural resource damages and restoration cost includes the diminution of use value prior to restoration, then natural resource damages will exceed the amount of money actually required for restoration. Since all the natural resource damages (except the damage assessment costs) must be used for restoration, the "extra" money implies restoration in excess of baseline levels.
4. The DOI regulations limit use values to "committed" uses, which are defined as current public uses or planned public uses "that have been financially, legally, or administratively documented" (51 Fed. Reg. 27680 [1986]).
5. The preamble to the DOI regulations defines existence value as "the dollar amount of the willingness to pay or willingness to accept of individuals who do not plan to utilize a resource now or in the future, but are willing to pay to know that the resource would continue to exist in a certain state of being" (51 Fed. Reg. 27692 [1986]). Similarly, option value is defined as "the dollar amount of the willingness to pay or willingness to accept of individuals who are not currently using a resource, but wish to preserve their option to use that resource in a certain state of being the the future."(51 Fed. Reg. 27692 [1986]).

6. Technically, the discount rate becomes a compounding rate for damages occurring in the past.

7. The *Ohio* decision also overturned DOI's hierarchy of assessment methods, whereby measures of damage based on market prices were given preference over measures based on appraised values, which were given preference over measures based on nonmarket valuation methods (such as the travel cost method). Since most natural resource services are not traded in markets, nor are appraised values for these services typically available, overturning DOI's hierarchy probably has little practical significance. In other words, the market–price and appraised–price methods would not apply to most natural resource services, which means that most damage assessments would rely on nonmarket valuation methods anyway.

8. We discuss the importance of this provision in the fourth section.

9. In contradiction to this statement in the OPA *Conference Report*, Section 6001(b) of OPA states, "an order, rule, or regulation in effect under a law replaced by this Act continues in effect under the corresponding provision of this Act until repealed, amended, or superseded". Accordingly, the proposed revisions in DOI's regulations pursuant to the *Ohio* decision indicate that trustees should use the DOI regulations until the NOAA regulations are promulgated (56 Fed. Reg. 19753 [1991]).

10. Under the Clean Water Act, the liability limit for oil tankers varied from less than $1 million to a maximum of $14 million depending on their size and the liability limit for onshore facilities was $50 million (Jones, 1989, 10333). The liability limits for offshore facilities was cleanup costs plus $35 million for damages under the Outer Continental Shelf Lands Act (Jones, 1989, 10335).

11. The Trans Alaska Pipeline Authorization Act, Deepwater Ports Act, and the Outer Continental Shelf Act created separate funds for oil spills involving relevant vessels and/or facilities. See Jones (1989) for more information on these funds.

12. An analysis of the changes in fines and penalties levied on businesses responsible for oil spills is beyond the scope of this paper. Furthermore, we ignore the role of the incidence of liability between insurance companies and responsible businesses for simplicity.

13. Actually, the Deepwater Port Act of 1974 allowed government agencies to recover natural resource damages from oil spills at deepwater ports. However, the applica–bility of this Act was extremely limited. See Breen (1989) for more details.

14. See Breen (1989) and Garre (1990) for discussions of the traditional common–law measures of damages.

15. As discussed above, the proposed revisions in the NRDA regulations do not formally operationalize the "grossly disproportionate" exception. Thus, the significance of this exception is not clear.

16. The "grossly disproportionate" exception was actually first used in the *Puerto Rico* v. *S.S. Zoe Colocotroni* case, in which 20 acres of mangroves were injured by a 1973 oil spill. See Mattson and DeFoor (1985, 299–301) for a discussion of this case.

17. See Dunford, Hudson, and Desvousges (1991) for a discussion of the relationship between restoration actions and the diminution of value under natural recovery and restoration.

18. For simplicity, the scenarios assume that no nonuse values are forgone as a result of the hypothetical oil spill.

19. Apparently, there was only one natural resource damage case involving an oil spill between 1977 and 1986—the *Zoe Colocotroni* case. In that case Puerto Rico settled with the tanker's insurers for $2 million for natural resource damages to 20 acres of mangroves. See Mattson and DeFoor (1985) for more details on this case. Breen (1989, 868) lists some early NRDA actions under CERCLA by the federal government and various states.

20 "Exxon agrees to $15 Million Settlement in New York Harbor Oil Spill'" *Wall Street Journal*, 21 March 1991.

21. The amount of released oil is not the only determinant of the resulting cleanup costs

and natural resource damages. Other potentially important factors include, but are not limited to: the type of oil released, weather conditions following the release, the distance of the release from the shore, the amount of oil that reaches the shore, the characteristics of the shoreline receiving the oil, the uses of this shoreline, the types of cleanup methods used, and the restoration actions selected. For simplicity, we assume that these other factors are similar for the three hypothetical spills, so that the amount of the oil released is the main determinant of cleanup costs and natural resource damages.

22.   As discussed above, most coastal states have no liability limit for oil spills. Since OPA did not preempt state liability laws, businesses responsible for oil spills may face a greater liability from a state than the federal government. However, the relationship between OPA and state liability laws is not clear. Presumably, a state trustee can use state law to recover any natural resource damages not obtained under OPA because of OPA's liability limit and/or OPA's per-incident ceiling on disbursements from the Fund. But, can money from the Oil Spill Trust Fund be used for natrual resource damages that are recoverable under OPA but are being sought solely under a state NRDA law? This and other questions about the relationship between federal and state liability laws remain to be resolved in regulations implementing OPA and/or furture court rulings. For a review of state NRDA laws, see Landreth and Ward (1990).

23.   Tanker owners can get $500 million in standard coverage, plus an additional $200 million in supplemental coverage, for oil spill costs/damages from the International Group of P & I Clubs See "P & I Clubs Add Surcharge to US Shipments'" *Oil Spill Intelligence Report,* 28 February 1991.

24.   "Danish Shipping Company Ending U.S. Oil Shipments", *Wall Street Journal*, 29 June 1990.

8. Lender Liability for Hazardous Waste Cleanup

Kathleen Segerson

INTRODUCTION

The possibility that banks and other lending institutions might be held liable for the cleanup of hazardous wastes at facilities in which they hold a security interest has sent shock waves through the financial community. In a recent court case, a lending institution was held liable simply by virtue of its capacity to influence the handling of hazardous waste at the contaminated facility, despite the fact that it had had no direct involvement with waste management at the site.[1] This ruling defines the potential for lender liability very broadly, and, since lenders tend to be "deep pockets", there is a fear that it will lead to greatly expanded financial risks for lending institutions.[2]

This chapter provides an overview of some of the issues related to lender liability for hazardous waste cleanup. It begins with a description of the institutional setting in which the potential for liability arises. The following section discusses some of the alleged impacts of holding lenders liable. Despite the concerns that have been raised, to date little formal analysis of these impacts has been conducted. The fourth section reviews a recent attempt to analyse some of these impacts using a simple economic model of the buying/selling/lending decisions involved in property transfers. The final section provides some concluding comments.

THE INSTITUTIONAL SETTING

Liability for the cleanup of hazardous waste is generally imposed under the Comprehensive Environmental Response, Compensation and Liability Act of 1980 (CERCLA), which is better known as Superfund.[3] Under CERCLA, potentially responsible parties can be required to finance cleanup of contaminated sites directly or to reimburse the federal government for costs it incurs in federal cleanup operations. The term "potentially responsible party" includes four categories: (i) current owners and operators of the site, (ii) owners and operators of the site at the time of the waste disposal, (iii) generators of the waste, and (iv) transporters of the waste.

The potential for lender liability arises from the first category of potentially responsible parties, since the security interest of a lending institution could theoretically make it a current owner or operator of the contaminated site. Recognizing this possibility, Congress included in CERCLA an exemption from liability for secured creditors who, "without participating in the management" of a site, hold "indicia of ownership" primarily to protect their security interest.[4] The extent to which the secured creditor exemption relieves lending institutions of liability has been the subject of several court cases. The main issue relates to the definition of "participation" in management that would invalidate the exemption.

In *United States* v. *Maryland Bank & Trust Company*,[5] the court found that the secured creditor exemption could not be invoked if the lending institution had actually taken title to the contaminated property upon foreclosure and held that title for an extended period of time (over four years in this case). Regardless of the degree to which the bank had "managed" the hazardous waste on the site, the bank was deemed an owner by virtue of having transformed a security interest into an investment. Thus, the question of the extent of participation allowed under the exemption arises only in the context of creditors who do not take title to the property or who dispose of the property shortly after taking title.

Even when a lending institution does not foreclose on a piece of property or disposes of it quickly, it can still be involved in the management of the property, particularly if that involvement is designed to improve the financial health of the debtor. In *United States* v. *Mirable*,[6] the court found that such management would not void the secured creditor exemption provided it was limited to the financial management of the property and did not include involvement in the day–to–day operations of the site. However, if the creditor influenced or participated in actual decisions regarding operation of the site, the exemption would not apply.

The need for actual participation in the operation of the site in order to trigger liability was rejected by the court in *United States* v. *Fleet Factors*.[7] In this case, the court found that the mere capacity to influence operational decisions was sufficient to trigger liability, even if the creditor had not actually exercised that influence. Clearly, this finding extends the scope for lender liability. As argued by Toulme and Cloud (1991, 136), it converts the secured creditor exemption from a source of protection for lending institutions to a source of increased liability, since the activities that trigger liability for creditors would now be broader than those applicable to operators.

While the secured creditor exemption is the primary means by which a lender can avoid CERCLA liability, a creditor might also be able to invoke the "innocent landowner" defense.[8] Although this defense seems geared primarily toward direct buyers, it could also be invoked by lenders who become landowners through foreclosure. The exemption relieves a defendant of liability if he (i) acquired the property after disposal of the waste, (ii) had no knowledge (and no reason to know) of the existence of contamination at the site at the time of purchase, (iii) exercised due care with regard to the hazardous substances, and (iv) took precautions against the foreseeable acts or omissions of any third party.

A key issue in invoking the innocent–landowner defense is establishing that the landowner had no reason to know of the contamination at the time of purchase. To establish this, the land–owner must undertake "all appropriate inquiry into the previous ownership and uses of the property". While the definition of "all appropriate inquiry" is left unspecified, it would presumably include at a minimum the conducting of an environmental assessment at the time of purchase. What else might be required is uncertain. Thus, conditions under which the innocent–landowner defense could be invoked by a landowner to avoid liability have yet to be clearly established (Dinan and Johnson, 1990).

There appears to be little judicial history regarding the interpretation of the innocent–landowner defense. In *State of New*

York v. *Shore Realty Corporation*,[9] the court simply confirmed that knowledge of contamination at the time of purchase is sufficient grounds for CERCLA liability even if the purchaser did not in any way participate in the waste–disposal activities. Several cases brought under state statutes have upheld liability exemptions for parties who were unaware of contamination at the time of purchase.[10] However, these cases do not directly test the "appropriate inquiry" requirement of CERCLA and thus provide little guidance regarding what is required in order to qualify for the exemption.

In response to concerns about the extent of lender liability and the inadequate protection provided by the secured–creditor and innocent–landowner exemptions, a number of bills have been introduced into Congress to limit that liability and define more explicitly what actions can and cannot be taken by creditors before CERCLA liability will be invoked. In addition, the Environmental Protection Agency (EPA) has issued proposed rules to define the scope for lender liability through regulatory means.[11] These attempts to limit lender liability are presumably based on a belief that the costs imposed by holding lenders broadly liable for cleanup outweigh any benefits that such a policy might have. The following section outlines some of those costs and benefits.

IMPACTS OF LENDER LIABILITY

In evaluating the potential for lender liability, a number of claims regarding its impacts have been made. Some highlight its beneficial effects while others emphasize its negative implications.

The main benefit from including lenders in the pool of potentially responsible parties is the incentives that such a policy creates for lenders to do what is within their power to reduce the risks of hazardous waste contamination. As noted by Dinan and Johnson (1990), lender liability creates an incentive for lenders to perform a "gatekeeping" role whereby the lender could induce appropriate hazardous–waste management by tying its financial support to appropriate management decisions. As such, lenders can effectively act as private regulators.[12] In addition, Dinan and Johnson argue that lenders may be better gatekeepers than direct buyers of property because of their "deep pockets". Private gatekeeping incentives will only be efficient if the gatekeeper has sufficient assets at risk to want to perform the gatekeeping role. If the buyer of a piece of property has limited assets, then his stake in inducing appropriate waste management will be limited. The stakes may be much higher for a lending institution, however, thereby creating a greater incentive for performing the gatekeeping role.

Clearly, part of the gatekeeping function is conducting environmental audits or assessments to detect existing environmental problems. To the extent that such investigations reveal contamination problems that can be contained or corrected early to avoid greater damages in the future, they reduce future cleanup costs. If lenders are potentially liable for those costs, they will have an incentive to insist on such investigations as part of the terms of a loan package.[13] In addition, if environmental assessments are a prerequisite to invoking the innocent–landowner defense, then the lender will have an even greater incentive to require them. Finally, if contamination-related costs are to be effectively capitalized into the purchase price of the land or the interest rate on a loan, then the extent of contamination needs to be known by all parties involved. This pro–vides still another incentive for lenders to require an environmental assessment at the time of the transaction.[14] Thus, environmental assessments will be performed more frequently as a result of lender liability.

In addition to the gatekeeping function of lender liability, it also ensures a larger pool of money from which cleanup can be financed, thereby reducing the amount of federal money that must be committed. While this may be an advantage from the perspective of the Federal government if its objective is to maximize the amount of cleanup that can be conducted with a limited pool of federal dollars, it is not clear that it is a social advantage of holding lenders liable. Aside from incentive effects regarding waste management and other related decisions, the question of who should pay for cleanup is a distributional question that hinges primarily on notions of fairness and/or risk–spreading. In fact, in terms of risk–spreading, it can be argued that financing cleanup through federal funds is more efficient than private financing.[15] Thus, what appears to be an advantage from the narrow perspective of the agency responsible for cleanup should not necessarily be viewed as a social advantage of lender liability.

While the proponents of lender liability have emphasized the positive incentive effects it creates, the critics have been very vocal regarding its detrimental effects. For example, the critics have argued that, as interpreted by the court in *United States* v. *Fleet Factors,* lender liability actually reduces the incentives for gatekeeping (Toulme and Cloud, 1991, 138). If a lender's liability will be triggered by either its capacity to influence or its actual influence over decisions regarding hazardous–waste management, then the lender will have an incentive to distance itself from those decisions to avoid liability. Thus, the ability to escape liability through lack of actual or potential involvement with waste management decisions provides an incentive for a "hands–off" policy by lenders. This suggests, however, that the problem is not lender liability *per se*, but rather the exemptions that have been granted to that liability and the lender's ability to influence whether or not it would qualify for an exemption.

A claim has also been made that the gatekeeping or monitoring function of lenders is socially costly and that it would be more efficient for debtors to monitor their own behavior (Mahue, 1990, 8). If all liability were to remain with the debtor, then presumably the debtor would face appropriate incentives to monitor his own behavior and would not need the outside (and costly) oversight of the lending institution. This argument ignores, however, the limitations on efficient monitoring incentives created by limited assets. If the debtor has limited assets, it may be able to avoid full liability. This possibility reduces the debtor's incentives to monitor its own behavior. As noted above, limited assets is likely to be less of an issue for lending institutions.

Another major criticism of lender liability is that it increases the cost of credit and decreases the availability of funds that could be used for land purchases and/or environmental cleanup or response (Toulme and Cloud, 1991, 138; Mahue, 1990, 8). As lenders seek to recoup the costs of environmental assessments and future CERCLA liability, the supply curve for credit will shift up. This will raise the equilibrium cost of credit, through increases in either loan–related charges or the interest rate, and decrease the equilibrium quantity. As a result, fewer land transfers will occur and expenditures on pollution control and other production–related expenses will be reduced. This is alleged to be a particularly severe problem for small businesses (Toulme and Cloud, 1991, 139).[16]

Despite these many claims for and against lender liability, to date little formal analysis of its implications have been conducted. Dinan and Johnson (1990) present an analytical framework for comparing the effects of Superfund liability with liability under New Jersey's Environmental Cleanup and Responsibility Act (ECRA) but do not consider the efficiency effects of lender liability *per se*. Such an analysis requires a comparison of resource allocation with and without lender liability. The following section describes an attempt to provide such a comparison.

AN ECONOMIC ASSESSMENT OF LENDER LIABILITY[17]

We focus here on two of the alleged impacts of lender liability, namely, its beneficial impact on the incentive to conduct environmental assessments at the time of purchase and its detrimental impact on the cost and availability of funds to finance property transfers. A simple economic model can be used to analyse the impacts of alternative assignments of liability on the decisions to conduct an environmental assessment and purchase/sell a piece of property. The decisions under the alternative liability regimes can then be compared to the decisions that are socially efficient to determine the effects of the different regimes on efficiency. To highlight some basic results, we focus first simply on the relationship between the buyer and the seller of the property. We then introduce the lender to illustrate the role of the lender and lender liability in property transfers.

Efficiency Conditions

Consider a piece of property with an existing but currently unknown level of contamination (possibly zero), which is being considered for possible purchase/sale.[18] The level of contamination can be revealed by conducting an environmental assessment. If such an assessment is done and reveals contamination, then steps can be taken to contain the contamination and prevent further damages or cleanup costs. Environmental assessments are costly, however. Clearly, it will be efficient from a social perspective to conduct an assessment if and only if the expected benefits of the assessment exceed its cost, where the expected benefit is the avoided incremental contamination minus any cost of containing or preventing it. Thus, it will not be efficient to conduct an environmental assessment for every potential property transfer, but only for those where the probability and/or magnitude of potential future damages justifies the cost of the assessment. For cases where subsequent damages are unlikely, an assessment is not warranted.

Regardless of whether an assessment is done or not, there are certain social benefits that would result from the use to which the potential buyer would put the land (exclusive of any potential environmental liability). Likewise, the land provides some social value if left in the hands of the seller. Since the sale of the property will not affect the existing level of contamination, it will be efficient for the seller to sell the property to the buyer if and only if the buyer will put the property to a higher social use than the seller, i.e. if and only if the social value of the land if the buyer buys it exceeds its social value if he does not.[19] Thus, not all property transfers are efficient. Rather, only those that result in an increase in the social value of the land should occur.

Given the efficiency conditions for conducting an environmental assessment and transferring a piece of property, we can then consider whether alternative liability regimes ensure that the private parties involved will undertake these activities when and only when it is efficient to do so. The results hinge on two key aspects of the problem. The first is the ability of one party to shift its costs onto other parties through price changes. In the context of the buy/sell transaction, this refers to the ability of the buyer (seller) to shift some of his expected liability costs on to the seller (buyer) through a decrease (increase) in the sale price of the property. For the lending transaction, it refers to the ability of the lender to shift its expected liability back on to the buyer through an increase in the cost of credit (e.g. the interest rate).

The second key aspect for determining the effect of alternative rules is the fact that some parties may be judgment–proof at the time that liability is ultimately imposed. The probability that a party will be judgment–proof depends on (among other things) the level of its assets and the ease with which it can be identified as a responsible party and brought to court. Thus, the probabilities of being judgment–proof may vary across the parties involved and depend upon whether a transaction occurs. For example, the probability that a seller will be judgment–proof may be different once he has sold the property than it would have been had he retained title, since he may have spent the money from the sale of the property (thereby reducing his assets) and/or simply be unidentifiable or inaccessible. Likewise, the probabilities may differ for the buyer and the seller (for example, because of different asset levels), which may in turn differ from the corresponding probability for the lender. As discussed below, the relative magnitudes of these probabilities play a key role in determining how the various parties "value" the liability that is imposed on them and thus the incentives they face to undertake environmental assessments or participate in property transfers.

Private Assessment Decisions

Consider first the seller's incentive to conduct an environmental assessment even if he does not sell the land. It will be in his interest to do the assessment if the private net benefits of doing so exceed the cost of the assessment. The private net benefit of the assessment is the reduction in expected incremental liability that would result from early detection and cleanup (or containment), minus the cost of that cleanup. If there is no chance that the seller will be judgment–proof, then the private benefit of the assessment will equal the social benefit since the expected incremental liability from failure to do an assessment will equal the actual amount of incremental damages that would result. In this case, the seller on his own will conduct environmental assessments when (and only when) it is efficient to do so. However, if there is some probability that the seller would be judgment–proof, then what he expects to pay in incremental liability will be less than the full social damages from failure to do an assessment. In other words, he will undervalue the assessment. Thus, there will be situations in which a private property owner will fail to do an assessment even though it is socially desirable to have one done. Note, however, that this does not imply that private owners will never do assessments on their own. Clearly, there will be some cases where even the private expected benefits are sufficient to justify the cost of the assessment.

Consider next the buyer's incentive to conduct an assessment in anticipation of purchasing the property. The buyer will do the assessment if the expected net benefits from the sale given an assessment exceed the expected net benefits from the sale without an assessment. Since the assessment will reveal the actual level of contamination, it will allow the sale price to be adjusted to reflect that level. Without the assessment, the price will simply reflect the expected level of contamination.

In either case, however, the sale price will also reflect the assignment of liability. Any increase in the buyer's share of liability will decrease the price he is willing to pay for the property and, to the extent that this implies a corresponding decrease in the seller's expected liability, a decrease in the price the seller will demand. Thus, any shift in liability from the seller to the buyer will translate into a lower purchase price (and vice versa). This translation will only be dollar–for–dollar, however, if both the buyer and the seller "value" the liability equally. For example, if the buyer is less likely to be judgment–proof than the seller, then a given amount of liability is actually more costly to the buyer than to the seller because of the higher probability that the buyer will actually have to pay it. In this case, the buyer would prefer to see the liability imposed on the seller, since the price "premium" that the buyer will pay because of the increased liability of the seller is less than the expected cost of that liability to the buyer if it were imposed directly on him.

When the purchase price of the land adjusts to reflect the assignment of liability in this way, the following conclusions regarding the buyer's incentives to conduct an environmental assessment can be drawn. First, if there is no chance that either the buyer or seller will be judgment–proof, then the buyer's incentives will be efficient regardless of the assignment of liability. In other words, there is no reason to use liability to encourage assessments. The buyer and seller will both value a given amount of liability equally and their incentives will thus be independent of who is legally liable for contamination since one party can always shift his liability onto the other party through an adjustment in the purchase price. In addition, their expected liability from not doing an assessment will equal the actual incremental damages. Thus, the incentives they face will also be efficient. If, however, as would generally be expected, there is some probability that at least one of the parties will be judgment–proof, then in general the buyer's incentives will depend on the liability regime.

Second, if one of the parties has no possibility of being judgment–proof but the other one does, then efficient incentives will result from the former party bearing the liability. For example, if the seller is unlikely to be judgment–proof, then the buyer will face efficient incentives even if all liability remains with the seller, i.e. even if the buyer is exempted from all liability. Alternatively, if it is the buyer who is unlikely to be judgment–proof, then his incentives will be efficient only if he becomes fully liable for any contamination.

Third, if the buyer and seller are equally likely to be judgment–proof, then a "negligence" approach to liability, under which the buyer becomes liable only if he failed to conduct "all appropriate inquiry" (here, an assessment) at the time of purchase, would be ineffective in encouraging assessments. Alternatively, if the buyer is less likely to be judgment–proof than the seller, then a negligence approach will encourage the buyer to do an assessment by increasing the private benefit of an assessment. However, such an approach could be too effective in the sense of encouraging assessments to be done when they are not socially justified. Thus, a negligence approach does not necessarily induce efficient buyer incentives.

Private Buy/Sell Decisions under Equity Financing

The assignment of liability can also potentially affect the private decisions regarding whether to buy/sell a given piece of property. The buyer will want to buy the property if and only if the purchase price is less than the net benefits he expects to receive from owning the land. Those net benefits equal the actual return from use of the land minus any expected liability costs the buyer will have to bear. The seller, on the other hand, will want to sell if and only if the price is such that the net benefits from selling the land exceed the net benefits from not selling, where each of these net benefits is adjusted to reflect any difference in his expected liability if he does or does not sell.

There are two potential sources of inefficiency in these private buy/sell decisions. The first stems from the ability of the seller to influence his liability simply by selling the property. If the probability of being judgment–proof depends on whether he sells the land, then the seller can influence (presumably reduce) his expected liability by selling. This creates a "false" incentive for him to sell, i.e. an incentive unrelated to the social merits of the sale. He will thus want to sell more often than is efficient.

A second potential source of inefficiency exists when the probabilities of being judgment–proof differ for the buyer and the seller. As noted above, this implies that the two parties will value liability differently. In particular, the party with the higher probability of paying will put a higher weight on the liability and thus undervalue the property relative to the other party. For example, if the buyer has a higher probability of paying than the seller, then the buyer will put an artificially low value on the property relative to the seller, thereby decreasing the likelihood of a sale.

Given these two potential sources of inefficiency, the following conclusions regarding the buy/sell incentives follow. First, if both the buyer and the seller are equally likely to be judgment–proof and the seller's likelihood is independent of whether or not he sells the property, then the buy/sell incentives will be efficient regardless of the assignment of liability. In this case, the seller cannot influence his liability by selling. In addition, the buyer and seller both value the liability equally. Thus, the purchase price is simply adjusted to reflect the assignment of liability and it has no effect on the buy/sell decisions. Those decisions are then based solely on the value to which the two parties can put the land and are thus efficient.

Second, with different probabilities of being judgment–proof, the buy/sell decisions will not generally be efficient. However, if the seller can decrease his likelihood of paying by selling the land and in addition the buyer is more likely to have to pay than the seller, then the two sources of inefficiency outlined above work in opposite directions. In particular, the seller's ability to reduce his expected payment by selling tends to cause too many sales, while the fact that he will overvalue the land relative to the buyer tends to cause too few sales.

Third, exempting the buyer from all liability will be efficient if and only if the seller cannot influence his expected payment by selling. With such an exemption, all liability remains with the seller. However, if the seller can influence his expected payment by selling, he will face a false incentive to sell, thereby resulting in too many sales.

Finally, a full transfer of liability to the buyer will be efficient if and only if the probability that the buyer will be judgment–proof is the same as the probability for the seller if he does not sell. When the buyer bears the full liability, his willingness to pay for the property will be reduced by an amount reflecting the probability that he will ultimately have to pay. Thus, if he sells, the seller also indirectly faces that same probability through a reduction in the sale price. In order for his sale decision to be efficient, he must also face that same probability if he does not sell.

The Role of the Lender

The discussion so far has focused simply on the incentives faced by buyers and sellers, without any consideration of the role a lender might play. When a purchase must be debt–financed, then a further condition for a sale to occur is introduced. Not only must the sale price be such that the buyer wants to buy and the seller wants to sell, but, in addition, there must be an interest rate at which the buyer wants to borrow and the lender wants to lend. Clearly, the interest rate at which the lender is willing to lend will reflect its expected cost, including any liability it might incur in the event of default. Thus, the equilibrium interest rate will depend on the lender's share of liability under default, the probability of default, and the value of the land (collateral) under default. In other words, the lender will be able to shift some (or all) of its liability costs onto the buyer in the form of a higher interest rate.

The net effect of the shifting of costs from the lender to the buyer is the creation of a "buyer/lender" entity that plays the role under debt financing that the buyer alone played under equity financing. For example, the key parameters in determining the efficiency of the buy/sell decision are no longer the probability that the buyer alone will be judgment–proof and the liability share of the buyer alone, but rather the probability that the buyer/lender combination will be judgment–proof and the expected liability share of the two combined. Of course, if the lender is truly a "deep pocket", then the probability that the buyer/lender combination will be judgment–proof is near zero, since, even if the buyer cannot pay the liability costs, the lender can. Likewise, if the lender simply assumes at the time of default any of the buyer's liability, then the expected liability share of the two combined is simply the buyer's liability share.

Given that the introduction of debt financing simply results in a replacement of the parameters for the buyer with the corresponding parameters for the buyer/lender combination, the results discussed above for equity financing can be easily extended to incorporate the existence of the lender. For example, since the buyer/lender combination is unlikely to be judgment–proof, efficient buy/sell incentives will exist if in addition the seller will not be judgment–proof regardless of whether he sells or not. Likewise, transferring liability to the buyer and subsequently to the lender will be efficient if and only if the seller will not be judgment–proof is he does not sell. As before, not transferring liability to the buyer in the first place is efficient if and only if the seller cannot influence his likelihood of paying by selling the property. The intuition for these results follows the same logic as for the corresponding results under equity financing.

In addition to the analogies with the results under equity financing, explicit introduction of the lender allows us to determine when, if ever, it might be efficient to transfer liability to the buyer but absolve the lender of liability in the event of default. With cost–shifting through the interest rate, such a policy merely reduces the expected liability share of the buyer/lender combination. The arguments above suggest that, in general, this is not efficient.[20] It does not eliminate the inefficiency due to the seller's ability to influence his expected payment simply by selling; nor does it eliminate the inefficiency due to the different values that the seller and buyer/lender would place on the expected liability because of different probabilities of being judgment–proof. Thus, in general, within the context of the effects discussed here, there is no efficiency justification for transferring liability to buyers but not subsequently to their lenders. However, if sellers cannot affect their probabilities of paying by selling, then efficient incentives can be maintained by exempting from liability not only the lender but also the buyer so that the combined share of the buyer and lender is zero. In this case, all liability would remain with the seller, who will face efficient incentives when he has no way to reduce his expected payments.

Although the attainment of efficiency may not be guaranteed through either allowing or disallowing a lender–liability exemption, the extent to which lenders are held liable for contamination can still affect the efficiency of buy/sell decisions. In general, the effect of increasing lender liability (*ceteris paribus*) is to reduce the likelihood of a sale by reducing the value of the land to the buyer/lender combination. Whether this increases or decreases efficiency depends on whether there are already too many or too few sales occurring. If the probability that the seller will be judgment–proof increases if he sells and that probability is greater than zero, then, as noted above, the two sources of potential inefficiency that were identified work in opposite directions and it is not possible to say whether too many or too few sales occur. Thus, without empirical estimates of the important parameters, it is not possible to determine whether the imposition of (or an increase in) lender liability would enhance or reduce the efficiency of sales. On the other hand, if the seller cannot influence his probability by selling or alternatively that probability decreases if he sells, then too few sales are occurring. In this case, any imposition or increase in lender liability will only reduce efficiency further.

CONCLUSION

The possibility that lenders will be held liable under CERCLA for the costs of hazardous waste cleanup at sites in which they hold a security interest has raised serious concerns within the lending community. Since lenders are often "deep pockets", they are particularly attractive targets for financing that cleanup. While the courts are still working out the interpretation of the secured–creditor and innocent–landowner exemptions that could provide some relief, legislators and regulators are seeking to clarify through other means the conditions that would and would not invoke liability.

Many claims have been made regarding advantages and disadvantages of extending cleanup liability to lenders. Among the strongest advantages are the incentives it allegedly creates for lenders to perform a "gatekeeping" role. In particular, it is thought to encourage the requirement of an environmental assessment as a precondition to securing a loan, thereby facilitating early detection and containment of waste problems. On the negative side, critics claim that it can encourage a "hands–off" policy by lenders in an attempt to avoid liability. In addition, it will increase the cost of credit, and as a result decrease funds available for use in cleanup or response and the financing of property transfers to below efficient levels.

To date, these claims have been subject to little analytical review. However, use of a simple economic model of property transfers suggests that under some conditions they may be unfounded. In particular, if the purchase price of the property adjusts to reflect the outcome of an environmental assessment, then the efficiency effects of lender liability depend crucially on the relative probabilities that the parties involved will be judgment–proof at the time that liability is imposed. For example, a buyer's incentive to conduct an environ-mental assessment will be efficient regardless of whether liability is transferred if there is no chance that he or the seller would be judgment–proof. If, however, the seller is more likely to be judgment–proof than the buyer, then assessments will be encouraged by a negligence approach under which the buyer is liable if he did not conduct an assessment at the time of purchase. It is possible, though, that such an approach will lead to too many assessments, i.e. assessments that are not cost–justified. Thus, while the claim that liability transfers encourage assessments is valid in some cases, it is not universally true and, even in those cases where it is true, the result may be the encouragement of unwarranted assessments.

With regard to its impact on the number of property transfers, similar results can be obtained. In particular, while lender liability will increase the cost of credit and reduce the incentives to purchase potentially contaminated property, this does not necessarily reduce efficiency. The effect of lender liability on the efficiency of transfers depends on whether there are currently two many or too few sales. This, in turn, depends on two potential sources of inefficiency that can exist in the buy/sell decision. First, if the probability that the seller will be judgment–proof increases if he sells the land so that by selling he can influence the probability he will actually have to bear any liability assigned to him, then he will face a "false" incentive to sell, thereby leading to too many sales. However, if the probability of being judgment–proof is higher for the seller than for the buyer, then the buyer will tend to undervalue the land (*ceteris paribus*) relative to the seller and too few sales will occur. Thus, depending on whether the combined effects of these two sources of inefficiency lead overall to too many or too few sales, the further reduction in sales resulting from the imposition of lender liability could increase or decrease efficiency.

The purpose of this chapter is not to provide a definitive analysis of the economic impacts of lender liability since clearly many issues have not been addressed. Rather, it is to suggest that the claims regarding the advantages and disadvantages of lender liability need to be subjected to more careful scrutiny within the context of economic theory to establish their validity. Given the current legislative and regulatory attempts to define the extent of lender liability, there is a clear need for these claims to be validated.

NOTES

1. *United States* v. *Fleet Factors*, 901 F.2d 1550, cert.denied, 1991 WL 139893 (US) (US, Jan. 14, 1991) (No. 9–504).
2. For discussions of the concerns regarding lender liability, see James (1988), King (1988), Peck (1989), Tom (1989), and Toulme and Cloud (1991).
3. 42 USC Sections 9601–9675 (1980). CERCLA was amended in 1986 by the Superfund Amendment and Reauthorization Act (SARA), Pub. Law No. 99–499 (1986).
4. 42 U.S.C. Section 9601(20)(A).
5. 632 F. Supp 573 (D. Md. 1986).
6. 15 Envtl. L. Rep. (Envtl. L. Inst.) 20992 (E.D. Pa. 1985).
7. 901 F.2d 1550 (11th Cir. 1990), cert. denied, 1991 WL 139893 (US) (US, Jan. 14, 1991) (No. 9–504).
8. See Sections 107(b)(3) and 101(35(A)–(B)) of CERCLA.
9. 759 F.2d 1032 (2d Cir. 1985).
10. See James (1988, 346) for a discussion of cases brought under state hazardous–waste statutes.
11. See Toulme and Cloud (1991, 146) for a brief overview of the legislative and regulatory proposals that have been introduced.
12. The ability of lenders to monitor the behavior of their debtors is also emphasized by Tom (1989, 931).
13. According to Toulme and Cloud (1991, 127), nearly all lending institutions now require such investigations for transactions involving any property that could potentially be contaminated. See also James (1988, 351).
14. In the absence of buyer and lender liability, capitalization would not occur.
15. See Segerson (1989) for a discussion of the tradeoffs between the risk–sharing and incentive effects of alternative means of financing hazardous–waste cleanup.
16. See also statement by Hon. John J. LaFalce, Congressional Record, US House of Representatives, Vol. 136 (40), 4 April 1990.
17. This section draws heavily on Segerson (1991), where the details of the model used to generate the results discussed here are presented.
18. Note that, by focusing on cases where the decisions leading to the initial contamination have already been made, we are restricting ourselves to consideration of cases where CERCLA liability is being imposed "retroactively", i.e. to cleanup associated with past disposal practices. This does not imply, however, that the total level of cleanup costs is exogenous, since incremental damages from past disposal can still be prevented if the current problems are discovered through an environmental assessment.
19. This assumes that both the buyer and seller face the same incentives regarding whether or not to conduct an environmental assessment and prevent subsequent damages. If the incentives for an assessment faced by the two parties differ, then the efficiency condition would have to be adjusted to account for the net benefits (if any) of the assessment. Since consideration of this asymmetry does not affect the results, we consider here the simpler case of symmetric incentives.
20. The outcome can be efficient if, by chance, the incentives created by the new combined share exactly offset any inefficiencies due to the seller's ability to influence his expected payment simply by selling the land. However, this requires a very specific allocation of liability between the buyer and the seller, which would depend on both the probability of default and the likelihood that the seller would be judgment–proof when he sells as well as when he does not sell.

PART III
Assessing the State of the Art

9. Environmental Enforcement

Clifford S. Russell

Standard models in the environmental monitoring and enforcement literature (e.g. Harford, 1978; Lee, 1984; Russell, 1990a; Malik, 1990) might be characterized as having abstracted the following elements from complex reality:

*   a "responsible agency" that does the monitoring and, in a looser sense, the enforcing;
*   a representative "source" of pollution that decides whether or not to violate environmental rules;
*   a probability of detection of those violations (sometimes complicated by acknowledgement of type I and II errors);
*   a fine for discovered violations that may or may not be related to the size of the violation or to a past record of violations.

The concerns of this standard literature include: the differential implications for the monitoring and enforcement problem of the choice of policy instruments (charges v. standards, for example); the implications of reflecting a past record of violations in current monitoring and enforcement actions; the implications of different marginal penalty structures; and the relative role of negligence (effort) as opposed to strict liability (result) in setting penalties.

I believe that the chapters on enforcement in this volume broaden our perspective by introducing to the problem setting some complexities that are generally eliminated. Perhaps most fundamentally, they make explicit the complicated relationship among government agency, regulated firm, and responsible agent. In particular, it becomes clear that envisioning the firm as a monolith, perfectly in control of its environmental performance, can be quite misleading. An overarching issue pushing this recomplication is the actual and appropriate place of criminal law and, most important, the uniquely criminal sanction of jail time for convicted violators, in the

enforcement of environmental laws. The complications that are put
back into the model of the overall problem are:

*   the possibility that the "fines–for–violations" approach gives an
    inadequate incentive to take care;
*   the possibility that the monitoring problem is more difficult
    than catching violations of a simple standard — that it may
    involve trying to gauge the extent to which care is taken;
*   the practical and philosophical difficulties (not the least of
    which are monitoring difficulties) created by recognition of
    the continuum of what we might call causal states of mind
    connected to violations: from passively or actively "negligent"
    through "knowing" to "willful" conduct.

And, at a slight angle to the main thrust of the other enforcement
chapters:

*   the possibility that in some circumstances the "responsible
    agency" notion should be expanded to include unofficial,
    private enforcers.

No one, least of all the authors of the chapters on enforcement,
would claim that they answer all the questions about the use of
criminal enforcement techniques and private approaches to
enforcement. Indeed, even this small set of authors would probably
not agree on what those questions are nor on how to rank their
importance. It is therefore with no illusions of completeness or
finality that I suggest the following version of where this train of
thought leads us.

To begin with, the notion of "violation" has almost always been
treated in the literature as better defined than it can possibly be in
practice. Only in a deterministic world, in which sources exercise
perfect control over their own actions and measurement techniques
exhibit no errors, does the notion of "a violation" lack ambiguity. As
soon as accidents can happen, agents can have different objective
functions from principals, or measurements occur with error, we find
that an observation of an event or action contravening a permit or
regulation is, in a sense, only the beginning — or only one of several
dimensions we should like to be able to observe. This is explicitly
recognized by the so–called "voluntary compliance" approach, which
effectively assumes the best about the apparent violator until
subsequent evidence shows that person or firm in a worse light (e.g.

Harrington, 1981). Thus, repeated violations or refusals to bargain in good faith about actions to resume compliance become observations on other dimensions that produce different interpretations of subsequent measured "violations". Cohen's chapter contains anecdotes that suggest related considerations influencing prosecutors, judges and juries: whether agents were fully and apparently persuasively instructed by principals in the environmental compliance policies of the firm; whether monitoring internal to the firm was in fact carried out; whether internal or external warnings were ignored.

Where the rubber of ambiguity meets the road of enforcement is exactly in the choice of enforcement technique and the severity of its application. As Cohen makes clear, the choice of fine size and, more importantly, the choice of criminal as opposed to civil or administrative enforcement route, is largely determined by the dimensions of "violation" that are not captured merely by the observation of an event. Indeed, even the size of the event (in barrels, gallons, pounds, or estimated dollars of damages, for example) is not a sufficient observation. Also of concern to those who pick the enforcement road are such observations (however imperfect) as to whether or not the source shows instant contrition and what we might call the source's causal state of mind. For this latter dimension Cohen identifies a continuum of possibilities from passive negligence, through "active" negligence, to "knowing", and finally "willful". So, while the use of criminal sanctions may suggest itself to economists as a way to produce compliance incentives when fines might not work because they might not even be paid by firms that would go bankrupt, the choice of enforcement penalty actually seems to be far more complex.

Thus, if we want to capture more of the richness of the environmental enforcement problem, we probably have to recognize that violations are multidimensional events and that enforcement is a multidimensional activity in which the notion of "marginal penalty" applies to more than fine size. At a sufficiently abstract level this is not a problem. Utility functions with arguments that match enforcement choices (money, jail time, probation, etc.) can be written down. And, while certainly more complicated, the choice of enforcement road and penalty type and size could formally be related to "observations" on the multiple dimensions of violation.

Whether such an exercise would be useful to more than the career(s) of the person(s) who undertook it remains to be seen. A minimal requirement would be that it allowed us successfully to predict what choices would be made in particular cases. Much tougher — perhaps impossibly so — would be the requirement that the theory lead to some useful normative conclusions about what those who decide such matters *ought* to do. (This would be to address Cohen's concern about *over*–criminalization and *over*–deterrence.)

A related matter that has received far too little attention in the literature on environmental enforcement is the to–encourage–the–others dimension. That is, enforcement choices are clearly made with one eye on the particular violator in the case at hand and the other on potential violators. Just as catching a violation must influence the subjective probabilities of being caught held by other potential violators, so very tough, unpleasant approaches must influence how they view the consequences of discovery (where "discovery" again involves multiple dimensions). Again, formal modeling of the Bayes–like processes can be imagined, but the empirical estimation of the relevant adjustment coefficients looks exceedingly tough. These are necessary, again, for normative if not for qualitative, positive, lessons to be drawn.

A second line of inquiry suggested involves "private enforcement". This amounts to recognizing the inadequacy of the "responsible agency" description of the enforcer. Again, there is no lack of evidence that private enforcement has played a role in the real world. US statutes actively encourage it, and in the early 1980s it seemed to many the only route open in the face of the Reagan administration's attack on the integrity of EPA. It would, however, be worth thinking hard about the proper as well as the actual place of private enforcement; and about how far the lessons of the US experience can be extended to other nations.

At the extreme, it is frighteningly possible to imagine an army of environmental zealots observing and reporting their neighbors for possible violations of the fine print on pesticide bottles or improper composting practices. Just as surely as we don't want that to come to pass, we sense that leaving everything to "the responsible agency" and prohibiting citizen involvement is unwise. In seeking some notion of a *via media* consider some examples of responsible agency failure:

* In the United Kingdom, the regional water authorities were, until privatized by Mrs Thatcher, responsible both for sewage treatment and for protection of ambient water quality (as well as for drinking water supply). Their record in enforcing existing pollution control requirements on their own treatment plants was apparently quite dismal, though it took a long time for this to become public knowledge because the water authorities managed to use ties into the national bureaucracy to keep a lid of secrecy on discharge monitoring data (Kinnersley, 1988).

* In the United States, some very serious environmental problems were created within and near Department of Defense and Department of Energy facilities. This illustrates that the problems that public agencies have in monitoring themselves tend to extend to between–agency relations.

These anecdotes suggest that one place to start in examining the role of private enforcement is the proposition:Private sources require public enforcement, while public sources require private enforcement.

This proposition in turn suggests that such groups are potentially more useful the more pervasive is government ownership of the sources of pollution (broadly defined). But there seems to be a strong correlation between having such a centralized economic system and having a closed, secretive, undemocratic, even authoritarian political system. This observation serves to highlight the problems of extending any version of private enforcement to other political systems and cultural traditions. Nonetheless, some foreign nongovernmental organizations (NGOs) have apparently found leverage at home through links to major U.S. environmental groups. This leverage operates through the influence of the U.S. groups on Congress and thus indirectly on the World Bank and International Monetary Fund (Rich, 1985; Vatikiotis, 1989). And NGOs are active in attempting to protect the environment in countries as different as Brazil, Japan, and Indonesia (e.g. Aden, 1975; Wickham, 1989; Findley, 1988; *Japan Times,* 1989).

Another major question about private enforcement has to do with private monitoring. Most US successes can be traced to the public availability of the results of required self–monitoring and reporting by sources. Although one occasionally sees reports of local efforts to measure or document environmental insults, most monitoring is necessarily expensive and technically difficult, and the application of many standard techniques requires access to source premises. This suggests that effective private enforcement can occur only where monitoring is either done by the sources or is so easy to do that lay volunteers can do it with minimal equipment and training.

The previous paragraph brings us back to monitoring, where much of the earlier discussion has also been pushing us. One of the features that makes the environmental enforcement problem so challenging is the complex linkage among:

* the nature of *violations* in particular contexts;
* the state of the art of our ability to *monitor* for any particular type of violation;
* the locus and severity of the *burden of proof*.

An example that I have used elsewhere to illustrate this linkage is the contrast between enforcing permit terms on fixed, point sources of air or water pollution and enforcing laws against midnight dumping (or any other form of illegal disposal) of small quantities of hazardous chemicals such as dry–cleaning solvents (Russell, 1988). In the first case the agency knows *where* to look for violations, and it can choose how often and with what precision to look. A particular source may have an option that allows it to change the timing of discharges — more likely in water than in air — but it is very unlikely to be feasible to change location. Small quantities of spent solvents, on the other hand, can be put in containers, shipped away from the plant (the site of their generation) and disposed of anywhere. Does the agency examine some fraction of trucks leaving the plant? Does it stop trucks at random on the highway? Does it try to watch potential disposal locations?[1] These questions, however, presume that it is necessarily the agency's responsibility to prove a violation. But when such proof is very difficult to obtain, why not think of rigging the incentives so that the generator (the source) will go to the trouble of proving compliance with some desired rule such as, "Bring all your spent solvent to recycling centers". To obtain that sort of compliance incentive it is necessary to reward the desired behavior — a payment, perhaps self–financed through an earlier deposit — for spent solvent, for example.

Another sort of environmental problem in which the conventional model seems quite inadequate is nonpoint source pollution, as from farms, golf courses, and commercial forests. Here the discharger cannot practically move the discharge but as a general matter there is no place at which to monitor because movement of nutrients, pesticides and herbicides occurs in sheet run–off or in percolation into ground–water. On the other hand, it is not obvious what would constitute acceptable proof of good behavior, either. (And "good behavior", in the sense of "best management practices", might well be different from one farm to the next, even in the same sub–basin.) This may be a problem in which only improved monitoring technology can make a real dent. It illustrates that the conventional model, however refined and extended with criminal penalties, for example, only represents potential solutions to part of the environmental enforcement conundrum. It also suggests that this is a wonderfully rich area for further research.

NOTE

1. Of course, what the RCRA manifest system tries to do is to make illegal disposal possible to detect once the paper trail has begun. But a serious violator would just not start the trail at all. There is currently no effort to check the concordance among generation, inventory, onsite disposal, and shipment.

10. Environmental Liability Law

Susan Rose–Ackerman[1]

Tort law is 'private' law. Regulation by statute is 'public' law. How should the two relate to each other in the environmental area where regulatory statutes are pervasive? Should statutes take on the colorization of tort law by permitting widespread private rights of action or should regulatory agency enforcement be the norm? Should the common law of torts be a substitute for statutory rules, or can it complement a statutory regime?

In recent decades there has been a remarkable convergence of tort law and statutory law in the environmental and the health and safety area. On the one hand, common law courts are regulating injuries allegedly caused by toxic chemicals such as asbestos and agent orange. The injured number in the thousands, the chains of causation are complex, and many years pass between exposure and injury. Chemistry, biology, epidemiology, and economics all play a role in understanding the issues and in fashioning remedies. The courts are taking on information–gathering and –processing tasks common to administrative agencies. They are overseeing remedies which require the creation of bureaucratic structures.

On the other hand, statutes in the environmental area permit private individuals to sue under the terms of the law.[2] Such suits are similar in many ways to common law tort suits, especially when damage remedies are available. They may provide the public with an opportunity to second–guess agency priority setting, or they may supplement agency enforcement efforts by providing an alternative route for the prosecution of violators. We need to consider whether such private rights of action are, on balance, constructive or whether they lead to overdeterrence or misplaced priorities.

To help evaluate these trends, I first consider the differences between archetypal common law tort claims and conventional regulatory statutes. Then I outline some of the ways in which tortlike features have been imported into modern environmental statutes. Next I discuss attempts to permit torts and statutes to coexist in some areas of substantive law. Finally, I point to two sources of potential tension: incentive–based regulatory reform efforts and tort law's traditional concern with compensation.

CLASSICAL TORTS VERSUS CONVENTIONAL STATUTES

The fundamental differences between tort law and conventional regulatory statutes center, not on substantive standards or on the distribution of benefits and harms, but on procedures. Conventional statutory regulation, unlike tort law, uses agency officials to decide individual cases instead of judges and juries; resolves some generic issues in rulemakings not linked to individual cases; uses nonjudicialized procedures to evaluate technocratic information; affects behavior *ex ante* without waiting for harm to occur; and minimizes the inconsistent and unequal coverage arising from individual adjudication. In short, the differences involve who decides, at what time, with what information, under what procedures, and with what scope.

Steven Shavell has developed a useful four–category schema to organize a discussion of alternatives (Shavell, 1987b, 277–90).   He distinguishes between *ex post* (backward–looking) and *ex ante* (forward–looking) options, and between privately initiated and state– initiated systems.   This framework produces four alternatives: tort liability (*ex post,* privately initiated), court injunctions (*ex ante,* privately initiated), command–and–control regulation or corrective taxes (*ex ante,* state initiated) and fines for harm done (*ex post,* state initiated).

Five factors, according to Shavell, should influence the choice between these approaches. First, state action is desirable when the harm is so diffuse that individuals have little incentive to sue on their own and cannot cheaply organize to sue as a group. Second, if injurers are too poor to pay for the harm they cause, a system based on *ex post* payments will not effectively deter them. Third, when harm can be demonstrated on a statistical, but not an individual, basis, regulations or taxes applied *ex ante* can shape behavior without a showing of causal links between particular parties.

Fourth, an *ex ante* regulatory system will be preferable when the same information about costs and benefits is relevant to many instances of harm. Fifth, administrative costs are an important consideration. If the probability of harm is low, *ex post* systems may be preferable since they only need come into play when damage occurs.

As Donald Dewees points out in his chapter in this volume, the five factors isolated by Shavell point toward the use of *ex ante* regulatory statutes for most environmental harms. Furthermore, the technical difficulty of many environmental issues also argues against reliance on the courts. Critics, such as Peter Huber (1988b) and W. Kip Viscusi (1984), point to the judiciary's incompetence concerning issues of health and safety — incompetence arising from lack of expertise, inadequate staff, and procedures ill–suited to the discovery of scientific truth. The common law of torts cannot be the primary legal tool for the regulation of environmental pollution.

Nevertheless, private causes of action brought under environmental statutes may have a useful secondary role to play.

The question raised by the chapters collected here is whether the advantages of private lawsuits can be grafted on to agency–administered statutes without undermining the benefits of government policy–making and enforcement. Can statutes charge agencies with the implementation of scientifically based regulation while using private suits constructively to provide additional incentives to regulatory agencies and regulated firms?

STATUTORY LIABILITY

When environmental statutes are drafted to include lawsuits as an integral part of the implementation scheme, policy–makers must resolve several key issues of statutory design. They must decide who can sue, who can be sued, what remedies will be available, who pays plaintiffs, legal fees, and whether or not suits under the statute will substitute for common law actions. Furthermore, if the agency promulgates rules, will these rules determine the standard of care in those common law suits which do go forward?

These questions must be answered in light of the purposes to be served by lawsuits. Four goals are common.

(i)   Citizen suits may seek to deter shirking by administrators not committed to the purposes of the laws they administer and may provide public input into the process of priority–setting within an agency.

(ii) Suits brought under the statute may supplement the enforcement activities of the agency.

(iii) Private suits might be used to enforce the statute directly, without the need for agency action.

(iv) The statute may have the open–ended goal of supplementing state tort systems, without interfering with common law adjudication.

The first, agenda–forcing, goal implies giving broadbased standing to citizens and organized groups, permitting suits against the administrator of the program, and providing for injunctive remedies which require the agency to take action within a specified time. Common law standards have little relevance to this type of private suit. While such suits may sometimes goad a recalcitrant bureaucrat into action, they seem a blunt instrument for public control. They risk disrupting the activities of conscientiously managed agencies. An agency with a limited budget which is charged with administering several statutes must set priorities.[3] It cannot do everything at once. Congress through appropriations acts and oversight hearings may provide some guidance on the relative importance they attach to the implementation of different statutes, but the agency will retain substantial discretion.

Lawsuits to force the administrator's hand will not generally be based on a comprehensive overview of the costs and benefits of various strategies. No entity except the agency has the information to make such judgements and even if outside groups have legitimate complaints, using nonexpert, generalist judges to decide the issue has little to recommend it. Thus suits must focus on a fairly clearcut agency responsibility which has not been met. If such suits are common, this will skew the agenda of the agency toward the mechanical fulfillment of specific directives while ignoring possibly more important, but less easily characterized, policy tasks.[4]

For example, the Clean Water Act permits suits to require the Administrator of the Environmental Protection Agency to fulfill nondiscretionary duties.[5] Since statutes are often vague about substantive policy, the easiest duties to challenge are deadlines which require the agency to take some action by a particular date. Such deadlines are often unrealistic and are frequently violated. One study found that the Environmental Protection Agency had met only 14 per cent of its deadlines under all the statutes it is charged with enforcing.[6] Once a deadline is past it, of course, cannot be complied with, but judicial decisions have the effect of requiring the EPA to give priority to programs with missed deadlines which have generated lawsuits.[7] Given the arbitrary nature of many deadlines and the further arbitrariness of which cases are brought to court, suits brought under these statutory provisions seem unlikely to have a beneficial effect. Statutory provisions of this sort should be repealed or at least narrowly interpreted by the courts. One possibility would be to use current appropriations acts as an indication of congressional priorities. If Congress has revealed that it does not take its own deadlines seriously, then the courts should not do so either.[8]

The second type of suit can serve a more constructive purpose. Under the most familiar version, private individuals and groups sue those who violate EPA rules or orders. The aim of such suits is to obtain compliance with the law. To be effective, liberal standing should be provided to anyone with the time and energy to locate violators and bring suit. The statute can facilitate such suits by requiring the regulated firms to supply data on their own discharges and by mandating that successful plaintiffs will have their legal fees paid by defendants.

Such a combination of mandated disclosure and fee–shifting has given environmental law firms an important role in enforcing the Clean Water Act.[9] These organizations look for violations by checking the public compliance records required of dischargers with EPA permits. Firms have an incentive to file truthful reports since false reporting leaves the firm and its officers open to criminal prosecution. The public–interest organizations seek injunctions requiring dischargers to comply with the law and, if successful, the plaintiffs have their legal fees paid by the defendants. While the enforcement cases are somewhat routine and do not give activists the satisfaction of making policy, they serve as a useful supplement for a budget–constrained agency.[10] They have the further advantage of forcing firms in violation to pay most of the cost of enforcing the law against them. The limited resources of public interest firms, however, counsel against too much reliance on private enforcement suits. The procedure can be effective only if the EPA and the polluters have borne most of the information–gathering costs before the suits begin.

In suits brought under the Clean Water Act, litigants seek to require dischargers to conform to their permits. While suits are encouraged by the fact that the legal fees of successful plaintiffs are paid by the defendants, no damages are available.[11] Successful suits, however, result in fines being paid to the EPA or to state environmental agencies. Cases that are settled out of court can produce financial payments divided between governments and environmental organizations.[12] In contrast, statutes could be written to permit class action suits with damage payments as well as fines. Remedies could be some combination of injunctions requiring compliance, fines included in the statutory scheme, and damage payments for the harm caused by past and present failure to comply.[13]

At the other extreme from private suits seeking injunctions, consider the inverse case of public agencies seeking damages. One method of enforcing CERCLA, for example, is for governments to collect cleanup costs and the value of damages to natural resources from those waste producers who used a particular site.[14] Similarly, as Richard Dunford explains in his chapter in this volume, businesses that spill oil in the marine environment are liable under the Clean Water Act and the Oil Pollution Act of 1990 for the harm they cause to natural resources and for cleanup costs.[15] Federal and state governments can bring the actions against tanker owners and collect damages.

In these cases the executive branch, not the courts, sets standards for damage assessment. While the federal courts reviewed the regulations for determining natural resource damages, and found fault with some aspects of them,[16] the basic responsibility for setting guidelines lies with the Department of the Interior. The important point here is not the details of the government's regulations but the fact that case–by–case damage assessments under several statutes will be governed by these rules.

The use of guidelines and the role of the government in acting as a trustee for natural resources has just begun to generate controversy. For example, in the wake of the 1989 oil spill from the *Exxon Valdez* in Alaska's Prince William Sound, several Native Alaskan villages have claimed the right to sue for natural resource damages.[17] Exxon claims that only the council formed to negotiate a settlement with Exxon can act as a trustee under the Clean Water Act. The council includes several federal government agencies and the state of Alaska. Exxon fears being required to pay several times over for natural resource damages if the suits are allowed to proceed. The Native Alaskans, while accepting Exxon's interpretation of the CWA, base their claims on CERCLA which has been interpreted as permitting local governments to sue for such damages.[18]

The third type of suit is a more complex and comprehensive variant of the second. It does not rely on prior agency action. Private individuals can sue for violations of the statute even though the agency has taken no action. Such suits are possible under CERCLA with recovery limited to the costs of cleanup. No damages can be awarded for property damage or personal injury.[19] Such suits are valuable only if the basic standards for judging hazards and evaluating cleanup methods are well understood. In areas of ambiguity the EPA needs to set general regulatory standards that can be applied by the courts to particular waste sites not on the EPA's own agenda. Otherwise the courts will be placed in the position of making choices which are essentially technical judgments — judgments they are poorly trained to make. Neither the courts nor the plaintiffs in such cases are likely to have the expertise or staff resources to substitute for the agency's basic responsibility to sort out the technocratic issues.

The open–ended enforcement actions which are possible under CERCLA raise questions about the way the threat of lawsuits controls corporate behavior. In a world where authority is spread among many actors from officers to shareholders to creditors, the question of who should bear legal responsibility is complex. The aim is to give firms an incentive to comply with the law so that future lawsuits will be unnecessary, but if we cannot figure out where responsibility lies, it will be difficult to design an effective pattern of liability.

For example, if the passage of time produces a bankruptcy and transfer of ownership to creditors, should these organizations be liable for harms caused by the corporation before it entered bankruptcy?[20] This is the topic of Kathleen Segerson's chapter in this volume. Under her approach the issue is similar to Shavell's problem of judgment–proof defendants. Suppose that a property may contain hazardous waste potentially subject to cleanup under CERCLA. Consider a voluntary transfer of ownership through sale. If neither buyer nor seller is judgment–proof, then any clear liability rule will induce the transacting parties to conduct an environmental assessment designed to discover hidden hazards. The threatened imposition of liability is not much of an incentive, however, if you lack assets or if the law permits you to shelter certain assets through bankruptcy. A site potentially subject to cleanup under CERCLA will be worth more to a financially insecure buyer than to a secure one. Furthermore, the incentive to finance a costly environmental assessment is less for the financially strapped buyer since he does not expect to have to finance any subsequent cleanup. Thus Segerson concludes that consideration should be given to imposing a higher share of CERCLA liability on the buyer if an assessment was not done.

High–risk buyers, however, are not likely to be able to purchase sites unless they can borrow money. If hazardous–waste cleanup liabilities are dischargeable in bankruptcy, banks and other lenders may be willing to extend credit with no costly evaluation of hazards. Thus the analysis points in the direction of expanding liability to include the creditors of bankrupt companies.

If a recent bankruptcy case is followed, however, creditors may insist on an environmental assessment of their own even under current law.[21] According to that case, the cost of a hazardous–waste cleanup under CERCLA is dischargeable only if there was a prepetition triggering event such as the release or threatened release of hazardous waste. However, in the absence of a prepetition event, any subsequent liability is not dischargeable. This opinion can create situations in which lenders insist on environmental assessments which, if they do reveal hazards, will place the liability on the seller. Thus the opinion, while seeming to protect lenders and impose more costs on the federal government, may actually induce the privately financed generation of more information and the imposition of costs on would–be sellers.

Whatever the subsequent developments in bankruptcy law, one should view Segerson's analysis with some caution, since she only discusses the incentives for generating information about hazards at the time of sale. Also of importance is the ongoing operation of a business which generates or disposes of toxic materials. Even the threat of liability might not induce creditors and diversified owners to monitor the behavior of managers. Creditors and shareholders may not oversee the actions of managers if the risk appears low and if the mechanisms for influencing managers are weak or expensive. Some commentators worry that increased liability for creditors would either generate unproductive meddling by lenders in all aspects of a firm's business or lead to a reduced supply and higher cost of credit without any change in behavior.[22] While one might suppose that insurance could resolve these problems, the development of an efficient private insurance market to protect passive creditors is restrained under current law by the inefficient insurance effectively supplied by Superfund.[23] Finding the right balance will be a difficult task.

An alternative to holding creditors and subsequent owners liable is the use of criminal sanctions. Mark Cohen in his chapter in this volume shows that criminal prosecutions against both individuals and polluting firms are on the rise. In the occupational health and safety area, states have prosecuted firms and their officers for injuring or killing their workers by exposing them to toxic chemicals.[24] As Cohen points out, however, criminal sanctions are not a cure–all. They imply that someone or some entity is "to blame" when the facts may point to a wide range of interlocking causes. Even when a clearcut case can be framed, the standards of proof are higher in a criminal case than in a civil case. Furthermore, the Federal Sentencing Guidelines, in an effort to impose more uniformity on the system, may reduce the flexibility needed to tailor remedies to harm caused. Thus for suits against corporations the criminal law has few advantages. For suits against individuals, where the stigma and the possibility of imprisonment loom large, assigning criminal responsibility may be daunting for many environmental harms.

However, according to Cohen, one familiar disadvantage of the criminal law — the lack of victim compensation — may be less important in the future. Under US Sentencing Commission guidelines, restitution payments and injunctive relief are both possible. In addition, the imposition of damages does not necessarily require that proof of harm be presented to the court.

The fourth sort of suit is not tied directly to a regulatory statute. Instead, private individuals bring private tort suits for damages and injunctive relief in spite of the statutory scheme. Preemption issues arise in this context. What is the role of regulatory agency standards in determining liability under tort principles? Are remedies such as punitive damages inconsistent with the statute? Even if state laws are asserted to be independent of federal regulatory statutes, overlap is inevitable. I develop these issues in somewhat more detail in the next section.

COMPLEMENTARITIES BETWEEN TORTS AND STATUTES

Ideally, tort law and regulatory standards work together to further deterrence and compensation goals. Torts and regulations can be complementary: (i) when tort doctrines are stopgaps which apply absent more stringent statutes; (ii) when regulatory standards are intended as minima which more stringent tort doctrines can supplement; and (iii) when a regulatory standard is set at the socially optimal level and tort doctrine imposes either strict liability or a standard of care lower than that required by the agency. However, when the regulatory standard is set optimally while the tort standard of negligence is interpreted to require an even higher level of care, conflicts can arise under a system of compensatory damages. Such conflicts are even more likely when punitive damages are available.

The first possibility seems a reasonable position for courts to hold, but it is not relevant when a statute exists. In the absence of a statute courts would see tort law as a stopgap pending future legislative action.[25] If a regulatory statute is then passed, courts would resolve conflicts between tort doctrines and regulatory principles by according priority to the statute.

Regulatory standards are sometimes designed to establish only a baseline. Then the second case holds. While violation of such standards usually amounts to negligence *per se* in a tort suit, compliance is merely evidence for the jury to consider in determining reasonable conduct. Note the asymmetry here. Because the standard sets a minimum, the plaintiff can argue that a higher standard should be imposed in a particular case, but the defendant cannot invoke special circumstances to justify its violation of the basic standard. The courts have viewed regulations as minima in many cases involving the safety of products and workplaces.[26] Similarly, tort suits involving automobile design are not preempted by regulatory statutes.[27]

While treating statutory standards as minima is sometimes appropriate, it destroys whatever uniformity the standard imposes and substitutes the judgments of judges and juries for the policy decisions of agencies. Only great skepticism about agency actions and great faith in courts might justify such a system. This justification, however, seems unpersuasive whether one views agency officials as technocrats or as politicians. If they are technocrats, it undermines their expertise by supposing that agencies can set lower, but not upper, limits on care levels. If they are politicians, their political compromises would be set aside by the supposedly apolitical courts, an outcome that violates the familiar administrative law norm that courts should not prefer their own policy judgments to those of agencies.

Careful statutory drafting can help prevent these conflicts. If the courts view environmental regulations as minima, there is no conflict if the agency itself has set a low standard in the belief that case–by–case adjudication is the best way to respond to the environmental problem. Although this may sometimes be a plausible strategy, the plaintiff should bear the burden of demonstrating that the legislature intended it. Without such a showing, an environmental statute should be taken to imply a legislative judgment that a comprehensive, state–centered, *ex ante* approach is the best way to deter harm. The difficulties of judicial standard–setting, especially in a complex area such as the environment, should lead judges to accept the stopgap role and to reject the notion that regulations are merely minima unless the legislature or agency has explained the regulations in these terms. If environmental regulations are indeed too lax, statutory or administrative reform is appropriate, not *ad hoc* judicial actions that respond to individual needs while producing system–wide inequities and inefficiencies.

Under the third form of complementarity, the doctrines of either negligence or strict liability can produce both a more consistent tort law and a more effective regulatory system. To accomplish this, however, courts must be prepared to surrender some of their independence in setting standards of care and assessing damages.

Consider a negligence rule which seeks to mimic the regulatory standard. In contrast to the asymmetric doctrine of negligence *per se*, the courts would also recognize a *per se* defense for dischargers who meet the regulatory standard. The wrongdoer could thus be punished twice: by whatever sanctions the state imposes through the regulatory process, and by paying damages to private litigants. While this may seem unfair to the wrongdoer, it is not inefficient even if the sum of the penalties exceeds the social costs of violating environmental standards. Convicted wrongdoers would pay "too much", but anyone can avoid this overcharge by simply conforming to the regulatory requirements. This optimistic view is true, however, only if agencies set clear standards, courts accept these standards in determining liability, and apply them competently to individual cases.

Suppose now that the tort standard is not negligence but true strict liability, which holds a discharger liable for all harm caused by its acts and only requires the court to determine causation, not to assess risks and benefits. True strict liability differs substantially from the "strict liability" of products liability law, which essentially requires the jury to make a negligence–like risk/utility calculation. Under true strict liability, torts and regulation need not conflict if damages are set equal to the harm caused by the tortfeasor. The possibility of a tort judgment will simply give the regulated entity an additional incentive to comply with the statute. The conditions assuring comple–mentarity, however, do not now exist. To achieve them would require substantial tort reform, yet attempts to reshape tort doctrine according to its behavioral effects would be difficult.

In contrast to the complementary options outlined above, tort law can work at cross purposes to environmental statutes when the regulatory standard is set at the socially optimal level of pollution control, but the courts impose a more stringent negligence standard. Two cases need to be considered: compensatory damages and punitive damages. Judges sometimes sharply distinguish the two, finding punitive damages "regulatory" and compensatory damages not. Justice Powell, for example, stated that: "There is no element of regulation when compensatory damages are awarded."[28] Under this view, the goal of compensatory damages is merely to make the victim whole, not to induce behavioral changes in potential injurers; thus compensatory damages cannot conflict with a regulatory purpose. If tort actions only provided compensation and if the agency's own enforcement mechanisms effectively assured compliance with its standards, this view might be correct. But these assumptions are always false where no statute exists (the stopgap case) and are often false even when one does.

To see the judicial error, suppose that a regulatory agency has set an environmental standard at the optimal level, but courts none the less find that complying firms have been negligent. A firm will then compare the extra costs of meeting the court's standard with the damages it must pay if it merely complies with the lower regulatory agency standard. If it can increase profits by complying with the court's negligence standard, the firm will do so. At this care level, however, it will surpass the optimal agency standard, and marginal costs will exceed marginal benefits.

Judges who distinguish between compensatory and punitive damages, however, are not completely misguided. Punitive damages also influence caretaking and the level of pollution discharged but may produce a different outcome than compensatory damages. If the courts impose a higher standard of care than is required by a socially optimal statute, economic distortions will occur. The regulated firm subject to punitive damages will choose one of two options (depending upon which is profit–maximizing): compliance with the tort standard where no damages are levied, or a level of environmental protection (somewhere between the socially optimal level and the tort standard) at which its marginal costs equal marginal punitive damages.[29]

THE REFORM OF ENVIRONMENTAL LAW

Commentators have long urged legislators and regulatory agencies to charge effluent fees set to reflect the risks created by polluting firms. Incentive–based reforms allocate environmental costs to those who can bear them most efficiently, encourage firms to search for innovative ways to reduce discharges, and force producers' prices to reflect the risks they impose on society. Well–designed reforms can improve the market's competitiveness and efficiency.

Incentive schemes require a fundamental rethinking of the relationship between tort law and statutory law. Following the conventional wisdom of economists and policy analysts, regulators have begun to use incentives and subsidies to affect behavior in lieu of command–and–control standards. The EPA has experimented with "bubbles", "offsets", and "banking".[30] The 1990 Amendments to the

Clean Air Act seek to control acid rain through a system of tradeable pollution rights.[31] Similar proposals exist to pay workers to use protective devices under OSHA and to establish marketable rights for water pollution.

Such reforms, however, could be undermined by an insensitive judiciary which treats only command–and–control regulation as behaviorally significant. Viewing environmental regulation as nothing more than standard–setting could have serious consequences in an era of regulatory reform. In a recent case, for example, the Superfund law was described as "not a regulatory standard–setting statute" because polluters pay for the cost of abating hazardous wastes "through tax and reimbursement liability".[32] This view is misconceived. Taxes, subsidies, and government–mandated liability regulate behavior as surely as direct orders.

How should courts handle claims by defendants that incentive–based environmental statutes preempt tort actions? Judges who view regulation as confined to standard–setting might allow tort actions on the ground that these statutes are not "regulatory" because they do not establish uniform standards but "only" create incentives. Yet the argument for preemption of tort law is even stronger in the case of incentive–based regulations than in the case of command–and–control regulation. With standard–setting based on either technology or performance, tort actions can complement regulatory agency activity if agency enforcement is not comprehensive or if the fines levied bear little relationship to damages. In contrast, if fee schedules have been set to reflect the social costs of the regulated firm's activities, then tort actions would be redundant at best and counterproductive at worst. A well–designed incentive system signals to a firm the social costs of its activities. A fee system resembles a tort liability system: no fixed standards are set, but firms respond to the cost of damages. The regulated entity must purchase the right to impose social costs in the same way that a tort judgment requires payment for harms. The main difference is the comprehensiveness of a fee schedule, which the state sets so that all firms are covered. A firm's liability does not depend on the contingency of private litigation and jury damage awards.

Tort judgments would undermine such a regulatory scheme, especially if courts applied a strict liability standard, the type of standard that some judges have found least "regulatory".[33] Thus incentive–based statutes should include a provision clearly preempting tort actions. For example, if the Environmental Protection Agency charges effluent fees, those damaged by the discharges that occur should not be able to sue since this would create inefficient caretaking incentives on the margin.[34]

The only remaining role for private individuals would be suits against delinquent regulated firms. Such suits might permit private recovery of damages for harm caused by lax enforcement. While environmental statutes do not permit recovery of damages, precedents do exist, at least on paper. The Consumer Product Safety Act permits suits for damages against firms that violate agency rules.[35] In situations where the damages are too diffuse to motivate private litigation, the recovery could be some multiple of fees that the agency could have exacted and could be paid to the Treasury with the public interest litigant recovering legal fees. Thus although ordinary tort actions would be preempted, certain specialized private remedies might supplement agency enforcement just as tort actions do that use government regulations as the standard of negligence.

COMPENSATION

Tort law provides more than a set of regulatory incentives; behavior modification is not its only legitimate function. It is also a compensa–tion system triggered by victims' complaints. If a regulatory statute bars private tort actions, those who were previously able to sue for damages will be disadvantaged, a result courts seem reluctant to permit. The Supreme Court permitted Karen Silkwood to sue in state court for punitive damages for exposure to radiation in spite of a federal statute that preempted state regulation of the nuclear industry. The Court noted that the statute did not provide for compensation and stated, "It is difficult to believe that Congress would, without comment, remove all means of judicial recourse for those injured by illegal conduct."[36] If compensation of victims is not addressed by a purely regulatory statute yet remains a policy goal, conflict may arise between the statute and tort law. Compensation–oriented courts may apply conventional tort doctrines that are at cross–purposes with regulatory policies. This problem is of more immediate importance in the area of product safety, however, than in the field of environmental protection. Because of the diffuse nature of many environmental harms, individually initiated tort suits are less common. Furthermore, some of the costs of pollution, such as natural resource damages, have no strong analogues in the common law of torts.

Where innocent victims exist, denying compensation is unjust and unwise. Yet retaining conventional tort actions in the face of regulatory statutes can undermine the behavioral impact of statutes. Other solutions must be found to the problem of providing compensation. If the victims are numerous and their losses fall into broad, easily identified categories, such as particular types of cancers, then the compensation goal could be served by direct subsidy programs like workers' compensation and the black–lung program.[37] In contrast, if the victims are few in number and their problems are idiosyncratic, the law should either permit private rights of action for damages, or allow tort actions under strict liability principles solely as a means of achieving compensation.

CONCLUSIONS

If Congress reforms environmental regulation to rely more heavily on incentives and on performance–based standards, the judicial role should be modest. Under incentive schemes requiring firms to pay for the damage they cause, statutes should preempt tort actions in order to avoid overdeterrence. Compensation should be effected through a separate system of social insurance. Private lawsuits would be permitted under environmental statutes only to compel those who discharge pollution to comply with existing regulatory standards.

But in environmental policy areas that have not yet been reformed, a limited role remains for tort law or, at least, for private causes of action embedded in statutory schemes. Negligence law can be complementary to command–and–control regulation if it adopts the agency's standard, not just as a minimum, but as the measure of due care. Conversely, a true strict–liability regime would obviate the need for a judicial risk–benefit calculation; courts would need to determine only causation. The choice between negligence and strict liability should then depend on how society evaluates the importance of giving victims an incentive to take care versus the distributive effects of initially shifting all losses to injurers.

In short, the widespread presumption favoring a vigorous tort system should be replaced, at least in the environmental area, with a more comprehensive view of the alternative ways to achieve both deterrence and compensation. Privately initiated lawsuits, brought either under tort principles or under regulatory statutes, should be quite limited and targeted on augmenting regulatory enforcement and responding to unusual situations that would be poorly resolved by broad–based regulations.

NOTES

1. Portions of this paper are derived from Rose–Ackerman (1991a, ch. 8), and (1991b).
2. Clean Air Act (CAA), 42 USC §§ 7401–7626 (1987); Resource Conservation and Recovery Act (RCRA), 42 USC §§ 6901–6992k (1987); Federal Water Pollution Control Act (FWPCA), 33 USC §§ 1251–1387 (1987 & Supp. IV 1990), as amended by Superfund Amendments and Reauthorization Act of 1986 (SARA), Pub. L. No. 99–499, 100 Stat. 1613 (1986); Oil Pollution Act (OPA) 33 USC § 2701 *et seq.* (1990).
3. See O'Leary (1989, 564–6), for evidence that lawsuits do influence priority setting within the EPA.
4. See O'Leary's (1989), study of the impact of the courts on the behavior of the EPA. As one example of misplaced priorities, she points to the $7.6 million and 150 staff work years spent over six years on one Clean Air Act case dealing with radionuclides. The resulting regulation was expected to prevent one cancer death every thirteen years (ibid. p. 562).
5. Federal Water Pollution Control Act, 33 USCA § 1365.
6. Environmental and Energy Study Institute and Environmental Law Institute (1985, ii). The number of deadlines totaled 300. In addition to the 14 per cent that were met on time, 41 per cent were completed after passage of the deadline; 27 per cent had not been completed; no information was available on 15 per cent, and 2 per cent were deleted or extended but not yet satisfied by 1985.
7. The courts' approach has been essentially to rewrite the statute to extend deadlines that have already passed. *National Resources Defense Council, Inc. (NRDC)* v. *Train*, 510 F. 2nd 692 (D.C. Cir. 1975); *Sierra Club* v. *Gorsuch*, 551 F. Supp. 785 (N.D. Cal. 1982); *New York* v. *Gorsuch*, 554 F. Supp. 1060 (S.D.N.Y. 1983); *Environmental Defense Fund* v. *Thomas*, 627 F. Supp. 566 (1986); *Delaney* v. *E.P.A.*, 898 F. 2d 687 (0th Cir. 1990). See Dickinson (1991) for a fuller discussion of the first three cases. Although the decisions differ in many details, Delaney is typical. The appeals court refused to accept the EPA's plan to give delinquent counties three years to carry out implementation plans under the Clean Air Act of 1977. The EPA argued that in spite of the clearly stated deadline in the 1977 Act, "Congress knew that some states would not attain by the 1982 deadline and did not intend that states implement draconian measures" (ibid. p. 690). The court did not accept this argument. However, since the deadline had passed, the most the court could do was require compliance as soon as possible using every available control measure.
8. See Dickinson (1991) who makes this argument. Federal courts seem not to accept this reasoning. Thus in *Kitlutsisti* v. *Arco Alaska, Inc.*, 592 Fed. Supp. 832 (D.

Alaska 1984), the EPA's claim that budgetary considerations had prevented issuance of an offshore oil drilling permit did not insulate oil companies from citizen suits. See also the cases cited in note 7 supra.

9.   FWPCA, 33 USCA §1365.
10. A challenge to the standing of public interest groups to bring such suits has been turned down. In *Public Int. Research of N. J.* v. *Powell Duffryn*, 913 F. 2d 64 (3rd Cir. 1990), Cert denied, 111 Sup. Ct. 1018 (1991), the third circuit ruled that a public–interest group could sue to enforce a water permit without showing that its members had been directly harmed by pollution. The Act itself states that any citizen may bring a suit where "citizen" is defined as "a person or persons having an interest which is or may be adversely" (33 USCA § 1365[g]).
11. *Middlesex Cty. Sewerage Auth.* v. *Natl. Sea Clammers Assoc.*, 453 U.S. 1 (1980) concluded that no damages were available to plaintiffs bringing suits under the FWPCA, 33 USCA §1365.
12. For example, a case brought by the New Jersey Public Interest Research Group against the Public Service and Gas Co. of New Jersey produced a $750,000 settlement, with $460,000 going to the US Treasury and rest being paid to various environmental organization. W. John Moore, "Citizen Prosecutors", *National Journal*, 18 August 1990, p. 2006. The legality of payments to environmental groups was upheld by the Ninth Circuit in *Sierra Club Inc.* v. *Electronic Controls Design Inc.*, 909 Fed 2d 1350 (9th Cir. 1990). In that case the Sierra Club had its attorney's fees paid by the defendant, and the rest of the settlement amount was paid to environmental organizations to maintain and protect water quality. The court upheld the settlement because it did not view the payments as civil fines since Electronic Controls had not admitted that it violated the law. The court did, however, require the Sierra Club to pay its own legal fees for the appeal to the ninth circuit.
13. The existence of damages remedies might, however, limit the standing of plaintiffs to those able to demonstrate that they had suffered harm.
     Two existing regulatory statutes not administered by the EPA provide for damage remedies. The Consumer Product Safety Act [CPSA] states (15 USCA §2072[a]):

> Any person who shall sustain injury by reason of any knowing (including willful) violation of a consumer product safety rule, or any other rule or order issued by the commission may sue any person who knowingly (including willfully) violated any such rule or order in [a federal district court]…, shall recover damages sustained, and may, if the court determines it to be in the interest of justice, recover the costs of suit, including reasonable attorneys' fees….

     The CPSA requires that manufacturers, distributors, and retailers of consumer products report to the agency "defects" that create a "substantial product hazard" (§2064[b]). A firm that fails to do so is subject to penalties (§2069). Several lawsuits have been brought alleging that such a failure should leave a firm open to suit for damages under §2072 (a). Given the paucity of CPSC rules, such a reading of the statute would considerably expand the scope of damage remedies under the statute. The federal courts have been unsympathetic to these writs, arguing that damages cannot be claimed for violations of the statue itself and that the rules issued by the Commission with respect to the reporting requirement are interpretive rather than substantive or legislative rules and hence are not independently enforceable. (*Drake* v. *Honeywell, Inc.* 797 F. 2d 603 [8th Cir. 1986]; *Benitez–Allende* v. *Alcan Aluminio Do Brasil, S.A.*, 857 F. 2d 26 [1st Cir. 1988]; *Kukulka* v. *Holiday Cycle Sales, Inc.*, 680 F. Supp. 266 [E.D. Mich. 1988]; and *O'Connor* v. *Kawasaki Motors Corp., U.S.A.*, 69 9 F. Supp. 1538 [S.D. Fla. 1988])
     The Surface Mining Control and Reclamation Act also contains a provision for damage suits [30 USCA § 1270 (f)], but a computer search found that it had not been used.

14. CERCLA, 42 USC § 9607(a).
15. FWPCA, 33 USC § 1321. OPA, 33 U.S.C. § 2706. The OPA is distinctive in providing up front money for damage assessments [§ 2706 (c)(5)(C)]. See Dunford *et al.* (1991).
16. *State of Ohio* v. *United States Department of the Interior*, 880 F. 2d 432 (D.C. Cir. 1989). The revised regulations are expected to be issued in the summer of 1991.
17. *Native Village of Chenega Bay* v. *Lujan*, 1991 U.S. Dist. LEXIS 2986 (D.C.D.C. 12 March 1991). Under OPA, 33 USC §2706, Indian tribes are explicitly permitted to act as natural resource trustees to obtain compensation for natural resource damages, but the act also includes a provision preventing double payment for the same damage.
18. Daily Report for Executives, May 21, 1991, p. A–3; 'Liability for Restoration is Looming,' National Law Journal, February 4, 1991.
19. CERCLA includes a provision that makes generators of hazardous waste liable for the "response costs" of "any other persons" (42 USC § 9607[a]). The courts have defined this term to exclude the costs of property damage, personal injury, or death (*Ambrogi* v. *Gould, Inc.*, 750 F. Supp. 1233, 1238, 1259 [M.D. Pa. 1990]). The provision has been read as giving these "other persons" a private right of action to sue generators or current owners of contaminated sites. As the judge wrote in *City of Philadelphia* v. *Stepan Chemical Co.*, 544 F. Supp. 1135, 1143 (E.D. Pa. 1982), the Act as a whole is designed to achieve one key objective — to facilitate the prompt cleanup of hazardous dumpsites by providing a means of financing both governmental and private responses and by placing the ultimate financial burden upon those responsible for the danger. The liability provision is an integral part of the statute's method of achieving this goal for it gives a private party the right to recover its response costs from responsible third parties which it may choose to pursue rather than claiming against the fund.

      See also *Walls* v. *Waste Resource Corp.*, 761 F. 2d 311, 317–318 (6th Cir. 1985), and *Tanglewood East Homeowners* v. *Charles–Thomas, Inc.*, 849 F. 2d 1568 (5th Cir. 1988). Federal appeals courts have found that suits may be brought even though there has been not prior government involvement in the site. (*Tanglewood* at 1575 which cites previous cases) Thus, unlike the CPSA, where suits are tied to prior agency action, CERCLA has been interpreted as permitting private suits for violations of the law.
20. The issue is a salient one. CERCLA exempts most secured creditors from liability by stating that an "owner or operator" does not include persons or entities who, "without participating in the management" of the facility, hold "indicia of ownership" primarily to protect a security interest [CERCLA 42 USC §9601 (20)(A)]. In *U.S.* v. *Fleet Factors Corp.*, 901 F. 2d 1551 (1990), cert. denied 111 Sup. Ct. 752 (1991), however, the 11th Circuit held that under CERCLA a creditor could be held liable for cleanup costs "if its involvement with the management of the facility is sufficiently broad to support the inference that it could affect hazardous waste disposal decisions if it so chose" [ibid. at 1558]. The EPA has drafted rules to limit lenders' liability to cases in which they participated in management. Legislative proposals also have been made to amend CERCLA to limit or eliminate the liability of such organizations. For a critical view of the Fleet Factors case and a summary of these proposals see Toulme and Cloud (1991). The American International Group Inc., an underwriter of commercial and industrial insurance, has proposed the creation of a fund with a surcharge on insurance premiums as a substitute for Superfund. W. John Moore, "Superfund Scrambling", *National Journal*, 16 March 1991, pp. 650–1.
21. *In re Chateaugay Corp.*, 112 B.R. 513 (S.D.N.Y. 1990). See also *In re Combustion Equipment Associates Inc.*, 838 F. 2d 35 (2d Cir 1988).
22. Toulme and Cloud (1991).
23. Oesterle (1991).
24. The New York State Supreme Court has ruled that the Occupational Safety and Health Act sets floors, not ceilings, and hence does not preempt state criminal prosecutions (*People* v. *Pymm*, 546 N.Y.S.2d 871 [A.D. 2d Dept. 1989]). The Michigan Supreme

Court found that state manslaughter charges against a supervisor whose employee died of carbon monoxide poisoning were not preempted. The court concluded that the Act was not comprehensive because of the low penalties for violations of its standards (*People* v. *Hegedus*, 432 Mich. 598; 443 N.W.2d 127 [Mich. Sup. Ct. 1989]). Similarly, the Illinois Supreme Court permitted criminal prosecutions to go forward against a corporation and its top officers for exposing employees to toxic chemicals (*People* v. *Chicago Magnet Wire Corp.* 534 N.E. 2d 962 [Ill. sup. Ct. 1989], cert. denied, U.S. Sup. Ct. Oct. 2, 1989).

25. *Larsen* v. *General Motors*, 391 F.2d 495, 506 (8th Cir. 1968); "[t]he common law standard of [reasonableness]...can at least serve the needs of our society until the legislature imposes higher standards." See also *Wood* v. *General Motors Corp.*, 865 F.2d 395, 402 (1st Cir. 1989).

26. They have ruled, for example, that the Food, Drug and Cosmetic Act does not preempt tort suits for damages. *Abbot* v. *American Cyanamid Co.*, 844 F. 2d 1108 (4th Cir. 1988); *Callan* v. *G.D. Searle & Co.*, 709 F. Supp. 662 (D.C. Md. 1989); *Kociemba* v. *G.D. Searle & Co.*, 680 F. Supp. 1293 (D.C. Minn. 1988); *Desmarais* v. *Dow Corning Corp.*, 712 F. Supp. 13 (D.C. Conn. 1989).

    Five circuits have held that the warnings required since 1965 by the Federal Cigarette Labeling and Advertising Act preempt state products liability suits against cigarette manufacturers. *Cipollone* v. *Liggett Group Inc.*, 789 F. 2d 181 (3d Cir. 1986), cert. denied, 479 U.S. 1043, (1987); *Roysdon* v. *R. J. Reynolds Tobacco Co.*, 849 F. 2d 230 (6th Cir. 1988); *Palmer* v. *Liggett Group, Inc.*, 825 F. 2d. 620 (1st Cir. 1987); and *Stephen* v. *American Brands*, 825 F.2d, 312 (11th Cir. 1987) In *Pennington* v. *Vistron Corporation*, 876 F. 2d 414, 417 (5th Cir. 1989), the Fifth Circuit judged that while claims involving failure to warn were preempted, claims that the product was unreasonably dangerous were not. The New Jersey Supreme Court, however, has permitted a case of inadequate warning, fraud in advertising, and design defect to go forward. (*Dewey* v. *R. J. Reynolds Tobacco Co.*, 121 N.J. 69; 577 A.2d 1239 [N.J. Sup. Ct. 1990]).

27. Cases involving the design of automobiles have left to the jury the question of whether compliance with a federal standard implied that an automobile was not defectively designed under principles of strict liability. (*Sours* v. *General Motors Corp.*, 717 F.2d 1511, 1516–1517 [6th Cir. 1983]; *Dawson* v. *Chrysler Corp.*, 630 F.2d 950, 958 [1980]; *Shipp* v. *General Motors Corp.*, 750 F.2d 418, 421 [5th Cir. 1985]; and *Pokorny* v. *Ford Motor Co.*, 902 F.2d 1116) The statute states explicitly: "Compliance with any Federal motor vehicle safety standard issued under this subchapter does not exempt any person from any liability under common law" (15 USC § 1397[c]). Air bags are a special case because the agency expressly permitted firms to select an alternative to air bags. See *Wood* v. *General Motors*, 865 F. 2d 395.

28. *Silkwood* v. *Kerr–McGee*, 464 U.S. 238, 276, n.3. See also *McDougald* v. *Garber*, 73 N.Y. 2d 246, 253–54 (1989):

    [A]n award of damages to a person injured by the negligence of another is to compensate the victim, not to punish the wrongdoer....[T]he temptation to achieve a balance between injury and damages...is rooted in a desire to punish the defendant [and] has no place in the law of civil damages.

29. Punitive damages may reflect not punishment of the tortfeasor but a correction for the fact that only a fraction of victims sue. If the courts set the damages multiplier to correct for this, the earlier analysis of compensatory damages applies.

30. For an overview see Dudek and Palmisano (1988, 223–44); Hahn and Hester (1989).

31. Clean Air Act Amendments of 1990, 104 Stat. 2399, Pub. L. 101–549, 15 November 1990, 101st Congress, S. 1630, Title IV, §401.

32. *State of New York* v. *Shore Realty*, 759 F. 2d 1032, 1041 (2d Cir. 1985).

33. *Silkwood* v. *Kerr–McGee*, 464 U.S. 238, 276 n. 3.

34. One argument often used to justify preemption, however, has little bite from a policy analytic perspective. Courts sometimes stress the need for uniformity as a reason to permit statutes to preempt tort law. Yet sophisticated proposals for incentive–based regulation do not aim at uniformity in the treatment of injurers. Instead, fee levels reflect the relative benefits of risk reduction in different areas. Effluent fees, for example, might be set at high levels in pristine areas where the cost of moving from no to some pollution could be very high, and at lower levels in other areas that are already industrialized. When health effects are the primary concern, fee levels should reflect differences in population density (Harrison, 1977). Thus the lack of uniformity introduced by tort suits is not in itself a reason to preempt tort actions. Rather, the argument must be that the variability in tort law bears little relation to variability in costs and benefits.

35. CPSA, 15 USCA §2072(a). The Surface Mining Control and Reclamation Act also contains an unused provision for damage suits [30 U.S.C.A. §1270(f)].

36. *Silkwood* v. *Kerr–McGee* 465 U.S. 236, 251.

37. See Viscusi (1983, 87–92, 159–160), for a suggested reform of the workers' compensation system.

References

Abel, Richard (1987), "The real tort crisis: Too few claims", *Ohio State Law Journal*, **48**.

Abraham, Kenneth (1988), "Environmental liability and the limits of insurance", *Columbia Law Review*, **88**, (5), June.

Abramson, Jill (1989), "Government cracks down on environmental crimes", *Wall Street Journal*, 16 February, p. B1.

Adams, Thomas L., Jr (1986), United States Environmental Protection Agency Memorandum, "Final EPA policy on the inclusion of environmental auditing provisions in enforcement settlements", 14 November.

Adams, Thomas L., Jr (1987), United States Environmental Protection Agency Memorandum, "Report on the implementation of the timely and appropriate enforcement response criteria", 15 January.

Adams, Thomas L., Jr (1987a), United States Environmental Protection Agency Memorandum, "Summaries of FY 1988 enforcement priorities", 16 April.

Adams, Thomas L., Jr (1987b), United States Environmental Protection Agency Memorandum, "Report on civil federal penalty practices", Compliance Policy and Planning, Office of Enforcement and Compliance Monitoring, July.

Adams, Thomas L., Jr (1988), "Report on the Implementation of the Timely and Appropriate Enforcement Response Criteria", US EPA, Compliance Policy and Planning Branch.

Adams, Thomas L., Jr and Braem, L. A. (1988), "EPA's enforcement priorities for fiscal year 1988", *National Environmental Enforcement Journal*, July.

Adams, Thomas L., Jr (forthcoming), US Environmental Protection Agency Memorandum, "Report on federal penalty practices", Compliance Policy and Planning, Office of Enforcement and Compliance Monitoring.

Aden, Jean Bush (1975), "The relevance of environmental protection in Indonesia", *Ecology Law Quarterly*, **4**.

Allan, Richard H. (1987), "Criminal sanctions under federal state environmental statutes", *Ecology Law Quarterly*, **14**, (1).

Arbuckle, G. *et.al.* (1989), *Environmental Law Handbook*, 10th edn, Rockville, MD: Government Institutes, Inc.

Arch, Mary Ellin (1987), "Plea bargain abruptly ends Orkin trial", *United Press International*, 30 July.

Arkin, Stanley S. (1990), "Crime against the environment", *New York Law Journal*, 9 August.

Arthur D. Little Inc. (1983), "Benefits to industry of environmental auditing", August, prepared for EPA's Regulatory Reform Staff.

Arthur D. Little Inc. (1984), "Benefits of environmental auditing, case examples", December, prepared for EPA's Regulatory Reform Staff.

Arthur D. Little Inc. (1985), *Annotated Bibliography on Environmental Management*, 1st edn, prepared for EPAs Regulatory Reform Staff, November.

Austin, Brent R. (1989), "The public trust misapplied: *Phillips Petroleum* v. *Mississippi* and the need to rethink an ancient doctrine", *Ecology Law Quarterly*, **16**.

Barnes, A. James (1986), Memorandum, "Revised policy framework for implementing state/EPA enforcement agreements", 26 August.

Barrett, Paul M. (1991), "Environmentalists cautiously praise $1 billion *Exxon Valdez* settlement", *Wall Street Journal*, 14 March.

Baumol, W. J. and W. E. Oates (1971), "The use of standards and prices for protection of the environment", *Swedish Journal of Economics*, **73**, March.

Baumol, W. J. and W. E. Oates (1988), *The Theory of Environmental Policy*, New York: Cambridge University Press.

Beavis, B. and M. Walker (1983), "Random wastes, imperfect monitoring and environmental quality standards", *Journal of Public Economics*, **21**, August.

Becker, Gary S. (1968), "Crime and punishment: An economic approach", *Journal of Political Economy*, **76**, March/April.

Block, Michael K. (1991), "Optimal penalties, criminal law and the control of corporate behavior", *Boston University Law Review*.

Bohm, P. and C. Russell (1985), "Comparative analysis of alternative policy instruments", in Allen V. Kneese and James L. Sweeney (eds), *Handbook of Natural Resource and Energy Economics*, Amsterdam: North–Holland.

Boland, John J. and Jerome W. Milliman (1989), "CERCLA natural resource damages: Uses and misuses of economic theory", *Hazardous Wastes & Hazardous Materials*, **6** (1).

Bratton, David and Gary Rutledge (1990), "Pollution abatement and control expenditures, 1985–88", US Department of Commerce, *Survey of Current Business*, **70** (11), November.

Breen, Barry (1989), "Citizen suits for natural resource damages: Closing a gap in federal environmental law", *Wake Forest Law Review*, **24**, December.

Breit, W. and K. Elizinga (1986), *Antitrust Penalty Reform: An Economic Analysis*, Washington, DC: American Enterprise Institute for Public Policy Research.

Brelis, Matthew (1989), "Guilty pleas in oil spill; agreement means $500,000 for R. I.", *Boston Globe*, **33**, 17 August.

Brennan, Douglas F. (1986), "Joint and several liability for generators under Superfund: A federal formula for cost recovery", *UCLA Journal of Environmental Law*, **5**.

Brennan, Troyen (1988), "Causal chains and statistical links: The role of scientific uncertainty in hazardous–substance litigation", *Cornell Law Review*, **73**, March.

Brennan, Troyen (1990), "Narrowing the wide open spaces: The role of torts in environmental law", mimeo.

Brenner, Joel F. (1974), "Nuisance law and the industrial revolution", *Journal of Legal Studies*, **3**.

Brickey, Kathleen F. (1984), *Corporate Criminal Liability*, Deerfield, IL: Callaghan.

Brodeur, Paul (1985), *Outrageous Misconduct: The Asbestos Industry on Trial*, New York: Pantheon.

Bryan, Gerald A. (1991a), United States Environmental Protection Agency Memorandum, "Draft report on the implementation of the Timely and Appropriate Enforcement Response Criteria", 6 May.

Bryan, Gerald A. (1991b), United States Environmental Protection Agency Memorandum, "Request for comments on: draft interim access and security procedures for EPA's recently developed Integrated Data for Enforcement Analysis (IDEA) capability", 31 May.

Bureau of the Census (1981), *County Business Patterns 1981*, Washington, DC: US Department of Commerce.

Butler, J. (1985), "Insurance issues and Superfund", hearing before the Committee on Environment and Public Works, US Senate, 99th Cong., 1st. Sess., 1985.

Carlson, Cynthia (1988), "Making CERCLA natural resource damage regulations work: The use of the public trust doctrine and other state remedies", *Environmental Law Reporter*, **18** (8).

Carson, Richard T. and Peter Navarro (1988), *Fundamental Issues in Natural Resource Damage Assessment*, Discussion Paper 88–10, San Diego, CA: UCSD Department of Economics.

Carter, Richard M. (1980), "Federal enforcement of individual and corporate criminal liability for water pollution", *Memphis State University Law Review*, **10**, Spring.

Charlier, Marj (1990), "Manville Trust, victims' lawyers plan payment pact", *Wall Street Journal*, 19 November.

Charlton, Thomas (1985), *Study of Literature Concerning the Roles of Penalties in Regulatory Enforcement*, Compliance Policy and Planning Branch, Office of Enforcement and Compliance Monitoring, September.

Clabault, James M. and Michael K. Block (1981), *Sherman Act Indictments, 1955–1980*, New York: Federal Legal Publications, Inc.

Coase, Ronald N. (1960), "The problem of social cost", *J. Law and Econ.*, **3**, October.

Coffee, J. C., Jr (1980, "Corporate crime and punishment: A non–Chicago view of the economics of criminal sanctions", *American Criminal Law Review*, **17.**

Coffee, J. C., Jr (1989), "Crime and punishment in the boardroom: Let's not shield corporations from criminal penalties", *Legal Times*, 13 February.

Coffee, J. C., Jr (1990), "For some companies, supervision is the best form of punishment", *Legal Times*, 19 February, p. 23.

Coffee, J. C., Jr (1991), "Does 'unlawful' mean 'criminal'?: Reflections on the disappearing tort/crime distinction in American law", *Boston University Law Review*.

Coffee, J. C. Jr, R. Gruner, and C. Stone (1988), "Standards for organizational probation: A proposal to the United States sentencing commission", *Whittier Law Review*, **10**.

Cohen, Mark A. (1987), "Optimal enforcement strategy to prevent oil spills: An application of a principal–agent model with moral hazard", *Journal of Law and Economics*, **30** (1), April.

Cohen, Mark A. (1989a), "Corporate crime and punishment: An update on sentencing practice in the federal courts, 1984–7", *American Criminal Law Review*, **26** (3), Winter.

Cohen, Mark A. (1989b), "The role of criminal sanctions in antitrust enforcement", *Contemporary Policy Issues*, **7**, October.

Cohen, Mark A. (1991a), "Corporate crime and punishment: An update on sentencing practice in the federal courts, 1988–1990", *Boston University Law Review*.

Cohen, Mark A. (1991b), "Optimal penalty theory and empirical trends in corporate criminal sanctions", Owen Graduate School of Management, Vanderbilt University.

Cohen, Mark A. and D. Scheffman (1989), "The antitrust sentencing guideline: Is the punishment worth the cost?", *American Criminal Law Review*, **27**.

Cohen, Mark A. and P. H. Rubin (1985), "Private enforcement of public policy", *Yale Journal on Regulation*, **3**, Fall.

Cohen, Mark A., Chih–Chin Ho, Edward D. Jones III, and Laura Schleich (1988), "Organizations as defendants in federal courts: A preliminary analysis of prosecutions, convictions and sanctions, 1984–1987", *Whittier Law Review*, **10**.

Coleman, Jules (1985), "Crime, kickers, and transaction structures", in J. Pennock and J. Chapman (eds), *Nomos XXVII: Criminal Justice*, New York: New York University Press.

Cooter, Robert (1984), "Prices and sanctions", *Columbia Law Review*, **84** (6), October.

Cooter, Robert and Thomas Ulen (1988), *Law and Economics*, Glenview, Ill.: Scott, Foresman.

Cordiano, Dean M. and Deborah J. Blood (1990), "Individual liability for environment law violations", *Connecticut Bar Journal*, **64**, June.

Cross, Frank B. (1989), "Natural resource damage valuation", *Vanderbilt Law Review*, **42**, March.

Crovitz, L. Gordon (1991), "Justice for the birds: Exxon forgot to get a hunting license", *Wall Street Journal*, 20 March, p. A23.

Cullen, Francis T., Bruce D. Link and Craig W. Polanzi (1982), "The seriousness of crime revisited: Have attitudes toward white–collar crime changed?", *Criminology*, **20**, (83), May.

Dau–Schmidt, Kenneth G. (1990), "An economic analysis of the criminal law as a preference–shaping policy", *Duke Law Journal*, **1**, February.

Desvousges, William H., Richard W. Dunford, and Jean L. Domanico (1989), *Measuring Natural Resource Damages: An Economic Appraisal*, Washington, DC: report prepared for the American Petroleum Institute, January.

"Developments in the law: Toxic waste litigation" (1986), *Harvard Law Review*, **99**, (7), May.

Dewees, Donald N., (1986), "Economic incentives for controlling industrial disease: The asbestos case", *Journal of Legal Studies*, **15**, June.

Dewees, Donald N. (1990a), "The effect of environmental regulation: two case studies", in M. Friedland (ed), *Securing Compliance: Seven Case Studies*, Toronto: University of Toronto Press.

Dewees, Donald N. (1990b), "The efficiency of the law: Sulphur dioxide emissions in Sudbury", *University of Toronto Law Journal*.

Dewees, Donald N. and M. J. Trebilcock (1991), "The efficacy of the tort system and its alternatives: A review of the empirical evidence", University of Toronto, Law and Economics Working Paper Series #1.

Dickinson, Nancy (1991), "Citizens' suits to force EPA compliance with statutory deadlines: Use of appropriations law in statutory interpretation", student paper, Yale Law School.

Dillard, Lee and Manik, Roy (eds) (1990), "FY 90 report on the Blackstone Project", Department of Environmental Protection and Environmental Management, Commonwealth of Massachusetts, 25 July.

Dinan, Terry and F. Reed Johnson (1990), "Effects of hazardous waste risks on property transfers: Legal liability vs. direct regulation", *Natural Resources Journal*, 30 (3), Summer.

Dower, Roger C. and Paul F. Scodari (1987), "Compensation for natural resource injury: An emerging federal framework", *Marine Resource Economics*, 4, (3).

Downing, P. and J. N. Kimball (1974), "The economics of enforcing air pollution controls", *Journal of Environmental Economics and Management*, 1, December.

Downing, P. and J. N. Kimball (1982), "Enforcing pollution control laws in the United States", *Policy Studies Journal*, 11, September.

Dudek, Daniel and John Palmisano (1988), "Emissions trading: Why is this thoroughbred hobbled?", *Columbia Journal of Environmental Law*, 13, (2).

Dunford, Richard W., Sara P. Hudson, and William H. Desvousges (1991), *Linkages between Oil Spill Removal Activities and Natural Resource Damages*, San Diego, CA: Paper presented at the 1991 International Oil Spill Conference, 4–7 March.

Edwards, T. and T. Kuusinen (1989), "Strategies for improving industrial compliance, a draft report", Regulatory Innovations Staff, Office of Policy, Planning and Evaluation, EPA, December.

Environmental and Energy Study Institute and Environmental Law Institute (1985), *Statutory Deadlines in Environmental Legislation: Necessary but Need Improvement*, Washington, D.C.

Environmental Law Institute (1980), *Six Case Studies of Compensation for Toxic Substances Pollution: Alabama, California, Michigan, Missouri, New Jersey, and Texas*, Washington, D.C.: Congressional Research Service, Library of Congress.

Environmental Law Institute (1986), "State civil penalty authorities and policies", report prepared for the US EPA, Compliance Policy and Planning Branch Office of Enforcement and Compliance Monitoring, 30 September.

Fadil, A. (1985), "Citizens suits against polluters: Picking up the pace", *Harvard Environmental Law Review*, 9, Winter.

Feller, D. A. (1983), "Private enforcement of federal antipollution laws through citizens suits: A model", *Denver Law Journal*, 60, Fall.

Ferrey, Steven (1988), "Hard time: Criminal prosecution for polluters", *Amicus Journal*, Fall.

Filar, Jerry A. (1985), "Mathematical techniques for optimization of enforcement strategies", Department of Mathematical Studies, The Johns Hopkins University, August.

Findley, Roger W. (1988), "Pollution Control in Brazil", *Ecology Law Quarterly*, **15**.

Fischer, Kurt (1987), "Environmental compliance and corporate culture: Methods and motivations", Draft workplan submitted to EPA's Office of Policy Planning and Evaluation, Tufts University, Center for Environmental Management.

Freeman, A. M. III (1990), "Water pollution policy", in *Public Policies for Environmental Protection*, Washington: Resources for the Future, Inc.

Garbade, K. D., W. L. Silber, and L. J. White (1982), "Market reaction to the filing of antitrust suits: An aggregate and cross-sectional analysis", *Review of Economics and Statistics*, **64**, (4), November.

Garber, Ellen J. (1987), "Federal common law of contribution under the 1986 CERCLA amendments", *Ecology Law Quarterly*, **14**.

Garre, Gregory G. (1990), "CERCLA, natural resource damage assessments and the DC circuit's review of agency statutory interpretations under Chevron", *George Washington Law Review*, **58**, June.

Garrett, T.L. (1986), "Pros and cons of citizen enforcement", *Environment Law Reporter*, **16**, July

Gaskins, Richard (1989), *Environmental Accidents*, Philadelphia: Temple University Press.

Gelpe, Marcia R. (1989), "Pollution control laws against public facilities", *Harvard Environmental Law Review*, **13**, Winter.

Gigliello, Kem (1990), United States Environmental Protection Agency Memorandum, "Pollution prevention–2% Set Aside Project", 11 December.

Gindler, Burton J. (1967), *Water Pollution and Quality Controls*, vol. 3 in the series: Robert E. Clark (ed), *Waters and Water Rights*, Indianapolis: Allen Smith Co.

Glass, Elizabeth (1988), "Superfund and SARA: Are there any defences left?", *Harvard Environmental Law Review*, **12**, 385

Government Institutes, Inc. (1991), *Oil Pollution Act of 1990: Special Report*, Rockville, MD, March.

Grad, Frank P. (1985), *Environmental Law*, 3rd edn, New York: Matthew Bender.

Grinder, R. D. (1980), "The battle for clean air: The smoke problem in post–Civil War America", in Martin V. Melosi (ed), *Pollution and Reform in American Cities, 1870–1930*, Austin: U. of Texas Press.

Grumbles, Benjamin H. (1990), "Major provisions, themes of the Oil Pollution Act of 1990", *Environmental Reporter*, **21** (27).

Guerci, Lloyd (1987), United States Environmental Protection Agency Memorandum, "Release of updated computer model for decision tree analysis of proposed Superfund settlements", 3 June.

Habicht, F. Henry II (1987), "The federal perspective on environmental criminal enforcement: How to remain on the civil side", *Environmental Law Reporter*, **17**, (12), December.

Hagerty, Kathleen *et al.* (1990), *Managerial Compensation and Incentives to Engage in Far–Sighted Behavior*, delivered at the Allied Social Science Convention, Washington, DC.

Hahn, R. W. (1989), "Economic prescriptions for environmental problems: How the patient followed the doctor's orders", *Journal of Economic Perspectives*, **3**, (2).

Hahn, Robert W. and Gordon L. Hester (1989), "Where did all the markets go? An analysis of EPA's emissions trading program", *Yale Journal of Regulation*, **6**, (1), Winter.

Hall, Jerome (1943), 'Interrelations of criminal law and torts', *Columbia Law Review*, **43**.

Harford, J. D. (1978), "Firm behavior under imperfectly enforceable pollution standards and taxes", *Journal of Environmental Economics and Management*, **5**, March.

Harrington, Winston (1981), *The Regulatory Approach to Air Quality Management*, Washington, DC: Resources for the Future.

Harrington, W. (1988), "Enforcement leverage when penalties are restricted", *Journal of Public Economics*, **37**, April.

Harris, Christopher *et al.* (1988), "Criminal liability for violations of federal hazardous waste law: The 'knowledge' of corporations and their executives", *Wake Forest Law Review*, **23**.

Harrison, David Jr. (1977), "Controlling automotive emissions: How to save more than $1 billion per year and help the poor too", *Public Policy*, **25**.

Hensler, Deborah (1987), "Trends in tort litigation: Findings from the Institute for Civil Justice's research", *Ohio State Law Journal*, **48**.

Holcomb, John M. (1991), "How greens have grown", *Business and Society Review*.

Holmstrom, Bengt (1979), "Moral hazard and observability", *Bell Journal of Economics*, **10**, (1), Spring.

Huber, Peter (1988a), "Environmental hazards and liability law", in Robert Litan, Clifford Winston (eds), *Liability: Perspectives and Policy*, Washington, DC: Brookings Institute.

Huber, Peter (1988b), *Liability: The Legal Revolution and Its Consequences*, New York: Basic Books.

Hutchins, Peggy (1991), "Environmental criminal statistics FY83 through FY90", US Department of Justice, Environmental Crimes Section, Memo, 11 February.

ICF, Inc. for the Office of Policy, Planning and Evaluation (1987), "Enforcement of the Clean Water Act: Theory, policy and practice", unpublished draft report, 31 January.

"Individual criminal liability of corporate officers under federal environmental laws", (1989), *Environment Reporter*, **6**, 9 June.

James, Walter D. III (1988), "Financial institutions and hazardous waste litigation: Limiting the exposure to superfund liability", *Natural Resources Journal*, **28**, Spring.

Japan Times (1989), "Japan begins to address global environmental problems", **24**, 29 April, p. 8.

Johnson, Barnes (1987), *Final Phase II Report, Stationary Source Inspection Modelling Project: Allocation of a State's Inspection Resources*, EPA's Office of Policy Planning and Evaluation, July.

Jones, Walter B. (1989), "Oil spill compensation and liability legislation: When good things don't happen to good bills", *Environmental Law Reporter*, **20**, (8).

Jordan, S. J. (1987), "Awarding attorneys fees to environmental plaintiffs under a private attorney general theory", *Boston College Environmental Affairs Law Review*, **14**, Winter.

Jorgenson, L. and J. Kimmel (1988), *Environmental Citizen Suits: Confronting the Corporation*, Washington, DC: The Bureau of National Affairs, Inc.

Kagan, Robert A. and John T. Scholtz (1984), "The 'criminology of the corporation' and regulatory enforcement strategies", Keith Hawkins and John M. Thomas (eds), *Enforcing Regulation*, Law in Social Context Series, Amsterdam: Kluwer–Nijhoff.

Kakalik, James S. and Patricia A. Ebener, William L.F. Felstiner, Micheal G. Shanley, (1983), *The Costs of Asbestos Litigation*, Santa Monica; Institute for Civil Justice

Kakalik, James S. and N. Pace (1986), *Costs and Compensation Paid in Tort Litigation*, Santa Monica, CA: Institute for Civil Justice

Kamenar, Paul D. (1990), "Proposed corporate guidelines for environmental offenses", *Federal Sentencing Reporter*, **3**, November/December.

Karpoff, J. and J. R. Lott, Jr (1990), "The reputational penalty firms bear from committing criminal fraud", Anderson Graduate School of Management, University of California, Los Angeles, Working Paper #90–11, 31 May.

Keeton, W. P., D. B. Dobbs, R. E. Keeton, and D. G. Owen (1984), *Prosser and Keeton on Torts*, 5th edn, St Paul, MN: West Publishing Co.

Kenison, Howard, Carolyn L. Buchholz, and Shawn P. Mulligan (1987), "State actions for natural resource damages: Enforcement of the public trust", *Environmental Law Reporter*, **17**, (11).

King, Susan M. (1988), "Lenders' liability for cleanup costs", *Environmental Law*, **18**, (2), Winter.

Kinnersley, David (1988), *Troubled Water: Rivers, Politics, and Pollution*, London: Hilary Shipman.

Kopp, Raymond J., Paul R. Portney, and V. Kerry Smith (1990), "Natural resource damages: The economics have shifted after *Ohio* v. *United States Department of the Interior*", *Environmental Law Reporter*, **20**, (4).

Kornhauser, L. A. (1982), "An economic analysis of the choice between enterprise and personal liability for accidents", *California Law Review*, **70**.

Kraakman, Reiner H. (1984), "Corporate liability strategies and the costs of legal controls", *The Yale Law Journal*, **93**, April.

Labaton, Stephen (1989), "Does an assault on nature make Exxon a criminal?", *New York Times*, 23 April.

Landes, William M. and Richard A. Posner (1987), *The Economic Structure of Tort Law*, Cambridge, MA: Harvard University Press.

Landreth, Lloyd W. and Kevin M. Ward (1990), "Natural resource damages: Recovery under state law compared with federal laws", *Environmental Law Reporter*, **20**, (4).

Laws, Elliott P. and Russell V. Randle (1989), "Enforcement and liabilities", in J. Gordon Arbuckle *et al.*, *Environmental Law Handbook*, 10 edn, Rockville, MD: Government Institutes, Inc.

Lee, D. R. (1984), "The economics of enforcing pollution taxation", *Journal of Environmental Economics and Management*, **11**, June.

Lewin, Jeff L. and William N. Trumbull (1990), "The social value of crime", *International Review of Law and Economics*, **10**, December.

Linden, A. M. (1988), *Canadian Tort Law*, 4th edn, Toronto: Butterworths.

Linder, S. H. and M. E. McBride (1984), "Enforcement costs and regulatory reform: The agency and firm response", *Journal of Environmental Economics and Managment*, **11**, December.

Lorant, Stefan (1964), *Pittsburgh*, Garden City: Doubleday.

Ludwiszewski, Raymond B. (forthcoming), United States Environmental Protection Agency Memorandum, "FY 1990 report on federal penalty practices", Compliance Policy and Planning, Office of Enforcement and Compliance Monitoring.

Lyon, Randolph M. (1990), "Regulating bureaucratic polluters", *Public Finance Quarterly*, **2**, April.

Macy, Johathan R. (forthcoming), "Agency theory and criminal liability of organizations", *Boston University Law Review*.

Magat, Wesley A. and W. Kip Viscusi (1987), "Project 2 report on economic efficiency of enforcement and enforcement related monitoring", unpublished draft report to EPA's Office of Policy, Planning and Evaluation, 30 March.

Magat, Wesley A. and W. Kip Viscusi (1990), "Effectiveness of the EPA's regulatory enforcement: The case of industrial effluent standards", *Journal of Law and Economics*, **33**, October.

Magat, Wesley A., W. Kip Viscusi, Richard Zeckhauser, and Peter Schuck (1986), "Project 1 report on economic efficiency of enforcement and enforcement related monitoring', unpublished draft report to the EPA Office of Policy Planning and Evaluation, March.

Mahue, Michelle A. (1990), "Environmental contamination and the rise of lender liability", Office of Real Estate research letter, University of Illinois at Urbana–Champagne, Fall.

Malik, Arun S. (1990), "Markets for pollution control when firms are non–compliant", *Journal of Environmental Economics and Management*, **18**, (2), March.

Maraziti, Joseph J., Jr (1987), "Local governments: Opportunities to recover for natural resource damages", *Environmental Law Reporter*, **17**, (2).

Martin, L. W. (1984), "The optimal magnitude and enforcement of evadable Pigouvian charges", *Public Finance*, **39**, (3).

Mattson, James S. and J. Allison DeFoor II (1985), "Natural resource damages: Restitution as a mechanism to slow destruction of Florida's natural resources", *Journal of Land Use and Environmental Law*, **1**, (3).

McElfish, James M. Jr (1987), "Waste hazardous waste crimes", *Environmental Law Reporter*, **17**.

McGarr, Frank J. (1990), "Inadequacy of federal forum for resolution of oil spill damages", a talk given at a conference on oil spills at Newport, Rhode Island, 16 May.

McLaren, John P. S. (1972), "The common–law nuisance actions and the environmental battle – Well–tempered swords or broken reeds?", *Osgoode Hall Law Journal*, **10**, December.

Meidinger, Errol, Barry Boyer and John Thomas (1987), "Analysis of environmental compliance theories", unpublished draft report submitted to EPA's Office of Policy Planning and Evaluation, June.

Meier, Barry (1985), "Dirty job: Against heavy odds, EPA tries to convict polluters and dumpers", *Wall Street Journal*, 7 January.

Miceli, Thomas and Kathleen Segerson (forthcoming), "Joint liability in torts: Marginal and infra–marginal efficiency", *International Review of Law and Economics*.

Michelman, David F. (1983), "Creative criminal prosecution", *Outlook Environmental Law Journal*, **3**.

Miller, Dale T. (1985), "Psychological factors influencing compliance", Study for the Federal Statutes Compliance Project, Ottawa: Department of Justice, 7 February.

Miller, J. G. (1983), "Private enforcement of federal pollution control laws – part I", *Environmental Law Reporter*, **13**, September.

Miller, J. G. (1984a), "Private enforcement of federal pollution control laws – part II", *Environmental Law Reporter*, **14**, February.

Miller, J. G. (1984b), "Private enforcement of federal pollution control laws – part III.", *Environmental Law Reporter*, **14**, November.

Naysnerski, Wendy and Tom Tietenberg (forthcoming), "The private enforcement of federal environmental laws", *Land Economics*.

Newman, Harry A. and David W. Wright (1990), "Strict liability in a principal–agent model", *International Review of Law and Economics*, **10**, December.

Oates, Wallace E. and D. L. Strassman (1978), "The use of effluent fees to regulate public–sector sources of pollution: An application of the Niskanen model", *Journal of Environmental Economics and Management*, **5**, (3), September.

Oesterle, Dale A. (1991), "Viewing CERCLA as creating an option on the marginal firm: Does it encourage irresponsible environmental behavior?", *Wake Forest Law Review*, **26**.

O'Leary, Rosemary (1989), "The impact of federal court decisions on the policies and administration of the US Environmental Protection Agency", *Administrative Law Review*, **41**, Fall.

Olson, Erik D. (1989), "Natural resource damages in the wake of the *Ohio* and *Colorado* decisions: Where do we go from here?", *Environmental Law Reporter*, **19**, (12).

Parker, Jeffrey S. (1989), "Criminal sentencing policy for organizations: The unifying approach of optimal penalties", *American Criminal Law Review*, **26**, Winter.

Peck, Laura E. (1988), "Viable protection mechanisms for lenders against hazardous waste liability", *Hofstra Law Review*, **18**, Summer.

Polinsky, A. Mitchell (1980), "Strict liability vs. negligence in a market setting", *American Economic Review*, **70**, (2), May.

Polinsky, A. Mitchell (1989), *An Introduction to Law and Economics*, 2nd edn, Boston, MA: Little, Brown.

Polinsky, A. Mitchell and Steven Shavell (1979), "The optimal tradeoff between the probability and magnitude of fines", *American Economic Review*, **69**, (5), December.

Polinsky, A. Mitchell and Steven Shavell (1984), "The optimal use of fines and imprisonment", *Journal of Public Economics,* 24, (1), June.

Polinsky, A. Mitchell and Steven Shavell (1989), *A Note on Optimal Fines When Wealth Varies Among Individuals,* John O. Olin Program in Law and Economics Working Paper No. 58, November.

Posner, Richard A. (1977), *Economic Analysis of Law,* 2nd edn, Boston, MA: Little, Brown.

Posner, Richard A. (1980a), "Optimal sentences for white–collar criminals", *American Criminal Law Review,* 17.

Posner, Richard A. (1980b), "A statistical study of antitrust enforcement", *Journal of Law and Economics,* 13, (365).

Posner, Richard A. (1985) "An economic theory of the criminal law", *Columbia Law Review,* 85, (6), October.

Posner, Richard A. (1986), *Economic Analysis of Law,* 3rd edn, Boston, MA: Little Brown.

Priznar, Frank J. (1990), "Trends in environmental auditing", *Environmental Law Reporter: News and Analysis,* 20, (5), May.

Rebovich, Donald J. (1987), "Policing hazardous waste crime: The importance of regulatory law enforcement strategies and cooperation in offender identification and prosecution", *Criminal Justice Quarterly,* 9, Fall.

Reich, Edward E. (1989), United States Environmental Protection Agency Memorandum, "Report on FY 1986–88 federal penalty practices", Compliance Policy and Planning, Office of Enforcement, April.

Reuter, Peter (1988), "The economic consequences of expanded corporate liability: An exploratory study", Santa Monica: The Rand Corporation, N–2807–ICJ.

Rich, Bruce M. (1985), "The multilateral development banks, environmental policy, and the United States", *Ecology Law Quarterly,* 12.

Riesel, Daniel (1985), "Criminal prosecution and defense of environmental wrongs", *Environmental Law Reporter: News and Analysis,* 15, (3), March.

Ringleb, A. H. and S. N. Wiggins (1990), "Liability and large–scale, long–term hazards", *Journal of Political Economy,* 98, (3), June.

Roberts, Leslie (1989), "A corrosive fight over California's toxics laws", *Science,* 243, (20), January.

Robilliard, Gordon A., William H. Desvousges, and Richard W. Dunford (1991), *Natural Resource Injury and Damage Assessment Response Guidance Manual, Volume 2: Reference Material and Appendices,* Final report for Petroleum Environmental Research Forum, June.

Rose–Ackerman, Susan (1991a), *Rethinking the Progressive Agenda: The Reform of the American Regulatory State,* New York: Free Press.

Rose–Ackerman, Susan (1991b), "Tort law in the regulatory state", in P. Schuck edn, *Tort Law and the Public Interest: Competition, Innovation, and Consumer Welfare,* New York, Norton, .

Russell, C. S. (1988), "Economic incentives in the management of hazardous wastes", *Columbia Journal of Environmental Law,* 13, (2).

Russell, C. S. (1990a), "Game models for structuring monitoring and enforcement systems", *Natural Resource Modeling,* 4, Spring.

Russell, C. S. (1990b), "Monitoring and enforcement", in Paul Portney (ed), *Public Policies for Environmental Protection,* Washington, DC: Resources for the Future, Inc.

Russell, C. S., Winston Harrington and W. J. Vaughan (1986), *Enforcing Pollution Control Laws,* Washington, DC: Resources for the Future, Inc.

Rutledge, Gary and Nikolaos Stergioulas (1988),"Plant and equipment expenditures by business for pollution abatement, 1987 and planned 1988", U.S. Department of Commerce, *Survey of Current Business,* **68**, (11), p. 26, November.

Sand, Peter H. (1991), "International cooperation: the environmental experience", in Jessica T. Mathews (ed), *Preserving the Global Environment: The Challenge of Shared Leadership,* New York: W. W. Norton.

Scholtz, John T. (1984), "Cooperation, deterrence, and the ecology of regulatory enforcement", *Law and Society Review,* **18**, (2).

Schuck, Peter (1986), *Agent Orange on Trial: Mass Toxic Disasters in the Courts,* Cambridge, MA: Belknap Press.

Segerson, Kathleen (1989), "Risk and incentives in the financing of hazardous waste cleanup", *Journal of Environmental Economics and Management,* **16**, (1), January.

Segerson, Kathleen (1990), "Liability for groundwater contamination from pesticides", *Journal of Environmental Economics and Management,* **19**, (3), November.

Segerson, Kathleen (1991), "Liability transfers: An economic assessment of buyer and lender liability", Working Paper, Department of Economics, University of Connecticut.

Segerson, Kathleen and Tom Tietenberg (1991), "The structure of penalties in environmental enforcement: An economic analysis", Colby College Working Paper, May.

Shavell, Steven (1979), "Risk–sharing and incentives in principal–agent relationship", *Bell Journal of Economics,* **10**, (1), Spring.

Shavell, Steven (1980), "Strict liability versis negligence", *Journal of Legal Studies,* **9**, (1), January.

Shavell, Steven (1984a), "A model of the optimal use of liability and safety regulation", *Rand Journal of Economics,* **15**, (2), Summer.

Shavell, Steven, (1984b), "Liability for harm versus regulation of safety", *Journal of Legal Studies,* **13**, June.

Shavell, Steven (1986), "The judgment–proof problem", *International Review of Law and Economics,* **6**, June.

Shavell, Steven (1987a), "The optimal use of nonmonetary sanctions as a deterrent", *American Economic Review,* **77** (4), September.

Shavell, Steven (1987b), *Economic Analysis of Accident Law,* Cambridge, MA: Harvard University Press.

Slavitt, Evan, (1990), "An overview of the tax implications of environmental litigation", *Environmental Law Reporter: News and Analysis,* **20**, (12), December.

Smilor, R. W. (1980), "Toward an environmental perspective: The anti–noise campaign, 1893–1932", in M. V. Melosi (ed), *Pollution and Reform in American Cities, 1870–1930,* Austin, TX: U. of Texas Press.

Stanfield, Richelle L. (1987), "Government polluters", *National Journal*, **19**, (13), March.

Starr, Judson W. and Thomas J. Kelly Jr. (1990), "Environmental crimes and the sentencing guidelines: The time has come...and it is hard time", *Environmental Law Review*, **20**, March.

Storey, D. J. and P. J. McCabe (1980), "The criminal waste discharger", *Scottish Journal of Political Economy*, **27**, February.

Straachan,J. L., D. B. Smith, and W. L. Beedles (1983), "The price reaction to (alleged) corporate crime", *Financial Review*, **18**.

Straube, Michael (1989), "Is full compensation possible for the damages resulting form the *Exxon Valdez* oil spill?", *Environmental Law Reporter*, **19**, (8).

Strelow, Roger and John H. Claussen (1988), "Liability management in practice: Waste generators", *Houston Law Review*, **25**.

Strelow, R. (1990), "Corporate compliance with environmental regulation: Striking a balance", *Environmental Law Reporter: News and Analysis*, **20**, December.

Strock, James M. (1990a), United States Environmental Protection Agency, Memorandum, "Report on FY 1989 federal penalty practices", Compliance, Policy and Planning, Office of Enforcement, March.

Strock, J. M. (1990b), "EPA's environmental enforcement in the 1990's", *Environmental Law Reporter: News and Analysis*, **20**, August.

Strock, James M. (1990c), United States Environmental Protection Agency Memorandum, "Final summary report: Enforcement effectiveness case studies", 6 December.

Strock, James M.(1991a), "EPA's enforcement priorities for fiscal year 1991", *National Environmental Enforcement Journal*, February.

Strock, James M. (1991b), United States Environmental Protection Agency Memorandum, "EPA policy on the use of supplemental environmental projects in enforcement", 12 February.

Strock, James M. (1991c), United States Environmental Protection Agency Memorandum, "EPA interim policy on the inclusion of pollution prevention and recycling provisions in enforcement settlements", 25 February.

Sugarman, Stephen (1985), "Doing away with tort law", *California Law Review*,. **73**, May.

Sullivan Allanna (1990a), "Exxon picks environmental watchdog, says selection raises priority on safety", *Wall Street Journal*, 11 January.

Sullivan, Allanna (1990b), "Oil firms, shippers seek to circumvent laws setting no liability limit for spills", *Wall Street Journal*, 26 July.

Sykes, A. O. (1981), "An efficiency analysis of vicarious liability under the law of agency", *Yale Law Journal*, **91**, (1), November.

Sykes, A. O. (1984), "The economics of vicarious liability", *Yale Law Journal*, **93**, June.

Thackery, T.O. (1967), "Pittsburgh: How one city did it", in *Controlling Pollution*, Englefield Cliffs, NJ: Prentice–Hall.

Tietenberg, T. H. (1988), *Environmental and Natural Resource Economics*, 2nd edn, Glenview, Ill: Scott, Foresman.

Tietenberg, T. H. (1989), "Indivisible toxic torts: The economics of joint and several liability", *Land Economics*, **65**, November.

Tietenberg, T. H. (1990), "Economic instruments for environmental regulation", *Oxford Review of Economic Policy*, **6**, (1), Spring.

Toensing (1990), "Corporations on probation: Sentenced to fail", *Legal Times*, February 23, p. 21

Tom, Roslyn (1989), "Interpreting the meaning of lender management particpation under section 101(20)(A) of CERCLA",*Yale Law Journal*, **98** (5), March.

Toulme, Nill V., and Douglas E. Cloud (1991), 'The *Fleet Factors* case: A wrong turn for lender liability under superfund', *Wake Forest Law Review*, **26**, (1).

Trost, Cathy (1985), "Bhopal disaster spurs debate over usefulness of criminal sanctions in industrial accidents", *The Wall Street Journal*, 7 January.

US Department of Justice (1984), *Bureau of Justice Statistics Bulletin*, January.

US Environmental Protection Agency (1984a), *Policy on Civil Penalties*, EPA General Enforcement Policy #GM – 21, 16 February.

US Environmental Protection Agency (1984b), *Agency–wide Compliance and Enforcement Strategy and Strategy Framework for EPA Compliance Programs*, May.

US Environmental Protection Agency (1986), *Annotated Bibliography on Environmental Auditing*, 6th edn, November, EPA's Regulatory Reform Staff.

US Environmental Protection Agency (1988a), *FY 1988 Enforcement Accomplishments Report*, Washington, DC: United States Environmental Protection Agency.

US Environmental Protection Agency (1988b), *Toxics in the Community: 1988*, Washington, DC: U. S. Government Printing Office.

US Environment Protection Agency (1989), Office of Enforcement and Compliance Monitoring, *Fundamentals of Environmental Compliance Inspections*, Rockville, MD: Government Institutes, Inc. August.

US Environmental Protection Agency (1990a), "Enforcement Four Year Strategic Plan: Enhanced environmental enforcement for the 1990's", Office of Enforcement, March.

US Environmental Protection Agency (1990b), "Summary of criminal prosecutions resulting from environmental investigations", Office of Enforcement and Compliance Monitoring, 30 September.

US Environmental Protection Agency (1990c), Office of Enforcement, *Enforcement Accomplishments: FY 1989*, WashingtonDC.

US Environmental Protection Agency (1991a), "Strategic direction for the US Environmental Protection Agency", pamphlet, April.

US Environmental Protection Agency (1991b), *National Penalty Report*, April.

US Environmental Protection Agency (forthcoming), *Enforcement in the 1990s Project*, Innovative Enforcement Workgroup Report.

US General Accounting Office (1979), *Air Pollution Improvements Needed in Controlling Major Air Pollution Sources*, Washington, DC: United States General Accounting Office.

US General Accounting Office (1990), *Improvements Needed in Detecting and Preventing Violations*, Washington, DC: United States General Accounting Office.

US General Accounting Office (forthcoming), "Effectiveness of EPA's enforcement policy", draft report

US House of Representatives (1990), *Conference Report on the Oil Pollution Act of 1990*, Report No. 101–653, Washington, DC.

US Sentencing Commission (1990a), "Draft guidelines for organizational defendants", 26 October.

US Sentencing Commission (1990b, *Guidelines Manual*, November.

US Sentencing Commission (1991), "Proposed sentencing guidelines: Chapter eight, Sentencing of organizations", Submission to the US Congress, 1 May.

Unterberger, Glenn L. (1991), "Citizen enforcement suits: Putting Gwaltney to rest and setting sights on the Clean Air Act", in *Environmental Reporter: Analysis and Perspective*, 4 January.

Vatikiotis, Michael (1989), "Pressure groups warned about overseas activities lobbying the donors", *Far Eastern Economics Review*, **24**.

Verespej, Michael A. (1990), "The newest environmental risk: Jail", *Industry Week*, 22 January.

Viscusi, W. Kip (1983), *Risk by Choice*, Cambridge, MA: Harvard Univeristy Press

Viscusi, W. Kip (1984), "Structuring an effective occupational disease policy: Victim compensation and risk regulation", *Yale Journal on Regulation*, **2**.

Viscusi, W. K. and R. J. Zeckhauser (1979), "Optimal standards with incomplete enforcement", *Public Policy*, **27**, Fall.

Wasserman, Cheryl. (1984), "Improving the efficiency and effectiveness of compliance monitoring and enforcement of environmental policies, United States: A national review", prepared on behalf of the Organization for Economic Co-operation and Development, Group of Economic Experts, 16 October.

Wasserman, Cheryl E. (1987), "Oversight of state enforcement", in *Law of Environmental Protection* ed. Sheldon M. Novick, Environmental Law Institute.

Wasserman, Cheryl E. (1989), "Environmental auditing provisions in consent decrees and riders", *Law of Environmental Protection*, ed. Sheldon M. Novick, Environmental Law Institute.

Wasserman, Cheryl E. (1990), "Overview of compliance and enforcement in the United States: Philosophy, strategies and management tools", Proceedings of the International Enforcement Workshop, Utrecht, The Netherlands, 8–10 May .

Weinrib, Ernest (1989), "Understanding tort law", *Valparaiso Law Review*, **23**, Spring.

Weisbrod, B. A. (1988), *The Nonprofit Economy*, Cambridge, MA: Harvard University Press.

Wickham, Trevor (1987), "Overview: institutions, WALHI: The Indonesian Environmental Forum", *Environment*, **29**, (7), September.

Wynne, Larry D. (1989), "A case for criminal enforcement of federal environmental laws", *Naval Law Review*, **38**.

Yang, Edward J. (1984), "Valuing natural resource damages: Economics for CERCLA lawyers", *Environmental Law Reporter*, **14**, (8).

Index

A & A Land Development, 106
Abbot v. American Cyanamid Co., 242
Abel, R., 140
Abraham, K., 146, 164
Abramson, J., 79, 87
acid rain, 236
Adams, T.L., 51
Aden, J.B., 219
Administrative Procedures Act, 71
Aerospace, 107
Agency Guidance, 28
Agency Vision Statements, 29
Agent Orange, 140, 146–7, 156, 223
    Vietnam, 146
air pollution, 128, 139, 151, 154, 158,
    160, 162, 220
air program, 28, 34, 36, 39, 44
Alaska, 170, 175, 229, 240
Allegheny County, 160
Alternative Fine Act, 87
Ambrogi v. Gould, Inc., 241
American International Group Inc., The,
    241
American Law Institute, 164
Amoco Cadiz, the, 13
Arbuckle, G., 136
Arkansas River, 89
Arkin, S.S., 105
Arthur Kill oil spill, 186, 190
Ashland Oil, 84, 87, 103, 106
Atlantic States Legal Foundation, Inc. v.
    Tyson Foods, Inc., 136
Austin, B.R., 145
automotive emissions, 163

Ballard Shipping, 84
Barnes, A.J., 51
Baumol, W.J., 136, 141
Beavis, B., 134

Beckenstein, A.R., 108
Beedles, W.L., 106
Benicia, city of, 185
Benitez-Allende v. Alcan Aluminio do
    Brasil, S.A., 240
Beshada v. Johns-Manville Products
    Corp., 164
Bingham, T., 191
black-lung program, the, 238
Blackstone Project, 51
Block, M.K., 105
Blood, D.J., 71
Bohm, P., 17
Boston Globe, The, 106
Bowles, C., 25
Boyer, B., 51
Bratton, D., 157
Brazil, 219
Breen, B., 192
Brelis, M., 106
Brennan, D.F., 152
Brennan, T., 151–2, 156
Brenner, J.F., 144, 164
Brickey, K.F., 105
Broadus, J., 191
Brodeur, P., 140
Bryan, G.A., 35, 39
Budget Reconciliation Act of 1989, The,
    178
Bureau of National Affairs, the, 135
Business Week, 107
Butler, J., 149

Callan v. G.D. Searle & Co., 242
Canada, 13, 142–4, 147, 149, 154, 161
    The Crown, 155
    Ontario, 155, 161
carbon monoxide, 158, 242
carcinogens, 152

Carter, B., 107
Carter, R.M., 75, 105
Charlton, T., 23, 51
Chemical Commodities, Inc., 90
Chemical Manufacturers Association, The, 159, 172
Chemical Week, 164
Chesapeake Bay Foundation v. Gwaltney of Smithfield Ltd, 51, 129, 135
chlor-alkali plants, 161
Cipollone v. Liggett Group Inc., 242
City of Philadelphia v. Stepan Chemical Co., 241
Claussen, J.H., 159
Clean Air Act 1977, 41, 45, 71, 77–8, 82, 94, 110, 115, 118, 128, 135–6, 236, 239, 242
Clean Water Act (CWA), 39, 44–5, 64, 67, 71, 77–8, 82, 94–5, 99, 114, 118, 127–8, 132, 135–6, 149–50, 165–6, 176–8, 180, 184, 190, 192, 226–9
Cloninger, D.O., 106
Cloud, D.E., 197, 200–201, 212, 241
Coase, R.N., 141, 147
Coffee, J.C., 76, 103, 106
Cohen, M., 9–10, 71–2, 75, 81–2, 86, 93–4, 97, 105–6, 134–5, 217–18, 231
Coleman, J., 76
Collins, J.C., 92
Comprehensive Environmental Response, Compensation, and Liability Act of 1980 (CERCLA), The, 5, 13–15, 77–8, 82, 87, 140, 147–9, 159, 162–4, 166, 169, 172–3, 177–8, 192, 195–8, 200, 210, 212, 228–30, 241
Conn, D.C., 242
Conservation Law Foundation, 122
Consumer Product Safety Act (CPSA), 237, 240–41, 243
Contractor Listing Authority, 45
Cooter, R., 140
Cordiano, D.M., 71
Corporate Crime Reporter, The, 105–6

Crime Control Act of 1984, 98
Criminal Fine Enforcement Act of 1984, 64, 84–5, 91, 103, 106–7
criminal penalties, 75–108
civil penalties, 76
criminal liability, 76–9, 96, 105
enforcement programs, 101
environmental offenses, 76, 82, 85, 95, 102, 105
sanctions, 80–81, 83, 90–93, 97–8, 101–2, 104–5
crop damage, 161
Crovitz, L.G., 77

Dalkon shield, the, 155
Dawson v. Chrysler Corp., 242
DC Circuits, 172
Deepwater Port Act, 176, 192
DeFoor, J.A., 192
Delaney v. E.P.A., 239
Delaware, 179
Delaware River, 71
Department of Defense, 219
Department of Energy, 219
Department of Interior (DOI), The, 14, 165–6, 169, 171–5, 177, 180–85, 190–92, 228
DES, 155
Desmarais v. Dow Corning Corp., 242
Desvousges, W.H., 171–2, 191–2
"Developments in the law: Toxic waste litigation", 148, 151–3
Dewees, D., 13, 139, 151, 153, 155, 158, 161, 225
Dewees paper, the, 12
Dewey v. R.J. Reynolds Tobacco Co., 242
Dickinson, N., 239
Dillard, L., 51
Dinan, T., 197–8, 201
dioxin spill, 159
Diver, C.S., 25
Domanico, J.L., 171–2
Downing, P., 134
Drake v. Honeywell, Inc., 240
dry-cleaning solvents, 220

Dudek, D., 242
Dunford, R., 14–15, 150, 165, 171–2, 191–2, 228, 241

Eagle Picher, 87, 102, 106
East Bay Regional Park District, 185
Edwards, T., 51
ELI study of toxic pollution (1980), the, 155
Elizabeth, New Jersey, 186
emissions control systems, the, 158
enforcement, private, 109–36
 civil penalties, 117
 cost-effective emission reduction, 126
 criminal penalties, 124
 discharge standards, 127
 enforcement and compliance incentives, 120–25
 marginal expected penalty curve, 122–3
 private litigation, 110, 113
 public enforcement, 109, 113–14, 122–4, 126, 129, 131–3
Environment Reporter, 106
Environmental and Energy Study Institute, 239
environmental audit provisions, 45
environmental contamination, 9
Environmental Defense Fund v. Thomas, 239
environmental enforcement, 215–21
 criminal penalties, 221
 private enforcement, 218–20
 public enforcement, 219
 sanctions, 217
Environmental Law Institute, 42, 144, 150, 155, 239
environmental laws, 4, 12, 21, 29, 32, 45, 47, 53–4, 58, 101, 128, 131, 164, 216, 227, 235
environmental liability law, 223–43
 causation, 223, 234, 238
 classical torts, 224
 compensation, 237–9
 conventional statutes, 224
 efficiency conditions, 202

environmental management, 2
 equity financing, 206, 208–9
 sanctions, 231
 statutory liability, 225
environmental policy, 1–3, 5–6, 11, 22, 27, 110, 125, 127–8, 131–3, 238
 civil penalties, 4, 8
 criminal monetary penalties, 4, 8–10
 ecological systems, 1
 emission taxes, 2
 emissions trading, 2
 enforcement, 4–7, 9, 12
 penalty structures, 7
 policy innovations, 4
environmental pollution, 34, 146, 156, 225
environmental programs, 21, 22, 28, 35, 41, 114, 159
Environmental Protection Agency (EPA), 26, 28–30, 35, 37–9, 41–7, 51, 54–5, 63, 68, 71, 75, 78, 80, 87–92, 106, 114, 118–19, 122, 124, 135, 139, 148, 158, 198, 218, 226–9, 235, 237, 239–41
 discharge monitoring reports (DMRs), 118
 Office of Criminal Enforcement, 75
EPA's Consolidated Rules of Practice, 71
EPA's Penalty Policy 1984, 43
EPA's Regions, 29, 35
EPA's water discharge standards, 127
environmental protection policy, 16
environmental risks, 2, 27, 29, 32, 50, 58, 61–3, 65–6, 69, 149
Environmental Science and Technology, 164
environmental standards, 4, 134
Europe, 134–5
European Economic Community, 131, 134
Exxon Corporation, 72, 76–7, 99, 103, 105, 185, 192, 229
Exxon Valdez, 72, 76–7, 92, 99, 105, 107, 175, 228–9

Fadil, A., 118
FDA, 92
Federal Bureau of Investigation (FBI), 44, 81
Federal Cigarette Labeling and Advertising Act, 242
Federal Civil Penalty Practices, 48
Federal enforcement, theory and practice, 21–51
  bubble approaches, 33
  civil penalties and other sanctions, 40–41
  credibility, 22
  effectiveness, 22
  efficiency, 22
  enforcement programs, 21, 23–4, 26–7, 30, 37, 46–8
  equity, 22, 50
  game theory, 25
  market-based approaches, 33
  multiplier effect, 23–4, 26, 47, 50
  offset approaches, 33
  operations research, 25
  state/federal relationship, 46
Federal Insecticide, Fungicide and Rodenticide Act (FIFRA), 64, 78, 82, 93
federal law, 79
Federal Register, 27, 51
Federal Rules of Civil Procedure, 154
Federal Sentencing Guidelines, 231
Federal Water Pollution Control Act (FWPCA), 239–41
Federal Water Quality Act of 1987, 71
Feller, D.A., 114
Filar, J.A., 25
Findley, R.W., 219
Finishing Corp. of America, 107
fiscal years (FY), 39, 43, 44, 68, 71, 81
Food, Drug and Cosmetic Act (FDCA), 242
Fortune, 107
Fortune 500 Companies, 108
Four Year Strategic Plan, 29
France, 13
Freeman, A.M., 136

Gabel, H.L., 108
Garbade, K.D., 106
Garber, E.J., 148
Garre, G.G., 192
Garrett, T.L., 130
Gaskins, R., 146
gasoline, 158
Gelpe, M.R., 136
General Accounting Office (GAO), 36, 43
General Electric Co., 106, 159
Gigliello, K., 51
Gindler, B.J., 145
Glass, E., 148
Government Institutes, Inc., 179
Grad, F.P., 144–5, 151, 162
Grand Canyon, 168
Great Britain, 144, 160, 164, 219
  regional water authorities, 219
Grinder, R.D., 160
ground-water contamination, 157
Gruner, R., 106
Guerci, L., 40

Habicht, F.H., 75, 80
Hahn, R.W., 17, 136, 242
Hall, J., 76
Hamker v. Diamond Shamrock Chemical Co., 135
Harford, J.D., 134, 215
Harrington, W., 17, 134, 217
Harrison, D., 243
Hazard Communication Standard, 164
hazardous chemicals, 152, 220
hazardous waste, 13, 34, 75, 78, 82, 87, 89–92, 94–5, 98, 105, 147–8, 155–7, 159, 230, 236, 241
hazardous waste cleanup, lender liability for, 195–212
hazardous waste program, 28, 35, 39, 51
Helmerich & Payne, 94
Hensler, D., 156
herbicides, 221
Hester, G.L., 136, 242
Holcomb, J.M., 90
Huber, P., 149, 153, 155–6, 164, 225

Hudson, S.P., 192
Hutchins, P., 75, 78, 81, 83
hydrocarbons (VOCs), 158

Illinois Supreme Court, 242
incarceration, 4, 7–11, 25, 42, 45, 53, 64–8, 70, 80, 91, 99
'Individual criminal liability of corporate officers under federal environmental laws', 79, 105
Indonesia, 219
Industry Week, 105
Integrated Data for Enforcement Analysis (IDEA), 35, 48
International Convention on Civil Liability for Oil Pollution Damage (CLC Convention), The, 179
International Convention on the Establishment of an International Fund for Compensation for Oil Pollution Damage (Fund Convention), The, 179
International Group of P & I Clubs, 193
International Monetary Fund, 219

James, W.D., 212
Japan, 219
Japan Times, 219
Johnson, B., 36
Johnson, F.R., 197–8, 201
Jones, C., 71, 191
Jones, W.B., 178–9, 192
Jorgenson, L., 135

K.V.P. Company Limited, Act, 1950, 164
Kagan, R.A., 51
Kakalik, J.S., 154
Kamenar, P.D., 99
Karpoff, J., 106
Kaye, J., 106
Keeton, W.P., 143–6
Kelly, T.J., 71, 75, 107
Kimball, J.N., 134
Kimmel, J., 135
King, S.M., 212
Kinnersley, D., 219

Kitlutsisti v. Arco Alaska, Inc., 239
Kociemba v. G.D. Searle & Co., 242
Kopp, R.J., 171, 180
Kornhauser, L.A., 58
Kraakman, R.H., 64
Kukulka v. Holiday Cycle Sales, Inc., 240
Kuusinen, T., 51

Labaton, S., 105
LaFalce, J.J., the Hon., 212
land contamination, 159
Landes, W.M., 140–41, 147
Landreth, L.W., 193
Larsen v. General Motors, 242
Lee, D.R., 134, 215
liability law, 3, 4, 5, 6, 13, 15, 17
Linden, A.M., 143
liquid wastes, 139
Little, A.D., 51
Lorant, S., 160
Los Angeles Times, 106–7
Lott, J.R., 106
Love Canal suit, the, 156
Ludwiszewski, R.B., 51
lung cancer, 152
Lyon, R.M., 72

Magat, W.A., 36, 134
Mahue, M.A., 200
Malik, A.S., 215
Manik, R., 51
Maraziti, J.J., 180
Marshall, D.V., 105–6
Martin, L.W., 134
Martinez, California, oil spill, the, 185, 190
Massachusetts, 51
Mattson, J.S., 192
McCabe, P.J., 134
McDougald v. Garber, 242
McGarr, F.J., 14
McKie et al. v. The K.V.P. Co. Ltd., 164
McLaren, J.P.S., 164
Meidinger, E., 51
mercury, 161
Miceli, T., 72

Michigan Supreme Court, 241–2
*Middlesex City, Sewerage Auth. v. Nail.
    Sea Clammers Assoc.*, 240
Miller, D.T., 51, 114, 136
Minn, D.C., 242
Moeller, A.P., 189
Monongahila River, 84, 87
Monsanto, 159
Moore, W.J., 240–41

National Journal, 240–41
National Law Journal, 241
National Municipal Enforcement Policy,
    43
*National Pollutant Discharge Elimina-
    tion System (NPDES)*, 39, 118
*National Resources Defense Council,
    Inc., (NRDC) v. Train*, 239
National Wildlife Federation, 172
Native Village of Chenega Bay v. Lujan,
    241
Natural Resource Damage Assessments
    (NRDA), The, 149, 166–8, 172–5,
    177, 180, 183–93
Nature Conservancy, the, 135
Naysnerski, W., 11, 12, 109, 134–5
Naysnerski-Tietenberg analysis, the, 11
New Jersey, 186
*New Jersey Public Int. Research Group
    v. the Public Service and Gas Co.
    of New Jersey*, 240
New Jersey Supreme Court, 242
New Jersey's Environment Cleanup and
    Responsibility Act (ECRA), 201
New York City, 186
New York State, 179
New York State Supreme Court, 241
New York Times, 107
New York v. Gorsuch, 239
Newman, H. A., 58
nitrogen oxides, 158
NOAA, 183–4, 189–90, 192
nongovernmental organizations (NGOs),
    219
nutrients, 221

*O'Connor v. Kawasaki Motors Corp.,
    U.S.A.*, 240
O'Leary, R., 239
Oates, W. E., 72, 136, 141
Occupational Safety and Health Act, 241
Oesterle, D. A., 241
Office of Price Administration, 25
Ohio decision, the, 14, 172–5, 180–84,
    190–92
*Ohio v. United States Department of
    Energy*, 136
Oil Pollution Act (OPA) of 1990, 5, 14–
    15, 149–50, 165, 175–84, 186–93,
    228, 239, 241
    Conference Report, 177, 192
Oil Spill Intelligence Report, 193
Oil Spill Trust Fund, 15, 178, 186–9,
    191, 193
Oil spills, 13–15, 101, 149–50
oil spills, natural resource damages from,
    165–93
Olanoff, B., 107
Olcott, Inc., 135
Olson, E. D., 184
Opaluch, J., 71
Oregon, 170
Orkin, 93
OSHA, 152, 236
Outer Continental Shelf Lands Act, 176,
    192

Pace, N., 154
Palmisano, J., 242
Paperwork Reduction Act, The, 35
Par Pharmaceuticals, 92, 107
Peck, L. E., 212
Pennington v. Vistron Corporation, 242
Pennwalt Corporation, 79, 87, 89, 102
People v. Chicago Magnet Wire Corp.,
    242
People v. Hegedus, 242
People v. Pymm, 241
Pest Control Company, 107
pesticides, 221
Pittsburgh, 160
Pokorny v. Ford Motor Co., 242

Policy Framework for State/EPA Enforcement Agreements, The, 37–8, 41–2, 46
Polinsky, A. M., 65, 66, 71–3, 140
Pollack, S., 135
pollution control, 2, 33, 125, 127, 139, 141, 157–8, 201, 219, 234
pollution damage, 141
pollution discharge, 140–41, 143, 147, 152, 156
pollution emissions, 158
Portney, P. R., 171, 180
Posner, R. A., 53, 71, 140–41, 147
Powell, Justice, 234
Pozsgai, J., 99
Priznar, F. J., 72
Public Int. Research of N. J. v. Powell Duffryn, 240
Puerto Rico v. S. S. Zoe Colocotroni, 192

radiation, 237
radionuclides, 239
Rand Corporation, 154, 158
Reagan, President, 135, 157, 166, 218
Rebovich, D. J., 17, 71
Refuse Act of 1899, 75, 77–8
Reich, E. E., 51
Resource Conservation and Recovery Act (RCRA), 39, 64, 77–8, 82, 114, 136, 221, 239
Reuter, P., 158
Rice Aircraft, 92
Rice, B., 92–3
Rich, B. M., 219
RICO, 77, 89, 92, 106
Riesel, D., 71, 78, 105
Ringleb, A. H., 72
river pollution, 151
Rivers and Harbors Appropriation Act of 1899, 105
Roberts, 108
Roberts, L., 135
Robilliard, G. A., 191
Rose-Ackerman, S., 223, 239
Royal Dutch/Shell Group, The, 189
Roysdon v. R. J. Reynolds Tobacco Co., 242

Rubin, P. H., 135
Russell, C., 17, 71–2, 134, 215, 220
Rutledge, G., 157

Safe Drinking Water Act, 78
Safe Rivers and Harbors Act, The, 45
San Francisco Bay, 185
sanctions, the efficiency of, 53–73
    civil penalties, 53
    civil proceedings, 55, 57–8
    corporate penalties, 62–3
    criminal monetary penalties, 53, 64
    criminal proceedings, 55, 58, 69
    environmental crimes, 56–7
Sand, P. H., 134
Scholtz, J. T., 51
Schuck, P., 140, 146
scienter requirement, 57, 72
Seattle Times, 107
Securities and Exchange Commission (SEC), 32
Securities Regulation and Law Report, 551, 107
Segerson, K., 7–9, 15–16, 53, 60, 71–3, 80, 96–7, 155, 195, 212, 229–30
Segerson-Tietenberg analysis, the, 9–10
Segerson-Tietenberg model, the, 98
Sellen Construction, Company, Inc., 89
Shavell, S., 17, 60, 65–6, 71–3, 140, 152, 224–5, 229
Shell Oil Company, 185
Shipp v. General Motors Corp., 242
Sierra Club Inc. v. Electronic Controls Design Inc., 240
Sierra Club Inc. v. Gorsuch, 239
Significant Non-Compliers (SNC), 28, 38–9, 46
Silber, W. L., 106
Silkwood, K., 237
Silkwood v. Kerr-McGee, 242–3
Skantz, T.R., 106
Slavitt, E., 71
Smilor, R. W., 160
Smith, D. B., 106
Smith, V. K., 171, 180
smoke pollution, 155

Social Sciences and Humanities Research Council of Canada, 164
soil contamination, 157
Solano County, 185
solid wastes, 139
Sours v. General Motors Corp., 242
Sovereign immunity, 124, 136
Spartan Trading Co., Inc., 91
SPIRG v. AT&T Bell Laboratories, 51
SPIRG v. Hercules, 51
St. Louis, 160
Standard and Poor's Register, the, 105
Stanfield, R. L., 72
Starr. J. W., 71, 75, 107
State of Alabama Department of Environmental Management, 92
State of New York v. Shore Realty Corporation, 197–8, 242
State of Ohio v. United States Department of the Interior, 241
statutory law, 223, 235
Stein, M., 135
Stephen v. American Brands, 242
Stergioulas, N., 157
Stone, C., 106
Storey, D. J., 134
Straachan, J. L., 106
Strassman, D. L., 72
Strelow, R., 135, 159
Strickland, T.H., 106
Strock, J. M., 28, 45, 51, 136
Student Public Interest Research Group v. Fritzsch., Dodge & Olcott, Inc., 135
Sugarman, S., 140
sulfur oxide emissions, 155, 161, 163
Sullivan, A., 72, 189
Summers, J. S., 107
Superfund Act, 5, 17, 40, 44, 146–8, 161, 166, 196, 231, 236, 241
Superfund Amendments Reauthorization Act (SARA), 148, 152, 212, 239
Supreme Court, 129, 135, 237
Surface Mining Control and Reclamation Act, The, 240, 243
Sykes, A. O., 58

Tanglewood East Homeowners v. Charles-Thomas, Inc., 241
Texaco, 94
Thackery, T. O., 160
Thatcher, Mrs., 219
Thomas, J., 51
Tietenberg, T., 1, 7–9, 11–12, 17, 53, 71–3, 80, 96–7, 109, 134, 136, 155
Toensing, V., 106
Tom, R., 212
tort law, 12–13, 66, 72, 76, 158, 223–4, 231, 233–8, 243
tort law, the deterrence of environmental pollution, 139–64
causation, 151–3, 156, 161
civil liability, 158, 163
market failure, 141
statutory liability, 147
Toulme, N. V., 197, 200–201, 212, 241
toxic chemicals, 159, 223, 231, 242
toxic substances, 144, 149, 153
Toxic Substances Control Act (TSCA), 64, 78, 82, 94–5
tradeoffs, 31, 40, 91, 212
Trans-Alaska Pipeline Authorization Act, 176, 192
Transit Mix Concrete Company, Inc., 89
Trebilcock, M. J., 158
Tufts University, 51

Ulen, T., 140
United Press International, 106–7
United States, 13–15, 21, 35, 57, 72, 75, 109, 131, 133, 135, 140, 142–5, 147, 151, 153–5, 159–61, 165–6, 178–9, 185, 188–9, 218–19
US Congress, 2, 10–11, 17, 30, 36, 57, 75, 98–9, 110, 119, 147, 149, 172, 175, 177, 179, 196, 198, 219, 226–7, 237–9
US Court of Appeals, 14, 165, 172–3, 175, 183–4, 239–43
US Department of Commerce, 177
US Department of Justice, 44, 51, 55, 68, 71, 75, 78–9, 80–83, 88–9, 99, 107–8

Environmental Crimes Unit, 75, 79, 81
US District Court for Southern New York, 92
US District Courts, 81
US Federal System of Government, The, 6
US House of Representatives 1990, 176–7
   1989 DC Circuit Court decision, 176
US Sentencing Commission, 10, 45, 81, 98–100, 102, 105–7, 231, 240
US Treasury, 116, 178, 237, 240
United States v. Fleet Factors, 197, 200, 212, 241
US v. Hoflin, 105
United States v. Johnson & Towers, Inc., 71
United States v. Maryland Bank & Trust Company, 196
United States v. Mirable, 196
US vs. Park, 79
US v. Roll Coaster, 51
US v. John W. Rutana, 107

Valmont Industries, 89
Vatikiotis, M., 219
Vaughan, W. J., 17, 134

Verespej, M. A., 105
Viscusi, W. K., 36, 134, 225, 243
volatile organic compound (VOC), 28

Walker, M., 134
Wall Street Journal, 192–3
Walls v. Waste Resource Corp., 241
Ward, K. M., 193
Washington, 170
Washington Post, The, 106, 136
Wasserman, C. E., 6, 21, 44, 51
water contamination, 159
water NPDES program, the, 34
water pollution, 71, 118, 139, 144–5, 151, 153, 159, 162–3, 220
water program, 39, 44
Weinrib, E., 140
Weisbrod, B. A., 111
Welco Plating, Inc., 92
Wetlands destruction, 145
White, L. J., 106
Wickham, T., 219
Wiggins, S. N., 72
Wood v. General Motors Corp., 242
World Bank, 219
World War II, 160
Wright. D. W., 58

Zeckhauser, R. J., 134